Political Communication

Media & Public Affairs
Robert Mann, *Series Editor*

Media & Public Affairs, a book series published by Louisiana State University Press and the Reilly Center for Media & Public Affairs at the Manship School of Mass Communication, LSU, explores the complex relationship between knowledge and power in our democracy. Books in this series examine what citizens and public officials know, where they get their information, and how they use that information to act. For more information, visit www .lsu.edu/mpabookseries.

The Manship School Guide

Political Communication

Edited by **ROBERT MANN**

and **DAVID D. PERLMUTTER**

Revised and Expanded Edition

Louisiana State University Press

Baton Rouge

Published by Louisiana State University Press
Copyright © 2011 by Louisiana State University Press
All rights reserved
Manufactured in the United States of America
LSU Press Paperback Original
FIRST PRINTING

DESIGNER: Amanda McDonald Scallan
TYPEFACE: Whitman
PRINTER: McNaugton & Gunn, Inc.
BINDER: Dekker Bookbinding

Library of Congress Cataloging-in-Publication Data

Manship School guide to political communication
Political communication : the Manship School guide / edited by Robert Mann and David D. Perl-
mutter. — Rev. and expanded ed.
    p. cm.
Includes index.
ISBN 978-0-8071-3789-5 (pbk. : alk. paper) — ISBN 978-0-8071-3790-1 (pdf) — ISBN 978-0-8071-
3955-4 (epub) — ISBN 978-0-8071-3956-1 (mobi) 1. Campaign management—United States. 2.
Political campaigns—United States. 3. Political consultants—United States. 4. Mass media—Po-
litical aspects. I. Mann, Robert, 1958– II. Perlmutter, David D., 1962– III. Manship School of Mass
Communication. IV. Title.
JK2281.M36 2011
320.01'4—dc22

                                                                                    2010054163

To our wives, Christie and Cindy

Contents

Contents

Constituencies

Acknowledgments

The editors are grateful to the Manship family, who generously funded a research professorship for the first edition of this book. The second edition benefited from research funding from the Professorship in Media & Public Affairs and the William K. "Bill" Carville Professorship of Communication and Political Empowerment at the Manship School of Mass Communication at Louisiana State University, Baton Rouge. We are also grateful to MaryKatherine Callaway and Alisa Plant of LSU Press for their support and encouragement. We wish to thank two graduate students from the Manship School—Katherine Knobloch and Paul Harang—who not only contributed chapters for this volume, but who also helped in many ways with its production and editing. Most of all, we wish to thank our spouses, Cindy and Christie, for their constant support, loyalty, and affection.

Acknowledgments

Political Communication

Introduction

DAVID D. PERLMUTTER AND ROBERT MANN

During the Iowa caucuses of the 2008 presidential campaign, then-Senator Barack Obama of Illinois defeated his rivals and immediately became the front-runner for the Democratic nomination. His victory in the Hawkeye State and his subsequent march to the White House also unveiled a new era of political campaigns. In 2003–2004, Howard Dean and the young political consultants, workers, activists, and Internet entrepreneurs of his campaign had pioneered a 1.0 version of online social-media interactivity between voters and their candidate. Like all prototypes, the initial model did not work exactly as planned or to the best effect. But the Obama version—heralded and championed by a candidate who looked, spoke, and acted like a technology innovator as well as a great communicator—created a 2.0 social-media campaign in 2007–2008 that transformed politics. Obama's team, in short, figured out how to marry the old and the new. Its get-out-the-vote strategy, which dates back at least to the voter-canvassing drivers of the early Roman Republic, was well coordinated with a MySpace outreach that allowed tens of millions of potential voters to contribute cash and time, and to build organization and enthusiasm for the candidate.

Political Communication: The Manship School Guide is about the processes, events, techniques, technologies, venues, theories, and applications of the modern world of political campaigns. It is also, at its core, about people: the actors who participate in and try to control their own destinies and those of their candidates. Two thousand eleven is a crucial time for a new edition of the original *Manship School Guide,* first published in 1999, because those key power players are currently rethinking and recasting their strategies and

1

tactics to try to adapt and survive in the new era. Back in our 1.0 edition, one of the editors was able to confidently state that the "political process today is consultant driven: where once party bosses were kingmakers, now political consultants determine much of campaign and election strategy and are even influential in the making of public policy." He was also able to point out that the phenomenon is hardly new. The courts of Ramses II, Julius Caesar, Charlemagne, and Elizabeth I swarmed with counselors offering tips on how to improve public goodwill and secure power. What is different today (at least in the annals of American history) is that instead of being background confidants, political consultants are public—some even say independent—players. Their appearances come in many forms, from the Hollywood screen to the MSNBC studios, from the op-ed pages of the *New York Times* to the "results" sections of academic papers. Perhaps more ominously, thousands of young women and men are setting out from college each year hoping to place the title "political consultant" on their business cards. But now, as our authors assess early twenty-first-century electioneering, online and elsewhere, we must take into account a new potential power player: the people themselves. Today people are measured not just by votes, attendance at rallies, or donations, but by their own voices, especially those heard loudest on social media such as blogs, Twitter, Facebook, YouTube, and other venues.

A point that will be developed and noted in many of the essays to come: once upon a time, the face and voice of a candidate belonged to him or her, the campaign, the press, and maybe the opponent. That gave you, as candidate, some control over who heard you and saw you, when and where. One of the editors of this book recalls an incident that typified the old situation. He followed his employer, a United States senator, to a speech at a senior center, a very standard political event. Suddenly, an older gentleman in the front row collapsed, sounding like he might be having a heart attack. The senator leaped from the podium and administered CPR until an ambulance arrived. That evening, the editor was surprised to see no mention of the incident on the news, nor was it in the paper the next morning. At work, he learned that the candidate, a truly modest and decent man, had specifically asked for this golden publicity moment to be censored, saying, "I just did what anybody would have done and I don't want to profit by it."

Such incidents might still happen, but now it would not be up to a politician or news organization to suppress video and reports of the event. Likely half the crowd, including young campaign workers, would pull out their PDAs or cell phones, recording the excitement and posting footage and commentary on their blogs or Twitter feeds even before the EMT sirens could be heard. In short, it is even more important now than it was in 1999 to uncover the roles people play—both as insiders and outsiders—in the confusing world of politics.

Hence the task of this book: to go beyond the blarney and blather and to discuss what consultant-driven and social media–enhanced political communication for campaigns and elections is and can be in the second decade of the millennium. Although some of the essays criticize aspects of the process, most simply try to explain what political communication is, what it is not, and how it is done; we invite the reader to retain a critical eye in this light. The contributors range from academics to journalists to political professionals. They are concerned with such diverse enterprises as recounting the history of political consulting in the republic, obtaining free media for their cause or candidate, designing television ads, profiling the Hispanic voter, understanding how the Constitution covers paid political speech, and diagnosing the sometimes tender, sometimes testy relationships between consultants and clients. The essays were solicited from people who have demonstrated considerable expertise in their subjects. Each contributor was mandated to explain in brief but also in detail how a process works. We hope that even so-called experts in one part of the political sphere might learn something from another writer's piece. Keep in mind, however, that the opinions expressed and the methods advocated are those of the individual authors. The reader is encouraged to research a particular topic further before coming to a definite conclusion about it.

But this book is not solely a how-to primer. One goal—not necessarily shared by all the contributors—was to try to establish some facts and truths in an arena of argumentation that often lends itself to hyperbole and fantasy. All would agree that many Americans of varying political persuasions have lost faith in the political system. Simply put, something needs to be done. But before reforms can move forward, we think it necessary to identify the problems we face. Unfortunately, inhibiting the process of problem-solving are several myths about politics and the media. Most of these myths are false at their core, but—like all tall tales—their really interesting feature is their widespread currency.

The first myth is that of the political money-monster. Once upon a time, in this hoary tale, American politics was driven by virtue and reason. Then came the bad money men, and now politics, especially campaigns and elections, is weighed down by filthy lucre. Politicians spend huge sums on television and other media, and special interests have bought control of the government. The ordinary person can no longer influence political events or hope to seek office.

Indeed, there is some truth here. It is extremely difficult to run for higher office in America without an enormous war chest filled with one's own money or that of wealthy friends and partisans. In almost all other aspects, however, the myth is groundless. First, there are more than five hundred thousand elected officials in the United States, which is probably a higher ratio of elected officeholder to citizen than in any other country in the history of the world. To run for offices that matter to a great number of people—school board representative, for example—does not take a venture capital fortune. Moreover, the fact that any man or woman cannot run for the United States Senate on a whim and stand a good chance of being elected is hardly unfortunate. The ballots are already clogged and confused; if for each office we were asked to choose among hundreds of our neighbors, democracy would soon descend into Babel. Nor is it disastrous that Nazis, Know-Nothings, and Leninists cannot find media time and ballot prominence equal to that for Democrats or Republicans.

When people assert that mass-mediated politics costs too much, they do not take into account the relative amount Americans do spend. Much has been made of the fact that in 2008, one candidate, Barack Obama, raised and spent two-quarters of a billion dollars. The truth is that Americans allot more annually to many other consumer products, both indispensable and incidental. A few are worth reviewing, because one can judge the character of a civilization by where it spends its disposable income. In 2008, Americans spent $43.4 billion for books and maps; $20 billion on flowers, seeds, and potted plants; $9.3 billion for admission to motion pictures; $5.4 billion for TV and radio repair. And so on. We are stingy about funding our politics even by government spending standards. For example, in 2007 the United States spent $7.2 billion in foreign assistance to Afghanistan and $6.1 billion for Iraq (not counting military expenditures).

A more revealing comparative statistic is that each year Americans pay about $10 billion for pornography; thus, we spend about ten times as much every two years on porn as we do on campaigns and elections. As Nadine Strossen of the American Civil Liberties Union has wittily noted, this spending does not represent ten perverts shelling out $1 billion a year. In contrast, at most about a third of the billion dollars annually spent on campaigns is directly donated by individuals, which means that the average American gives no more than $2 a year to the political process. In addition, many of the spending restrictions that politicians and consultants work under do not account for more than thirty-five years of inflation, and the spending power of one dollar in 1972 is now about a quarter. We the people are, in a word, underfunding democracy.

Why, in an age of a vastly expanded population that can be reached only through mass media channels, do we still think that candidates can campaign with a couple of dimes, a buckboard, and a barrelhead? The answer is that we have a homespun conviction that politics shouldn't cost anything. A cultural historian might trace this notion back to the Revolutionary era and even earlier, arguing that the frugal American colonists revolted as much at the expenses associated with aristocracy as at unreasonable taxes. Similarly, we as a nation have bridled at Richard Nixon's overdressed White House doorkeepers, Nancy Reagan's new china, and Michelle Obama's trip to Spain. We display equal ire at the expense of $36 million for a New Jersey seat in the United States Senate.

In being outraged, we forget that we are no longer a nation concentrated along the East Coast in thirteen lightly populated states. Mass communication, likewise, no longer consists of the bulk printing of broadsides and their distribution by donkey. We are also slow to see how changes in campaigning—for example, campaign seasons starting ever earlier, super-combined primaries at the national level, demands by media to pay up-front costs for placing ads— have forced candidates to raise more money, sooner. We expect democracy to exist on the cheap, although we should know that it is the very lack of money that causes the most desperation and corruption. Ironically, political consultants bring ruthless efficiency to this impoverished process. They are able, for example, to create a television commercial with not-unpleasing aesthetic properties for about one one-hundredth of the money that the publicists of Toyota and Revlon expend.

That said, politics is and always has been about personality. In most campaign races—at least, those not involving ballot referendums—people vote for people, not for policies. The second-century Greek writer Dio Cassius observed in *Dio's Rome* that "all crowds judge measures by the men who direct them." If you tell, for example, a die-hard Barack Obama supporter that "President Obama recently proposed this," he or she will be more inclined to think favorably of the proposal—whatever it is—than if you introduce it as originating from Glenn Beck or Rush Limbaugh.

But another myth—the "Mr. Smith Goes to Washington" fantasy drawn from the deeper well of the Cincinnatus ideal—holds that these candidates should be what were once called "men of the soil" or "born in a log cabin," that is, unpolitical, unshaped, and unconsulted. Being natural folks, they should eschew modern media trickery and manipulations. We do not impose such primitivism and unprofessionalism on any other occupation, but that seems not to matter. The basic problem is that we live in a mass-mediated age, so compromise must be made with technology to be able to communicate politically. Ronald Reagan had a made-for-the-screen persona, but he always understood the need for memorizing the script, walking through the performance beforehand, and testing the lines. He knew that success in front of a camera was possible only because of the labor and organization of all the elements behind the camera. No one is "natural" on TV. Someone has to be director, gaffer, and best boy.

Then there is the myth of the "out of touch" politician who is beholden to lobbyists and pays no attention to his or her constituents. Anyone who reads these pages or is able to observe the inner workings of political campaigns may easily conclude that exactly the opposite is the case—although the consequences are equally dire. Barack Obama is a good example of the new model politician: he listens. Indeed, consultants and officeholders are very much concerned with what the people think and want. The result—leaders who will not jump ahead of the curve and will not lead in the old-fashioned sense—is problematic. Many important innovations in American democracy, such as civil rights for citizens of sub-Saharan African descent, would have never occurred if many politicians of the time had paid attention only to polls and the weight of constituent mail.

But in expressing cynicism that all politicians are corrupt, and in painting political consultants as viscous opportunists, we are not just casting aspersions but flattering ourselves. While consultants are to blame for much of what is wrong with politics, to say in turn that the people are victims is to subscribe to another myth perpetuated by the whole spectrum of American politics. Moralists on the right claim that Washingtonian immorality stands in stark contrast to the down-home virtues and honesty of the ordinary American. Those on the left contrast "the people" with corrupt politicos and corporate fat cats, as if greed and sloth were traits held only by the powerful. Politicians themselves play along, criticizing each other and even running against their own species with insincere anti-Washington rhetoric. Finally, the American press contributes to the demonizing of political players and their advisers, promoting a commensurate uplifting of the electorate.

In short, nobody dares turn the finger of accusation away from our leaders, journalists, and spinmeisters—the usual suspects—and back toward the ordinary citizens. As the literary scholar and cultural historian Paul Fussell once noted in the debate about high auto-insurance rates, blame will be cast against "greedy" insurance companies, lawyers, politicians, and so on, but no one will boldly suggest that people might try driving more safely. In many public issues, from Social Security to the environment to health-care reform, we demand solutions without sacrifice.

This unwillingness to fault "the people" is traditional and ubiquitous. Charles Mackay, writing in the nineteenth century, described the South Sea bubble—the speculative frenzy that had seized his country of England a hundred years previously—in just such terms. Masses of people, from dukes to butchers, had thrown away their life savings on the promises of unlimited wealth in gold and beaver pelts to be gathered from expeditions to the New World, without any evidence whatsoever that those riches were immediately obtainable. When the bubble collapsed and the English parliament began its investigation of the debacle, the directors of the South Seas Company were vilified. But as Mackay put it so acidly in his 1841 book *Extraordinary Popular Delusions and the Madness of Crowds,* "Nobody blamed the credulity and avarice of the people—the degrading lust of gain, which had swallowed up every nobler quality in the national character, or the infatuation which had made the multitude run their heads with such frantic eagerness into the net held out for them by scheming projectors. These things were never mentioned. The people were a simple, honest, hard-working people, ruined by a gang of robbers, who were to be hanged, drawn, and quartered without mercy." Demonization was—and is—preferable to self-criticism.

We live in analogous circumstances and hold similar prejudices today. Almost all the problems of politics that we decry and that political consultants seem to perpetuate could be solved in a fortnight by an invigorated and self-ennobled American people. If each of us gave $100 a year to the politicians and political causes of our choice, the so-called special interest money would be washed away in the tide, and the fat cats would grow lean on slim pickings. Even twenty hours a year of our time devoted to politics would make a difference when multiplied by the size of the voting population. (More people have attended at least one sporting event than have read a news editorial or voted.) Or, better yet, what if we all took democracy seriously and became an educated electorate, actually thinking about and researching our voting choices?

If we expend only a little money, thought, and time, perhaps we might have people running for office who took virtue, both fiscal and personal, seriously. The famous lament of Cicero was, "Oh, happy Marcus Cato, whom no one dares to try to corrupt!" The Roman senator he envied was legendary for his uprightness, an anomaly in his own time. But such exemplary men and women have always existed, and they can be found both in boardrooms and in bowling alleys. Their rectitude will only be nurtured, and their presence in political life encouraged, by a mass movement of public sentiment and private dollars.

This book, then, can be seen as a corrective to the many myths about modern political campaign communication. We discover in these pages that political communication is a business run mostly by serious and sober people. But we find something else, too. The reader will note the high level of enthusiasm these men and women have about their particular specialties, to the point of believing that "my constituency is the crucial swing vote," or "my campaign communication technique is the most effective." As editors, we toned down such boosterism but did not eliminate it; the reader may judge the wares in this collected marketplace of ideas. In fact, these people keenly believe in what they do: whatever their age, political philosophies, or area of expertise, they are aggressive partisans of their methods and the people they serve. These people are not guns for hire, nor do they engage in campaign practices that are simply the means to collecting exorbitant fees.

It is difficult to claim idealism in politics without inviting laughter. But in these pages you will find civic-minded ideas and commitment, and this is a social good. The solution to the problems of politics and media, if there is one, will not be from the top down. We cannot expect the powers that be to make things better for us, because their urge to satisfy our unreasonable cravings is largely the cause of the present difficulties. No popular movement for political reform can exist, however, without a vanguard of experienced political workers who understand the process and its problems and are willing to collaborate and change for the better. From among the ranks of political consultants, reformers will find opponents, but they will also find their greatest allies.

This book also has a more prosaic agenda. As several writers here mention, and others explore in detail, the pop-culture myth of the political consultant includes images of fame, sex, and cash obtained simply by being spontaneously clever. A quick tongue seems to buy MSNBC guest spots and invitations to Glenlivet-and-cigar parties with the rich and powerful. But these essays emphasize that whatever rewards come to successful political consultants, those rewards are based on the human activity most absent on television: work. In sitcoms about aspiring twenty-somethings in the big city, a preponderance of time seems to be spent chatting in coffeehouses. Likewise, political consultants on TV and in movies are largely represented as bullshit artists whose medium is spin. And spinning seems to be easy—short hours, no heavy lifting.

In outlining here in copious and comprehensive detail some of the varieties of campaign activities, a blow is struck against this myth. What is apparent is how much labor and thought must go into the vast minutiae of political campaign communication. Even if one disagrees with the style and substance of the result, the sweat of the process deserves notice and respect. No one who wastes August, September, and October indulging in the excesses of the seraglio could possibly retain the mental acuity and physical stamina necessary to win a race for one's candidate on the first Tuesday in November. If the reader recognizes this point—that consulting for political campaign communication is a business, and that this business requires industry, economy, concentration, preparation, deliberation, and discipline—then *Political Communication*'s mission is accomplished.

Understanding
the Industry

1

Consultants and Candidates

JOHN FRANZÉN

Political consultants are an unruly lot. We view ourselves as professionals and maintain a professional association, yet literally anyone can adopt the title of consultant and start soliciting clients. Although several universities have programs now in campaign strategy and management, most consultants have no academic training in the profession itself, and many would scoff at the notion that anyone could learn it in school. We've emerged, unlicensed and largely unregulated, from a thousand campaign headquarters, congressional offices, newsrooms, software shops, commercial ad agencies—you name it—united only in our conviction that we can successfully coax the electorate in the right direction, as we see it, and make a buck in the process.

Political consulting is a profession, in other words, that attracts all kinds—and that's as it should be. Our work is democracy, not dentistry, and in a democracy everyone has an equal right to participate.

But that's not to say that everyone is going to succeed. Political consulting is a Darwinian world, one of the few remaining truly free markets, where fortunes can rise and fall with breathtaking speed. No consultant's status is entirely safe, with a perpetual swirl of upstarts promising to do things better, faster, or cheaper. And it's in this boisterous, jostling marketplace that politicians go shopping for professional assistance. There are bound to be some bumps and bruises.

Politicians, of course, live in a state of nature, too. They succeed more by perseverance and cunning than by any formal training, and they can rocket even more spectacularly to fame or into oblivion. Facing the absolute reckoning of election victory or defeat, they go looking for professional guidance with a keen awareness of the stakes—an awareness that sharpens the judgment of some but makes others easy pickings for flimflam artists. In a process that proceeds mostly by word of mouth, smart politicians look for a record of election success and other objective evidence of the consultant's experience, creativity, and judgment. The others get caught up in gadgetry and giveaways, or simply go with who's hot.

Who Gets the Limelight?

We live in a carnival age. The same culture of celebrity that turns ball players into role models and actors into icons can also make stars of consultants. We've seen the awesome ability of television and the Internet to turn our political clients into household names, and it's hardly surprising that many consultants would put those tools to work for themselves.

Of course, going on TV or getting quoted in the paper isn't necessarily a bad thing for a political consultant to do. It's a free country, and all of us need to market ourselves. But our job as consultants is to make stars of our clients. We're paid to make *them* look good, to give *them* the credit, to advance *their* ideas and careers. How is it, then, that some consultants have become more famous than most of the people they work for?

The late, great movie director Alfred Hitchcock had a playful habit of appearing briefly in his own films. We glimpse him in the background, missing a bus in *North by Northwest* or winding a clock in *Rear Window*. But in a troubling number of political campaigns today, old Alfred just keeps showing up. He takes center stage. He explains at great length to the audience how he directed the actors, wrote their best lines, and thought up most of the plot.

Again, self-promotion has its place, but an important line is crossed when the political consultant gets quoted publicly explaining the campaign of his or her client, particularly when the campaign is still underway. Each instance of this becomes a reminder to the newspaper reader or TV viewer that the candidate in question is dependent on professional handlers, generally from out of town. Getting this kind of attention is easy for the consultant—it plays perfectly into the journalist's desire to reveal what's going on behind the scenes—but it reinforces the suspicion among voters that nothing the candidate says or does in public can be taken at face value. In fact, it insults and devalues the candidate and breeds further cynicism toward the political process.

As obvious as this problem ought to be, many politicians continue to hire and rehire consultants who thus discredit and disrespect them. It would make more sense for candidates to demand that their consultants remain essentially anonymous within the context of the campaign.

At the same time, it must be said, consultants can do great things for their clients by providing information and guidance to the press off the record or on background. Indeed, working the press anonymously is often an essential part of building a campaign's credibility and momentum. But the consultant worth hiring is the one who does all this to promote the reputation of the client. The client gets the credit—for the well-turned phrase, the bold strategic move, the sound policy idea—and gets shielded from blame for the mistakes.

Maintaining this self-effacing stance is no small feat. Political reporters today have very little interest in what politicians say on the stump, unless they commit a gaffe, and even less interest in their policy ideas. The words of the candidate or office holder are generally treated as a mere confection of professional advisers, spun from polling data and focus groups. In this atmosphere, the consultant needs extraordinary skill and self-control to be able to shift the focus away from the stage hands to the person out in the spotlight.

Client Overload

The sins of political consultants, unfortunately, don't end with self-aggrandizement. Perhaps our most common failing is to take on more work than we can handle. In political circles, horror stories abound of candidates who hired the big-name firm and then couldn't get that big name on the phone, or found that their TV spots were being produced by college interns. In an industry where the work is so seasonal and where success builds so rapidly on success, getting overextended is a serious occupational hazard.

The wise candidate will look at the consultant's list of clients, including the list from the previous campaign year, and do a little division. Let's see, this firm with three principals handled fifteen congressional campaigns in the last election. That's five campaigns per principal, which means each campaign, in effect, got one day of attention per week, or four days per month. Hmm.

Client overload is driven in part by price competition, which has grown far more intense in recent years as increasing numbers of consultants have entered the business. Consultants who sign up clients by low-balling their prices generally have to make their profit through volume, and the candidates who think they're getting a great deal, as the saying goes, generally get what they pay for. The thoughtful candidate shops for quality and is willing to pay for it, particularly if it comes with a guarantee that the consultant will turn new business away when the plate is full.

Things to Look For

What does quality look like? Again, the consultant's election success rate is a pretty good indicator, but it's not the only measure. A very high winning percentage doesn't mean much if the consultant has worked only for safe incumbents. A lost election may sometimes be viewed as a plus, if the loss was narrow and the odds were long.

It's also wise to scan the consultant's client list for patterns of repetition. If other politicians have hired the consultant back election after election, that's clearly an endorsement, while a string of one-timers is a danger signal. And of course the candidate seeking a consultant should get on the phone to the consultant's former clients—the winners and the losers—and ask for their frank opinion. It's amazing how many candidates don't bother to do this in a systematic way.

Many candidates focus with particular concern on the size of the consulting firm. Is it big enough, they wonder, to be able to handle their campaign and give them the kind of support they need? That's a good question, but it can't be answered simply by counting heads. As noted above, along with the number of individuals in the firm, one has to consider the number of other clients who will be competing for the firm's attention. Also, it's important to remember that a consulting business can be run quite effectively by assembling teams of freelance talent on a project-by-project basis—talent that doesn't appear on the letterhead or fill up space in the office.

This more free-form approach to the management of a consulting business has particular advantages if the consultant works in many different parts of the country. Why, for example, should a media consultant based in Washington, D.C., have to fly a salaried employee to California to scout locations for filming when California has hundreds of available scouts who actually know the territory? As a firm believer in the small-is-beautiful approach to political consulting, I've developed working relationships over the years with dozens of such freelancers around the country to whom I can turn on short notice. This not only helps me hit the ground running; it allows me to turn a profit without having to charge an arm and a leg to cover permanent overhead. Again, it's essential to talk with the consultant's former clients and ask whether they got the support and attention they needed, irrespective of how big or small the consultant's firm appears to be.

The most important factors in judging the quality of a consultant, of course, are also the hardest to quantify. In particular, there's the matter of creative talent. Like pornography, it can't really be defined but we recognize it when we see it—or at least we ought to recognize it. Candidates and campaign managers do have an unfortunate tendency to talk about "media" as if it were an undifferentiated commodity, like soybeans. To achieve a particular effect, it's said, you need to air this many gross rating points of media. But we know very well that some TV and radio ads have no impact at all, no matter how many times they're aired, while others can shift public attitudes dramatically with only a few repetitions. The candidate who hires mediocre creative talent in order to save a little money is generally wasting money by the bushel.

And finally there's the matter of personal chemistry and trust. Hiring a campaign consultant means placing a very large part of your life and career, and a whole lot of money, in someone else's hands. You'd better feel some basic confidence in that person's character and judgment. Together, you're going to walk through fire.

While there's no completely foolproof way to know that a consultant is a person of integrity, the careful checking of references is obviously a must. The campaign should also check to see whether the consultant is a member of the American Association of Political Consultants. Every AAPC member has pledged in writing to abide by the organization's code of professional ethics, which covers basic matters such as truth in billing and client confidentiality.

Foibles of Candidates

A campaign can be reduced to misery not only by inept or unprincipled consultants. Candidates and their staffs are human too, and their failings are just as numerous. The extraordinary pressure of an election campaign, with political life or death looming at the ballot box, often drives candidates crazy, particularly if it's their first time around.

A common candidate syndrome is the compulsive refusal to delegate decisions. Obviously, the candidate should insist on signing off on the big ones, such as which issues to run on, but a depressing number of candidates just can't resist rewriting the ad copy or niggling endlessly over the logo. I once had a candidate who personally had to choose the type fonts for the campaign brochure. At some point in such situations the consultant has to stop and ask: If you can do it better yourself, why did you hire me? And if the problem persists, the consultant should be prepared to resign. In an election campaign the most precious commodity of all, after money, is the candidate's time. It has to be conserved and directed toward things that only the candidate can do.

At the other extreme, and more rare, are candidates so stricken with the fear of defeat that they throw themselves blindly on the expertise of their handlers, expecting to be told at every turn what to say and do and believe. In all my years in the business, I've had to deal with only one serious case of this. The candidate asked me up front simply to create an image for him that would sell and he would go along with it. I did my best for him but the voters knew better, and he lost.

There are still other candidates who jump into a campaign and then realize they hate it, but can't bring themselves to back out. They decide instead to lose, and they proceed, either consciously or not, to do things that are clearly stupid and self-destructive. I've had three such candidates in my time. Two of them succeeded in losing. The third we were able to surround and protect from himself. Once in office, he decided he liked it and became a pretty good legislator.

A variation on deciding to lose is the candidate who refuses to raise money. This is a widespread syndrome, and one with which I can sympathize. I wouldn't trust a candidate who actually enjoys begging for money from people who generally want to see some specific benefit in return, and I think our campaign finance system should be radically reformed to break the hold that big contributors now enjoy. But until we achieve that goal, candidates must work within the system we have and must face the fact that contributors expect to be asked by the candidate. It's standard procedure in any campaign to assign large, daily blocks of time on the candidate's schedule to fundraising, but simply putting those phone calls on the schedule is no guarantee that they're going to be made. The reluctant candidate can find endless excuses to avoid them. In campaign after campaign, in my experience, staff members and fundraising consultants have had to dog the candidate endlessly in order to make the calls happen.

The unpleasantness of this exercise can lead candidates and their fundraising assistants to resent the staffers and consultants who get to spend the money. Why should you have all the fun, they seem to say, while we go through this ordeal? They often harbor the suspicion that the money they've raised through blood, sweat and tears is being wasted—which sometimes, unfortunately, is true.

And finally, no discussion of candidate foibles would be complete without a mention of the occasional candidate's spouse (or brother or uncle or other family member) who uses that privileged position to keep the campaign in perpetual chaos and crisis. Over late-night drinks at the bar, political consultants vie to top each other with these stories. The father of one of my candidates, who had held public office himself a generation earlier, became so convinced that his son's strategy and message were mistaken that he sneaked into campaign headquarters one day and carted away all the literature. Other consultants tell of candidate spouses who repeatedly sabotaged the campaign by wandering wildly off message out on the stump. Human nature being what it is, some of this rogue behavior is probably inevitable, but candidates can help to minimize it by carefully working things through with their families before ever deciding to run and by making it abundantly clear to them who's going to be managing the campaign.

It must also be noted that a candidate's spouse can be a huge campaign asset. Bill Clinton would never have survived the New Hampshire presidential primary in 1992, when stories of his alleged philandering and Vietnam-era draft avoidance erupted, if it hadn't been for the steely resolve of his wife, Hillary. And he did his level best to return the favor in 2008—sometimes overdoing the public enthusiasm, perhaps, but raising the millions of dollars from his fundraising network without which her campaign could not have continued beyond its crushing defeat in the Iowa caucuses.

Money Troubles

With campaigns having grown so expensive, it's not surprising that many of the difficulties that arise between consultants and their clients revolve around money. Misunderstandings can often occur simply because the terms of the candidate/consultant relationship have not been spelled out clearly in advance. It's also important for the candidate to have some understanding of how the consulting business works. I don't have the space here to explicate every branch of the profession, but a brief look at the financial side of my own branch may be helpful.

A political media consulting firm is essentially an advertising agency, and we tend to charge for our services in the same three ways that agencies do. First, there are creative and consulting fees. Some media consultants will bill these fees on an hourly basis or a fee-per-spot basis, but most will simply set a fixed creative fee at the beginning of the campaign, payable in regular installments, sometimes with a victory bonus.

Second, there's the commission on the airtime buy. The standard agency commission is 15 percent of the gross airtime cost—the TV or radio station bills the agency based on the gross rate and expects payment of the "net," which is 85 percent of the gross. But that 15 percent differential isn't written in stone, and high-dollar campaigns can often persuade the consulting firm to reduce its commission and plow the savings back into the campaign.

Finally, there are production mark-ups. It's a common practice for ad agencies to mark up their production and other expense reimbursement billings by a certain percentage, although some agencies will conveniently neglect to identify this charge as a separate line item. As with fees and commissions, however, there's no absolute rule governing whether or how to charge mark-ups. In my own firm, we generally don't charge them to candidates. Some media consultants, I'm told, do charge but manage to hide them.

So clearly there's no one correct formula for structuring the media consultant's compensation package. The three ways of billing should be seen as interdependent variables. But it is essential to understand the options and to spell out the arrangement in writing.

Of course, getting it in writing doesn't exempt a campaign and its consultants from any further difficulties over money. The spending of large amounts of cash very rapidly in what amounts to a life-or-death struggle is inherently stressful. While every good campaign begins with an agreed-upon budget, that document is only a starting point. Candidate campaigns are tremendously fluid, requiring dozens of revisions of the budget based on fast-breaking political developments and uneven rates of fundraising success, and these decisions must always involve a certain amount of guesswork. All the more important, then, that candidates hire consultants who've been through this experience before and whose former clients can attest to their skill and judgment.

Getting Paid

A common money problem for consultants in campaigns is the basic matter of getting paid. Just because there's a signed contract saying the consultant will receive X dollars on a specific schedule doesn't necessarily mean it's going to happen. Again and again one hears of the consultant who gets caught up in the spirit of a difficult race, extends some credit and then some more, and in the end the candidate loses. At that point, the candidate can't raise money, the campaign committee shuts down, and the consultant is left high and dry.

How is it possible that so many consultants who seem otherwise bright and resourceful get caught so often in this position? The principal reason, I think, is that most people in political consulting simply aren't motivated, or at least weren't motivated originally, chiefly by business considerations. I know this runs counter to the stereotype of consultants as sharks and high-rollers. But the truth is, most of us got into politics to advance a particular cause or point of view, and we discovered only later and to our surprise that people might actually pay us to do this. Having entered in that frame of mind, it's not surprising that we sometimes have trouble with the realities of operating as a business.

At any rate, the wise consultant will do some things to make payment a whole lot more likely. One can specify, for example, that some part of the fee must be paid in advance, and the subsequent installments can be structured to make the final payment come due before the end of the campaign—before the last of the work is due. This will give the consultant some leverage for prying loose that final payment, which is often the big one. The consultant can also insist on receiving payments in advance to cover major expenditures, such as TV production. The process of obtaining an advance, which generally involves the presentation of a budget, will also help to ensure that the client really understands what's involved in the production effort—reducing the likelihood of complaints at the end of the line that a particular item wasn't approved or seems way too expensive.

But perhaps the most effective thing consultants can do to ensure that they're going to get paid is to get the personal signature of the candidate on the contract. Losing campaign committees generally go out of existence. Losing candidates don't. The smart consultant always insists on having the candidate's personal commitment, in writing, to fulfill the payment terms if the campaign committee is unable to do so. This little addendum to the contract has a wonderful way of focusing the candidate's attention on the campaign's payment obligations and can actually help motivate fundraising.

Occasionally, it must be noted, a consultant doesn't get paid because the client sincerely believes that payment isn't deserved. The work was shoddy, perhaps, or it arrived late, or the consultant mishandled funds. And occasionally, too, an unprincipled client simply decides to stiff the consultant—authorizing a major expenditure, for example, with an assurance that the check is in the mail when it isn't. Far more often, however, the client who fails to pay the consultant does so with the best of intentions. It's simply a matter of the dynamics of the campaign having gotten out of hand, with the campaign manager or the consultant or both having allowed their high hopes to overrule their better judgment. In the well-run campaign, the manager and the consultant are making regular reality checks and adjusting their spending plans accordingly in order to keep from falling short.

Working Together

A campaign, after all, is a collaborative enterprise, and it's far more likely to succeed when there's an atmosphere of mutual trust and respect. The odds of maintaining such an atmosphere are greatly increased when lines of decision-making authority have been clearly established up front and when consultant, candidate and campaign manager have a clear appreciation of each other's roles and responsibilities.

There's a natural tendency for on-site managers and other campaign staff to feel some suspicion or even resentment toward the consultant who comes in from the airport and tells the locals what to do. The locals, very often, are working outrageous hours for very low pay, while the consultant makes comparatively big bucks. But if the candidate and staff don't feel the consultant is worth the bucks, they should hire someone else who is, not go around griping about the unfairness of it all. They should also bear in mind that the consultant works long hours, too, and has to pay rent, staff, and other overhead that continues beyond the election. Many's the consultant who ends a campaign season feeling quite fat but who's starving by the start of the next one.

But the great sweetener in this process—the thing that smoothes out the bumps and heals the bruises of a stressful, exhausting campaign—is the prospect of ultimate victory. Achieving that goal makes everyone feel like a hero and has a wonderful way of erasing bad memories of turf battles and arguments over money. Working together and giving everything you've got to succeed in a noble cause may not be the only thing in life, but it does beat everything else.

2

A Brief History of Political Advertising on Television

DARRELL M. WEST

Television advertising in presidential campaigns got its start in 1952. Simplistic by contemporary standards, early political spots often took the form of footage from press conferences or testimonials from prominent citizens. Many of Eisenhower's "I Like Ike" and his "Talks to America" commercials were reels in which the candidate looked straight into the camera and spoke for thirty or sixty seconds, without any cuts, graphics, animation, or mixing of many shots from different locations and events.

Contemporary ads, in contrast, are visually exciting. Technological advances allow ad producers to use colorful images and sophisticated editing techniques to make spots more compelling. Images can be spliced together to link one visual image with another. Animated images can visually morph one person into another in a split second. It is the norm to use catchy visuals, music, and color to capture the viewer's attention and convey political messages.

These changes have generated a dramatic growth in the use of advertising as a communications tool. Ads now constitute about 60 percent of the budget for major presidential candidates. Not only are television spots the largest single expenditure in campaigns, they are a major source of information for voters and a tool for influencing the way reporters cover political races.

Ads can be used for a variety of purposes, from undermining political opponents by associating them with unfavorable visual images to enhancing the candidates' appeal by associating them with positive images such as flag and family. In addition, ads influence patterns of media coverage. One of the most striking developments of recent years has been the increasing coverage of political advertising by reporters. The increase in news coverage of advertising has blurred or even eliminated the past division between the free (news) and paid (advertisement) media representations of campaigns and elections.

It is now common for network news programs to rebroadcast ads that are entertaining, provocative, or controversial.

Ads that are broadcast for free during the news or discussed in major newspapers have a clear advantage over those aired purely as commercials. Viewers traditionally have trusted the news media—far more than paid ads— for fairness and objectivity. William McGuire has shown that the credibility of the source is one determinant of whether the message is believed. Because of the high credibility of the media, ads aired during the news have an important advantage over those seen as overt commercials.

Johnson's "Daisy" Ad in 1964

Nothing illustrates the emergence of advertising as an effective political tactic better than the 1964 Daisy spot, which is arguably the most infamous ad in television history. The ad, designed by Tony Schwartz, opens with a little girl standing in a meadow plucking petals from a daisy. After she counts "1, 2, 3, 4, 5, 7, 6, 6, 8, 9, 9," an ominous voice begins its own countdown: "10, 9, 8, 7, 6, 5, 4, 3, 2, 1, 0." At zero, the picture of the child dissolves and a mushroom cloud fills the screen. President Lyndon Johnson's voice closes the ad by warning, "These are the stakes. To make a world in which all of God's children can live, or to go into the dark. We must either love each other or we must die."

This ad aired only once, during NBC's *Monday Night at the Movies* showing of *David and Bathsheba* on September 7, 1964. Condemnation of the spot came almost immediately. Bill Moyers, then Johnson's press secretary, recounted, "The president called me and said, 'Holy shit. I'm getting calls from all over the country.' Most of them said that it was an effective ad. Others said they didn't like it." Press reaction was swift. According to Lloyd Wright, an advertising strategist for Johnson, "The first night it aired, it created such a media flap that the next night it was used in its entirety on the newscasts on all three networks."

Even though the spot was never rebroadcast as a commercial, news reporters included it in news stories and thereby assured it a wide audience. In conjunction with other Democratic ads suggesting that Barry Goldwater, the Republican candidate for president, was an unstable extremist not to be trusted with America's future, the Daisy ad helped Johnson achieve a landslide victory. The effort dramatically demonstrated the emerging new era of campaign communications.

Bush's "Revolving Door" Ad in 1988

George Bush's Revolving Door ad illustrates how, in conjunction with clever stage management, commercials can take an issue at the edge of public concern and make it the focal point of a campaign. Visually, the ad was simple but striking: criminals entering and then immediately exiting a prison through its revolving door. CBS first covered this commercial in its broadcast on October 7, 1988. (News stories about convicted criminal Willie Horton—who had been released on a prison furlough program and shortly thereafter arrested for a newly committed crime—had been broadcast on September 22.) The story described the commercial as an ad that highlighted the prison furlough policy of Massachusetts governor Michael Dukakis. Clifford Barnes and Donna Cuomo, victims of an assault by a convict who had been released on a weekend furlough, were reported to be participating in a speaking tour with a pro-Bush group. Bush, meanwhile, was shown campaigning with police officers.

A related CBS story followed on October 20, this time detailing Horton's crime record and supplying background on the Bush ad. Bush was shown campaigning in New York City at a police union rally. It was not until October 24 and 25—almost three weeks after the commercial first appeared—that critics of the Revolving Door ad appeared on the news to claim that it contained racist undertones. But in keeping with the horse-race mentality of the media, a second story on October 25 also quoted Tony Schwartz as saying that Bush's ads were successful and that the Revolving Door ad was particularly effective.

The contrast with the coverage of Johnson's Daisy ad was stark. Whereas the 1964 ad was immediately condemned and removed from the airwaves, reporters in 1988 treated the furlough ad as a genuine news story. Criticisms came late and were never solidly addressed; the spot was not pulled off the air. More important, news stories during that election season emphasized the effectiveness of negative ads or commented on how such ads were increasingly acceptable to the public. Finally, some analysts even attributed Bush's lead in the polls to the success of his negative commercials and the lack of an appropriate and timely response by Dukakis.

This tolerance of negativity, combined with the grudging respect reporters accorded to effective GOP ads, created a pattern of coverage that assisted Bush. Whereas reporters in 1964 had condemned the Daisy ad, journalists in 1988 did not complain when the Revolving Door commercial stayed on the air. They even rebroadcast the ad repeatedly throughout the last month of the campaign. This treatment gave Bush more air time and therefore lent him more credibility than any campaign organization alone could have managed. The news media helped make Bush's 1988 advertising campaign one of the most effective efforts of the past twenty years.

Clinton Contrast Ads in 1996

By the 1990s, after several elections filled with attack ads, voters were growing weary of campaign negativity. Ever sensitive to changing voter sentiments in this regard, the Bill Clinton campaign made effective use of contrast ads, which simultaneously criticized Clinton's opponents and explained how Clinton would address voters' concerns.

Both Clinton and Robert Dole, each having wrapped up his party's nomination, aired commercials throughout March, April, May, and June attacking each other. Clinton tied Dole to Newt Gingrich and accused the pair of gutting Medicare, Medicaid, education, and the environment. Dole, for his part, questioned the president's trustworthiness in light of the Whitewater allegations concerning Clinton's real estate and financial transactions in Arkansas.

Clinton won the spring phase of this campaign. By June 1996, according to a CBS News/*New York Times* poll, he had a lead of 54 to 35 percent among registered voters and was viewed more favorably than Dole. Whereas 48 percent viewed the president favorably and 33 percent viewed him unfavorably, Dole had a favorability rating of 29 percent and an unfavorability rating of 35 percent. By early October, Dole's unfavorability rating had risen to 41 percent, while his favorability rating remained at 29 percent. Clinton was viewed favorably by 47 percent and unfavorably by 36 percent. His lead was 53 to 36 percent.

But more surprising was how well Clinton did in the blame game. When asked in May 1996 whether the candidates were spending more time explaining their views or attacking the opponent, 32 percent of voters said that Dole was explaining his views and 48 percent believed he was attacking his opponent. In Clinton's case, 53 percent thought he was explaining his views and only 28 percent felt he was attacking his opponent.

By the last week of the campaign, 55 percent felt that Dole was attacking his opponent, 21 percent believed Clinton was doing so, and 21 percent thought Reform Party candidate Ross Perot's ads were attack spots. When asked who was most responsible for the negative campaigning that year, 52 percent cited Dole, 13 percent Clinton, and 6 percent Perot.

As they had done successfully in 1992, the Clinton team used an inocula-tion strategy to warn people that Republicans would launch "a relentless at-tack" of negative advertising and misinformation. Speaking before a thousand Democratic women at Emily's List (a women's pro-choice political caucus), First Lady Hillary Clinton predicted: "Get prepared for it and don't be sur-prised by it. When you've got no vision of how to make the world a better place for yourself or your children, then you go negative." After Dole did go negative in the fall, Clinton adviser George Stephanopoulos explained Dole's public persona to a newspaper reporter: "All you ever see him doing on TV is carping, attacking, whining."

The Clinton staff shielded themselves from the backlash against negative campaigning by employing contrast ads. Recognizing that voters did not ap-prove of negative advertising, the Clinton ads combined negative and positive appeals. One example is an ad Clinton ran as a response to Dole's attack on Clinton's drug record. The ad criticized both Dole for opposing the creation of a drug czar and Congress for cutting monies for school drug prevention programs, but it then went on to explain that Clinton had sought to strengthen school programs and had expanded the death penalty to include drug kingpins. By using attack ads as a surgical tool, not as a sledgehammer, the Clinton cam-paign attached negatives to the opponent while sheltering itself from blame by voters upset about highly critical ads.

Bush and National Security

The 2004 campaign agenda focused on terrorism and national security. American elections typically center much more on domestic than foreign policy considerations. But the September 11, 2001, terrorist attacks in New York City and the subsequent wars with Afghanistan and Iraq placed foreign policy directly onto the political agenda. In terms of campaign-related topics, President George W. Bush attempted to portray Democrat John Kerry as a flip-flopping liberal out of touch with the American mainstream.

In early advertising, Bush complained that Kerry would penalize drivers with a 50-cent-a-gallon gasoline tax, would "raise taxes by at least $900 billion," would "weaken the Patriot Act used to arrest terrorists," opposed "body armor for troops in combat," and "opposed weapons vital to winning the war on terror: Bradley Fighting Vehicles, Patriot missiles, B-2 stealth bombers, F-18 fighter jets." A Bush spokesperson justified these attacks by saying that "Kerry sailed through the Democratic primary process with little or no scrutiny. In order to make an informed judgment about whether Kerry is a suitable choice for president, voters need to have this information." The Kerry campaign saw a more nefarious motive. Strategist Michael Donilon complained that Bush staffers "have decided that the only way to win this election is to destroy John Kerry."

In the fall, Bush attempted to maintain the focus on terrorism. One of his more provocative ads was called "Wolves." In it, a wolf runs through a forest, while a female announcer warns, "In an increasingly dangerous world, even after the first terrorist attack on America, John Kerry and the liberals in Congress voted to slash America's intelligence budget by $6 billion. Cuts so deep they would have weakened America's defenses. [Image of a pack of wolves resting on a hill.] And weakness attracts those who are waiting to do America harm."

Not to be outdone by animal imagery, Kerry started broadcasting an ad featuring an eagle and an ostrich. The voiceover said, "The eagle soars high above the earth. The ostrich buries its head in the sand. The eagle can see everything for miles around. The ostrich? Can't see at all. . . . Given the choice, in these challenging times, shouldn't we be the eagle again?"

Within a day, individuals outside the Kerry campaign had put up a new website entitled WolfpacksforTruth.org, which advertised the "real story" on Bush's Wolves commercial. Taking on the voice of the wolves, the site explained that the wolves were tricked by George W. Bush: "They told us we were shooting a Greenpeace commercial! When the camera crew showed up, we wondered why they were all driving Hummers. . . . Little did we know we were being tricked into this vicious campaign attack ad! We are not Terrorists! . . . We are a peaceful pack of wolves. All we want in life is: Live in tree-filled forests. Drink clean water from our rivers and streams. Breathe fresh and clean air."

By election day, though, it was clear how much Bush's effort at focusing the agenda on terrorism and moral values had paid off for him. National exit polls revealed a clear tie between seeing particular issues as most important and voting for the president. Bush won 85 percent of the votes of those who cited terrorism as their most important issue, compared to 15 percent for Kerry. Seventy-eight percent of those naming moral values as their most important consideration in the election cast ballots for Bush, compared to 19 percent who did so for Kerry. In contrast, Kerry's top issues were the economy and jobs (he received 81 percent of the vote of individuals saying this was their most important issue), education (76 percent of their vote), and Iraq (75 percent).

It's Still the Economy, Stupid

The 2008 agenda saw the country's financial meltdown and weak economy return to the forefront. In the spring of that year, when asked to identify the most important problem then facing the country, Americans named the economy, followed by the war in Iraq, health care, and high gas prices. But by October, when the market slid into negative economic growth, all eyes centered almost solely on the domestic economy.

Barack Obama's early ads focused on his record as having emphasized ethics reform and having worked in a bipartisan fashion. One spot, known as "America's Leadership," focused on the then-senator's bipartisan work with GOP senator Richard Lugar of Indiana. Obama's commercials complained that the Republican nominee, Senator John McCain of Arizona, had accepted contributions from big oil companies and then had turned around and proposed major tax cuts for them. His ad "Pocket" ended with the memorable tagline, "After one president in the pocket of big oil, we can't afford another."

By October, though, Obama had shifted to traditional Democratic issues such as the economy, health care, and education. With the stock market having fallen by more than 40 percent and unemployment rising, his campaign broadcast ads showing how voters in large industrial states such as Ohio and Pennsylvania were suffering from hard times. People's health care benefits were suffering, and jobs were being shipped overseas. Complaining about McCain's shifting stance on fiscal matters, Obama's ads argued that McCain was "erratic" and had "careened from stance to stance." The result, according to the Illinois senator, was that his counterpart from Arizona had "poured gasoline on the economic mess."

For his part, McCain sought to distract people from the dismal economic news by tying Obama to controversial figures such as alleged 1960s-era terrorist William Ayres, convicted Chicago financier Tony Rezko, and Chicago political machine fixture William Daley. The spot ended with the tagline of "With friends like that, Obama is not ready to lead." Another McCain commercial, called "Dangerous," alleged that Obama was a somewhat dodgy individual who did not support American troops. An announcer ominously claimed that Obama was "too risky for America."

By the end of the campaign, McCain employed a man named Joe Wurzelbacher, who he called "Joe the Plumber," to make the point that taxes would increase for middle-class workers if Obama were elected president. One ad took footage of an encounter between Obama and Wurzelbacher to criticize Obama's response that he would "spread the wealth" around and benefit everyone. This ad ended by saying, "Barack Obama: Higher Taxes. More Spending. Not Ready." However, these attacks were not successful, and Obama ended up winning a comfortable victory.

Internet Ads

Recent elections have introduced a new type of political communication: information and ads delivered via candidate websites on the Internet, where interested browsers could read full-text speeches, detailed biographies, discussions of policy positions, and copies of press releases.

All of the candidates in 2000 used video-streaming technology to post television spots on their websites, allowing viewers with video players and sound cards to watch ads that were broadcast over the airwaves. Many of the candidates even placed video from speeches and webcasts onto their websites for later viewing by voters. These website ads displayed the same mix of positive and negative advertising as found on television. This was a significant change from 1996, when website ads tended to be more positive than television spots.

By 2004, candidates were using their websites in the same way as they did television spots: to present a blend of attacks on the opposition along with positive statements about their own programs. The biggest shift from earlier years was in the large number of attack ads featured on both the Bush and Kerry websites. Both candidates used the Internet to publicize hard-hitting attacks on the opposition.

As with television advertising, though, the organizations running the most negative websites were the mainstream political parties and special-interest groups. For example, the RNC had a "Kerryopoly" game on its site, in which players moved pieces around a board showing Kerry's five homes and various luxury possessions. Meanwhile, the DNC had a feature called "Bush Record Exposed" on its website that listed his "Top 10 Lies," "Top 10 Flip-Flops," and "Top 5 Scandals."

In a twist on past elections, Bush's site presented a "Kerry Gas Tax Calculator" that estimated how much more money people would pay at the pump if Kerry's 50-cent-a-gallon proposal were enacted into law. The calculator asked people in which state they lived and how many miles they drove in an average week and then computed how much a gas tax increase would cost them. People could also forward a link to the calculator to someone else via e-mail so that individual could determine his or her own increase.

Bush's website also had an animation game called "John Kerry's Flip Flop Olympics," in which players were asked to name Kerry's positions on improving education, tax relief, and Iraq. After allowing visitors to indicate how Kerry had voted and what statements they believed he had made on these issues, the game listed what it said were Kerry's contradictory positions over the years.

Kerry's website emphasized "A Fresh Start for America." It explained how to volunteer for his campaign, recruit fellow voters, and organize local events. Visitors could contribute to campaign blogs and learn about a Kerry's position on a variety of issues. There also was a Rapid Response Center on the site, which provided answers to GOP criticisms of and attacks on Kerry. Another section featured a link titled "Bush-Cheney: Wrong for America," which accused Bush of leading one of the most negative campaigns in history.

Neither candidate devoted much money to running ads on commercial websites. According to a study by the Pew Internet & American Life Project, Kerry and Bush spent less than $2 million on Internet advertising, a small proportion of their overall campaign expenditures. Kerry spent around $1.5 million, or about three times as much as Bush, who expended around $500,000.

The 2008 presidential contest became America's first truly digital campaign, much as 1960 represented our first television election. Digital communications came into their own, in both good and bad ways. On the positive side, the candidates (especially Obama) used the Internet to raise record amounts of money. Both nominees also placed nearly all their advertisements on their websites, allowing voters to see the spots either on television or online. This helped free campaign communications from television stations and gave candidates much greater freedom over paid advertising. It helped to nationalize campaign advertising since voters were no longer dependent on local television stations for candidate commercials but could see ads at the candidate websites as well as a variety of news and entertainment outlets (including YouTube.com).

Another charge that came up in regard to Obama was that he was a tax-and-spend liberal who would raise middle-class taxes. In the closing weeks of the general election, McCain repeated this complaint repeatedly in ads and debates, as well as on the campaign trail. One ad, called "Tax Cutter," showed footage of Obama claiming that "I'm a tax cutter." The voiceover rejects that characterization, claiming that Obama voted 94 times for higher taxes. The spot then showed newspaper headlines describing higher taxes and spending by Democrats. It closed by saying, "Congressional liberals. The truth hurts . . . [long pause] you."

Obama defended himself from the higher taxes argument by setting up a website with a tax-cut calculator. On this site, he asked people to enter their income, marital status, and number of children. The calculator then generated voters' estimated tax amounts under his plan versus that of McCain. This website, TaxCutFacts.org, generated thousands of hits during the closing days of the campaign and helped Obama rebut the tax increase claim. By the end of the campaign, national polls showed that Obama successfully had reduced the confidence gap between him and McCain on the tax issue.

SUGGESTED READINGS

Franz, Michael, Paul Freedman, and Kenneth Goldstein. *Campaign Advertising and American Democracy.* Philadelphia: Temple University Press, 2008.

Geer, John. *In Defense of Negativity: Attack Ads in Presidential Campaigns.* Chicago: University of Chicago Press, 2006.

Graber, Doris, Denis McQuail, and Pippa Norris, eds. *The Politics of News.* Washington, D.C.: Congressional Quarterly Press, 2008.

McGuire, William. "Persuasion, Resistance, and Attitude Change." In Ithiel de Sola Pool, ed., *Handbook of Communication.* Chicago: Rand McNally, 1973.

Robinson, Michael. "Public Affairs Television and the Growth of Political Malaise." *American Political Science Review* 70 (1976): 409–32.

West, Darrell M. *Air Wars: Television Advertising in Election Campaigns, 1952–2008.* 5th ed. Washington, D.C.: Congressional Quarterly Press, 2009.

West, Darrell M., and Burdette A. Loomis. *The Sound of Money: How Political Interests Get What They Want.* New York: Norton, 1999.

3

Political Communication Center

LYNDA LEE KAID

The Political Communication Center (PCC) is an interdisciplinary unit at the University of Oklahoma that coordinates academic degree programs in political communication, facilitates research projects, sponsors conferences, oversees archival collections, and provides service to the academic and professional communities interested in political communication, political advertising, and political debates.

The PCC sponsors the Josh Lee Lecture Series, which focuses on the art of oratory. It honors Josh Lee, a former U.S. senator from Oklahoma and former chair of the university's Department of Communication.

The archival collections of the PCC serve as important historical repositories for political materials. Containing over 90,000 items, the Julian P. Kanter Political Commercial Archive is the world's largest collection of political radio and television commercials. The major purpose of the archive is to preserve these valuable historical materials and to make them available for scholarly and professional use.

Originally founded in 1956 by a private collector, Julian P. Kanter, and housed at the University of Oklahoma since 1985, the archive collects, preserves, and catalogs an ever-increasing number of political commercials and related materials. It maintains a strict preservation and access environment for the materials it preserves, including climate and humidity controls for preservation and adherence to Library of Congress cataloging standards. The collection has operated for many years with the endorsements of the National Archives, the Library of Congress, the American Film Institute, the American Association of Advertising Agencies, the Republican and Democratic national committees, and the American Association of Political Consultants.

The PCC also maintains collections of other political communication materials, including an archive of televised political debates, a collection of international political television programs, and a small number of print political advertising items.

Contents of the Collections

The commercials in the archive date back to 1936 for radio and 1950 for television. All levels of races are included: presidential, U.S. senatorial, U.S. congressional, gubernatorial, state legislative, other statewide offices, county and municipal, judicial, school board, and so on. The archive has materials from all 50 states and some foreign countries. It also contains advertisements for and against ballot issues (or propositions) and an increasing number of advocacy commercials that deal with public and social-policy questions, commercials by political action committees, and advertisements sponsored by corporations and special-interest groups on public issues. Many of the items in the archive are one-of-a-kind copies and are no longer available through any other source.

The commercials vary in length from very short spots to program lengths of 30 or 60 minutes. The original masters of the spots are on a number of formats, including audio tape, 16mm film, 2-inch videotape, 3/4-inch videocassette, 1-inch videotape, and 1/2-inch videocassette.

The televised debate archive contains copies of debates from all presidential elections, as well as from many state and local campaigns. The international collections includes political programs and debates from Britain, Germany, France, Italy, Romania, Bulgaria, Japan, Korea, Chile, Poland, Russia, Turkey, Thailand, and many other countries.

Access to the Collections

Users can locate items in the collections in one of four ways. First, the PCC has published a printed catalog, *The Political Communication Center: A Catalog and Guide to the Archival Collections*, by Lynda Lee Kaid, Kathleen J. M. Haynes, and Charles E. Rand (Norman: University of Oklahoma, Political Communication Center, 1996). Second, the PCC sends electronic versions of its holdings, according to Library of Congress cataloging standards, to the OCLC Union Catalog. These listings are available in libraries throughout the world. The catalog and OCLC access provide general information on the holdings for a particular candidate or entity, and these listings only include material up to the early 1990s. Third, an online catalog is available at the PCC's website: ou.edu/ pccenter/catalog.htm. In the online catalog, campaign spots can be located through an alphabetical listing of candidates. In addition, the catalog includes the election year the spot aired, the state and office for which the candidate was running, the candidate's party, and other identifying information. Fourth, the PCC maintains an on-site computer database for more detailed analysis of each item in the collection. The on-site database details the characteristics of each individual commercial or program by candidate, political party, year, state, type of election, type of commercial, issues contained in the commercial, gender of the candidate, and many other attributes.

Because the University of Oklahoma is a public educational institution, its collections are open and available for use on-site during the normal operating hours of the University of Oklahoma. However, the archive does adhere to any restrictions placed on access to specific materials by the donor of those materials. Very few archival holdings are subject to such donor restrictions. No spots or other holdings are available for online access.

For most users, access is available only to copies of the materials and primarily on-site. No originals are available for routine usage. For this reason, advance consultation with the archive staff can provide information on the most efficient methods of providing for a particular user's needs. This is particularly true if a user's needs involve extensive compilations of materials that span several time periods or campaigns. In unusual cases, copies of materials may be rented to off-site users at a cost necessary to cover staff time, equipment usage, and supplies. Such off-site compilations usually contain no more than 20 spots and no more than 5 spots for any one candidate. All usage and copying of archive materials are subject to adherence to federal copyright laws. Additional fees and restrictions apply for commercial users who wish to re-broadcast spots.

When the archive provides materials for off-site use, the user is given rental copies of the materials only, and these copies must be returned within the specified time, usually 30 days. The user must provide assurances to the archive that materials will not be used in any unauthorized ways. It is the express policy of the archive that its materials will not be used in any way to bring disrespect, ridicule, or misrepresentation to the candidates or producers of the commercials it preserves.

For further information about the Political Communication Center or the archives, interested users should contact:

Political Communication Center
University of Oklahoma
610 Elm Avenue, Burton Hall 113
Norman, OK 73019-3141
Telephone: (405) 325-3114
Fax: (405) 325-1566
ou.edu/pccenter

Laws and Regulations

4

Political Advertising and the First Amendment

LOUIS A. DAY

During the 2007 Louisiana gubernatorial campaign, the state's Democratic Party aired a television spot accusing Republican candidate Bobby Jindal, a Catholic, of calling Protestants "scandalous, depraved, selfish, and heretical." The ad precipitated a political firestorm and calls from the GOP to take the ad off the air. Even veteran political commentators, usually impervious to the incivility of modern political campaigning, questioned whether the ad went too far and whether it accurately reflected Jindal's religious views. Republicans and the head of a national Catholic organization labeled the ad a smear.

A year earlier, Democratic incumbent Michael Dvorak, the public prosecutor for St. Joseph County, Indiana, sought an injunction against his Republican challenger, Greg Kauffman, to halt a 30-second television ad that Dvorak claimed falsely accused him of violating the law by hiring his wife to work in his office. Dvorak maintained that hiring his wife was not illegal because he did not directly supervise her. The judge, apparently believing that the most effective remedy for false speech is more (hopefully truthful) speech, rejected the prosecutor's request. The judge concluded that the ad, even if inaccurate, was constitutionally protected speech and that Dvorak was free to counter his opponent's ad with one of his own.

These two anecdotal snapshots are emblematic of modern political campaigns, which are played out against a backdrop of negative and sometimes false and defamatory political advertising, cleverly packaged for an increasingly cynical electorate that lacks the time and resources to assess the quality and accuracy of the campaign rhetoric being thrust upon them. And yet voters display a certain moral ambiguity about such negative campaigning, often ranting and raving about how they are turned off by it, even as studies continue to show that voters are paying an increasing amount of attention to negative ads. In short, negative ads appear to work.

Indeed, they work so well that the *Cleveland Plain Dealer,* in assessing the quality of television advertising surrounding the 2008 presidential campaign between John McCain and Barack Obama, observed that "outright falsehoods in candidates' ads may be reaching a level not seen since TV commercials entered presidential politics as the primary pipeline to voters in 1952." This is happening, the *Plain Dealer* said, because of the relative absence of legal sanctions and because "truth becomes a relative and disputable term in the alternate reality of partisan politics." It seems that each new campaign is accompanied by calls to scale back on negative political advertising, particularly on ads containing false statements of fact. Given such perennial concerns with false political speech and its corrosive effect on channels of political communication, it is fair to ponder a few questions: Has the quality of political campaigns degenerated to such a point that our confidence in the marketplace of ideas as the final arbiter of political truth been severely eroded? If so, should government have a role in restoring some degree of decorum to political campaigning? How far can government go in regulating false and deceptive political advertising without running afoul of the First Amendment?

History is a stern taskmaster when it comes to adding perspective to contemporary campaign techniques. The brutality of American political campaigns did not begin with the current genre of attack ads employed by some campaign strategists. George Washington, for example, was accused of having monarchial aspirations, Thomas Jefferson was described as an illegitimate atheist and madman, and Abraham Lincoln was described variously as a fiend, a lunatic, and a traitor. What has changed in the modern era is that politicians are less inclined to ignore such attacks than their predecessors. Some have responded with aggressive campaigns of their own, including attack ads; a few have taken more drastic measures by invoking state libel laws or campaign falsity statutes.

Since censorship is anathema to democratic systems and yet the democratic process depends on a reliable flow of truthful information, the issue of how to deal with deliberate falsehoods or other communications strategies within a constitutional framework is a persistent paradox. In the United States, political falsehoods are dealt with primarily through libel laws and state campaign falsity statutes. Although defamatory falsehoods are the stuff of private litigation, and campaign falsity statutes involve government regulation, the two are not entirely discrete venues. As we shall see, the Supreme Court has "constitutionalized" libel law—a legal revolution that has informed legislative efforts to deal with false campaign rhetoric.

Arguments For and Against the Regulation of False Political Ads

There are compelling arguments both in favor of and against the regulation of false political ads. Although these concerns are pertinent to all false campaign speech, they are particularly relevant to political advertising because of the Madison Avenue approach to packaging and marketing candidates through a diversity of media platforms that reach millions of potential voters. Critics of deceptive campaign speech point to several specific harms that it produces.

First, false statements can distort the electoral process by misinforming voters. Since democracy is premised upon an informed electorate, deceptive ads undermine the electoral process and corrupt the channels of political communication. Second, attack ads based upon false statements can lower the quality of political discourse by requiring opponents to respond to the spurious attacks, often with attacks of their own, thus marginalizing a serious discussion of the major campaign issues. Third, political falsehoods can lead to voter alienation and distrust of the political process, which in turn decreases voter turnout. As a consequence, political decisions often mirror the preferences of a few rather than a true democratic majority. Fourth, attacks upon a candidate's character can inflict reputational and emotional injury, which is inimical to the common good and, unchecked, may discourage other potential candidates from seeking public office.

The arguments against regulating false political ads are just as engaging. First, the harms attributed to false political speech may be overblown. Deception, it might be noted, does not really corrupt the political process because voters frequently do not believe what they see and hear. Many voters consider it an article of faith that politicians are not restrained by truth and accuracy. Moreover, there is always an opposing candidate poised to respond to factual misstatements. Second, government restrictions on campaign speech, even false and defamatory speech, are in tension with the Constitution's free-speech guarantee. Political speech lies at the core of the First Amendment, and relying upon an unfettered public square to sort out competing claims is preferable to a system of government sanctions. Third, sanctioning false political advertising may be an ineffective means of informing the public, since adjudicating such claims often exceeds the election cycle. Fourth, in the rather untidy world of political campaigning, the question of whether a statement is viewed as true or false often depends upon context, perspective, and motivation, thereby opening the door to partisan abuse. Whether administrative agencies or even courts can be sufficiently insulated from this pressure to render fair and nonpartisan decisions is problematical. Fifth, the use of civil litigation or government regulatory oversight can turn the mechanisms of government into political pawns, because such actions may have less to do with correcting the record or restoring one's reputation than with inflicting political damage. A lawsuit, for example, can engender dramatic news coverage that detracts from the campaign issues and keeps the alleged political falsehoods in the public consciousness long after the election itself.

Defamatory Falsehoods in Political Advertising

Defamation is defined as a false statement of fact that is likely to injure someone's reputation. To prevail in a defamation suit, a candidate must prove, among other things, that the charges are false and that they involve questions of fact, not mere opinion. In addition, the accusations or representations must be of a kind that are not merely critical of a candidate's performance, political views, or voting record but are likely to injure the candidate's reputation.

The claim that the regulation of calculated political falsehoods implicates free speech concerns is not self-evident; indeed, until the second half of the twentieth century, the Supreme Court considered defamatory falsehoods to be "unprotected speech." Within this framework, defamation was essentially an equal-opportunity tort. The common law of libel did not distinguish between public officials and private parties in establishing the burden of proof. But in 1964, the Court, for the first time, recognized the constitutional dimensions of libel law and raised the barriers significantly against libel suits by public officials. In reversing a $500,000 libel judgment in favor of an Alabama public official, the Court held in *New York Times v. Sullivan* that the First Amendment limits the authority of states to award libel damages to public officials unless they can prove that the defamatory falsehoods are published with actual malice, that is, the knowledge that they are false or demonstrate a reckless disregard for the truth of the publication.

The euphoria surrounding the Sullivan decision in 1964 obscured the fact that the Court's reasoning had less to do with the constitutional value of falsity than with providing "breathing space" for protected expression to avoid chilling political debate, especially press coverage during the heat of a campaign. In fact, just ten years after its *Sullivan* opinion the Court reaffirmed its long-held skepticism toward the constitutional value of false statements of fact, which "are no essential part of any exposition of ideas, and are of such slight social value as a step to truth that any benefit that may be derived from them is clearly outweighed by the social interest in order and morality." However, under Sullivan, the media are protected against liability for defamatory falsehoods contained in political advertisements unless they know the claims are false or publish with reckless disregard of whether the information is false.

Government Regulation of Campaign Advertising: Political or Commercial Speech?

Any meaningful discussion of government regulation of false political advertising must begin with the realization that political ads are really a hybrid of the two most prominent forms of speech in American society: political speech (that which informs our public debate) and advertising, or, as the Supreme Court refers to it, "commercial speech." In their most noble moments, such ads can service the political system by providing valuable information about a candidate's views and platform and can enrich the voters' arsenal of political knowledge during a campaign. Yet there is an unmistakable resemblance between commercial and political advertising in their format and techniques—so much so that political ads are frequently referred to derisively as the "packaging" of candidates.

From a legal perspective, whether political ads, which are designed to sell candidates to the electorate, are considered commercial or political speech is significant. In the United States, false political speech, even defamatory falsehoods, receives some constitutional protection—not because falsity has "value" (as noted previously) but because some falsehoods are inevitable in political discourse and a vibrant public square requires protection for a broad spectrum of political content. In addition, the rhetorical hyperbole and political huckstering in some ads is balanced by more temperate and informative issue-oriented advertising produced by some campaigns. In contrast, states and the federal government are free to regulate false commercial advertising without any serious constitutional consequences. Commercial advertising is constitutionally protected only when it embodies a truthful message for a lawful product. The selling of toothpaste, it seems, doesn't command the same respect as the day's political intelligence. But when political speech is combined with commercial speech—or, to put it more indelicately, when candidates are packaged like shaving cream or Hormel sausage—some interesting legal questions are posed, the most significant of which is: For the purpose of government regulation, should campaign ads be treated like political speech or commercial advertising?

The Supreme Court has left little doubt as to where political ads fall in the constitutional scheme of things. As early as 1964, in the *Sullivan* decision, the Court rejected the argument that speech that communicates information of public interest loses its constitutional protection simply because it is conveyed in the form of an advertisement. Thus a voter who believes that he or she has been misled by a political ad has no recourse before the courts, the Federal Trade Commission, or the Better Business Bureau.

Nevertheless, campaign reform is perennially attractive to voters, and some state legislatures have not awaited the Supreme Court's benediction in attempting to impose some decorum on the political process. In so doing, they have had to walk a tightrope between regulating the most egregious abuses of political advertising and protecting the public square from the oppressive hand of government regulation.

State Regulation of False Political Advertising

About a third of the states (seventeen) have statutes that prohibit or regulate deceptive campaign speech, which of course includes false political advertising. There are two distinct governmental interests furthered by these statutes: (1) protection of a candidate's reputation, and (2) protection of the integrity of the electoral process. These laws differ significantly in their scope and purpose. For example, seven states regulate only false statements about a candidate in an election. Nine states have laws regulating false statements about candidates and ballot measures. One state, South Dakota, regulates only false statements about ballot measures. Some state laws also differ according to the form of political communication. Statutes in nine states apply to both written and oral communications. The other eight states regulate only false political speech in written form. Three specifically limit the type of written statement covered.

For example, Minnesota's statute restricts only paid political advertisements, campaign material, and letters to the editor. North Dakota limits false political ads and news releases, whereas Tennessee restricts only campaign literature. The remaining campaign falsity statutes make no distinction as to the type of written false statement prohibited.

In addition to a threshold showing of falsity, several statutes demand proof of additional elements as a prerequisite to a violation. Both the Nebraska and Oregon laws, for example, require that the false statement relate to a material fact. In Alaska, Mississippi, and Montana, statutory violations are limited to those that are defamatory under the common law, that is, those that are injurious to a person's reputation. A majority of the states with campaign falsity statutes (ten) require that the false statement be designed or have the tendency to affect the vote on a candidate or ballot question. The sanctions for statutory violations, as might be expected, vary from state to state. In Louisiana, for example, in addition to a misdemeanor penalty, an affected candidate or voter is entitled to an injunction against future violations of the law. Several states provide for the invalidation of an election or the removal from office of the winning candidate if he or she is found to have knowingly made a false statement during the campaign. Even here, however, there is one significant exception. Every state has a constitutional provision similar to Article I, Section 5 of the U.S. Constitution, which provides that the legislature is to be the sole judge of the qualifications of its members. Thus, courts have no jurisdiction in this area because of the separation of powers doctrine.

Despite what appears to be an impressive regulatory scheme for false political speech, the overall effectiveness of such statutes is dubious. The line between fact and opinion and truth and deception is not always clear, from a legal perspective, and for this reason courts have been sensitive to the dangers of censorship under state campaign falsity statutes. Since all of the statutes are directed at false statements of fact (rather than opinion or commentary), some courts have gone to extraordinary lengths to construe political statements as opinion or commentary rather than assertions of fact. A case in point is a decision from the Wisconsin Supreme Court. When a candidate for sheriff suggested that his opponent was a "love pirate" and a "demoralizer of homes" because the opponent allegedly had written a questionable letter to a married woman, the court decided the statements fell within the field of political commentary.

Statutory construction aside, opponents of state regulation of false political speech (including advertising) argue that such statutes are unconstitutional. In 1998, the Washington State Supreme Court seemed to agree when it struck down as unconstitutional its statute banning false political advertising, even though the law required that malice be proven by a "high standard of proof." One justice, dissenting from the majority's 5–4 decision, lamented, "Today the Washington State Supreme Court becomes the first court in the history of the Republic to declare First Amendment protection for calculated lies."

However, the Washington court's liberal construction of the state's statute is an anomaly. The U.S. Supreme Court has never specifically addressed the issue, but it is fair to say that false political-speech statutes are probably constitutional as long as they include, in recognition of the *Sullivan* decision, a requirement of a showing of actual malice before a court imposes sanctions. Indeed, one lower federal court that did consider the question held "any state regulation of campaign speech must be premised on proof and application of [the *New York Times's*] 'actual malice' standard to be in compliance with the requirements of the First Amendment."

Indeed, the few state statutes that target false political advertising appear to conform, either in the language of the statute or through judicial construction, to the actual malice standard set forth in the Sullivan decision—that is, violations of law occur only when political messages are communicated with the knowledge that they are false or with reckless disregard of whether the statements are true or false.

A case in point is a 1994 House race in Minnesota, during which Republican candidate Tad Jude ran an ad that was reminiscent of the notorious "Willie Horton" ads run against Democratic presidential candidate Michael Dukakis in the 1988 presidential election. The Jude ad cited the case of a woman and two daughters who were abducted and raped repeatedly during a two-day ordeal by a man who, despite two prior convictions, had been released from prison on a weekend furlough. Jude had introduced a bill in an earlier legislative session that would have prevented such early releases, and the ad charged that the rapist might never have been released and "this crime never committed" if Jude's campaign opponent, Democratic state senator William Luther, had not blocked the bill. The ad was false, and Jude and his campaign manager were indicted under a Minnesota statute that outlawed false political advertising, despite Jude's testimony to the grand jury that he believed the ad was true. However, the trial judge threw out the case, and the Minnesota Court of Appeals refused to reinstate the indictment, holding that the law was too broad because it allowed someone to be charged for only having "reason to believe" that an ad they prepared was false. The court held that Supreme Court rulings required a higher standard of proof, namely actual malice.

Political Advertising and Media Access

State legislatures have focused most of their attention on campaign falsehoods rather than ensuring a candidate's access to the public square through advertising. While such statutes would appear to enhance rather than abridge the First Amendment's intent of ensuring an unfettered political marketplace, in 1974 the Supreme Court held that a governmentally mandated right of access to the print media is unconstitutional. A different constitutional paradigm is applied to the electronic media, however, which is governed by the Federal Communications Act of 1934, as amended. Section 315 of the act requires that when a broadcast licensee allows a "legally qualified" candidate for a given office to "use" his or her facilities, the licensee must provide "equal opportunity" to all other candidates for that office. Section 315 applies to all appearances by a political candidate except during bona fide news programs and interviews. The exact meaning of equal opportunity has been the subject of adjudication by the Federal Communications Commission (FCC), but it essentially means that all candidates for the same office must be treated alike. For example, if state senatorial candidate "A" purchases fifty minutes of airtime on Channel 10, all other candidates must be provided with the opportunity to buy an equal amount of time (hence the common reference to Section 315 as the "equal time" law, although the term never appears in the statute). Similarly, if Candidate A seeks maximum exposure by scheduling all of his spots in prime time, all of Candidate A's opponents must be afforded the same opportunity. And so on.

Section 315 does not obligate a broadcast licensee to sell or otherwise provide time to candidates for any given race at the state and local levels, but Section 312 of the act requires broadcasters to provide "reasonable access" for candidates for federal elective office. In other words, a broadcaster may not, as a matter of policy, refuse to make time available (either through commercial spots or otherwise) to candidates for Congress or president and vice president.

Does the equal-opportunities requirement apply to supporters of political candidates? In 1970, in response to an inquiry from a congressional staff member named Zapple, the FCC declared that when a station provides time to supporters of a candidate during a campaign, the station is obligated to offer equal opportunities to supporters of opposing candidates. Two years later, however, the commission limited this requirement to the major party candidates, thus relieving broadcasters of the obligation to accommodate requests from supporters of minor party or fringe candidates. Interestingly, while the FCC requires that groups who do "issue ads" (such as supporters of candidates) must document the accuracy of their claims, candidates themselves are not subject to such restraints. Because of recent changes in FCC policies, the National Association of Broadcasters has expressed doubts as to whether the Zapple doctrine is still in effect, but the FCC has not directly addressed this issue.

Campaign Reform and Political Advertising

Each session of Congress, it seems, brings renewed calls for campaign reform. Some reform statutes have emerged from Congress, each with its predictable assortment of loopholes, which in turn precipitates another round of ethical hyperbole and calls for further improvements. An exploration of the complicated morass of campaign-reform legislation is beyond the scope of this chapter, but there are a couple of ways in which political broadcast advertising has been linked to campaign reform.

The first of these is directly linked to the cost of political campaigning. Because broadcast licensees might be inclined to keep candidate use to a minimum by charging higher-than-normal advertising rates, Section 315(b) of the Communications Act prohibits broadcast stations from charging rates that exceed that of other users during most of the year. However, during the 45 days preceding the date of a primary or primary runoff election and during the 60 days preceding the date of a general or special election in which a person is a candidate, the candidate must be charged the station's "lowest unit" rate for the "same class and amount of time for the same period." In other words, while commercial advertisers must purchase a certain number of commercials to qualify for the lowest unit rates, political candidates are entitled to such discounts automatically, regardless of the number of spots they purchase. In addition, to qualify for such rates, candidates for federal office must include a statement in each commercial that they approved the broadcast.

The second link between political advertising and campaign reform is the so-called McCain-Feingold campaign-finance law enacted by Congress to ban soft-money fundraising and spending by the national political parties. One provision of the law prohibits "electioneering communication," including broadcast ads that name a candidate paid for from corporate or union treasuries, 30 days before a federal primary election or 60 days before a federal general election. In 2002, the Supreme Court upheld the law, but in June 2007 it struck down the advertising provisions, in part holding that such restrictions amounted to censorship of core political speech unless those advertisements explicitly urge a vote for or against a particular candidate. "Where the First Amendment is implicated," Chief Justice John Roberts wrote, "the tie goes to the speaker, not the censor."

Conclusion

Money alone, of course, does not win elections, but well-crafted political messages do resonate with voters and can even exert a profound influence on voter preferences. Studies suggest that negative political advertising is often effective, but when the ads are false or deceptive the integrity of the channels of political communication is at stake. Under the circumstances, government sanctions are sometimes viewed as the most effective remedy for false and deceptive political ads. However, as an article in the November 2004 issue of the University of Pennsylvania Law Review cautions, "Sanctioning deceptive campaign messages [may be] supported by sound policy considerations, but the First Amendment concerns triggered by such regulation are also compelling. After all, campaign speech by its very nature is tumultuous, provocative, and prone to overstatement; and investing the government with the power to proscribe campaign speech, in any form, raises the most serious First Amendment concerns."

SUGGESTED READINGS

Fueroghne, D. K. *Law and Advertising.* Chicago: Copy Workshop, 1995.

Hall, J. A. "When Political Campaigns Turn to Slime: Establishing a Virginia Fair Campaign Practices Committee." *Journal of Law and Politics* 7 (1990–91): 353–77.

Kruse, Becky. "The Truth in Masquerade: Regulating False Ballot Proposition Ads through State Anti-Speech Statutes." *California Law Review* 89 (2001): 129–81.

Marshall, William P. "Symposium: The Law of Democracy: New Issues in the Law of Democracy: False Campaign Speech and the First Amendment." *University of Pennsylvania Law Review* 153 (2004): 285–323.

Neel, R. F., Jr. "Campaign Hyperbole: The Advisability of Legislating False Statements out of Politics." *Journal of Law and Politics* 2 (1985): 405–24.

William, Williams A. "A Necessary Compromise: Protecting Electoral Integrity through the Regulation of False Campaign Speech." *South Dakota Law Review* 52 (2007): 321–54.

Winbro, J. "Misrepresentation in Political Advertising: The Role of Legal Sanctions." *Emory Law Journal* 36 (1987): 853–916.

Wright, J. S. "Money and the Pollution of Politics: Is the First Amendment an Obstacle to Equality?" *Columbia Law Review* 82 (1982): 609–45.

5

Electronic Media and Congressional Politics

RON GARAY

In late 2008, according to the Nielsen Company, there were approximately 290 million television viewers occupying some 114.5 million U.S. households with at least one television. Since citizens have access to radio in the home, in the automobile, and in the workplace, the radio medium saturates nearly the entire U.S. population. This vast audience of electronic media consumers relied on roughly 4,600 TV stations and 14,800 radio stations to access daily programming. Added to these were the ancillary program sources of cable TV's nearly 6,100 local systems and the video and audio sources of national direct broadcast satellite (DBS) providers.

Like traditional TV and radio broadcast stations, cable-TV systems and DBS providers produce or originate some of their own programming but rely heavily on network or individual program services to fill most of their daily schedules. Among the most popular cable TV and DBS program services are those providing news and information, such as CNN, FoxNews, MSNBC, and others. With the exception of public radio, local radio stations, as a rule, have de-emphasized news programming in the last few years, but many cities now have at least one or two stations that specialize in some variation of a news/talk/information format. In fact, the number of stations in 2008 airing such a format ranked second only to stations airing a country music format, according to Arbitron.

Added to all of these audio and video electronic media are a growing array of "new platform" services that supplement as well as compete with traditional media by furnishing viewers and listeners a wide assortment of alternative programming and program options. Web-based news sites are among the most heavily used options. Among the most popular sites in late 2007, according to Nielsen Online, were Yahoo News, MSNBC, CNN, AOL News, and the *New York Times.*

Such potent media—with nearly universal access to the eyes and ears of Americans—provide invaluable means for members of the U.S. Congress to reach the public. Dating from nearly the beginning of the electronic media revolution in this country, Congress has relied on radio and television to convey information about the institutional business of the U.S. Senate and House of Representatives. Individual members of each chamber also have come to rely on radio and television as a means of addressing their constituents with their own messages, whether regarding positions on legislative or public policy matters or during election or reelection campaigns.

Keeping in Touch: The Institution

Radio was first considered as a means for Congress to speak directly to the American public in 1922. Radio broadcasting was not yet widespread (America's first radio station, KDKA in Pittsburgh, had begun operations only in 1920), but several congressmen nonetheless introduced legislation aimed at broadcasting House and Senate floor proceedings to listeners nationwide. The effort failed, due primarily to technical barriers and cost, and little serious attention was given to the matter for the next quarter of a century. During that period, however, the two major radio networks, NBC and CBS, maintained standing policies of allowing free air time upon request to members of Congress.

With the arrival of television as a mass medium, attention returned to congressional broadcasting in the post–World War II years. Congress's more relaxed view toward electronic coverage, coupled with the television industry's eagerness to experiment with programming ideas, meant that the time was ripe for Americans to have their first electronic peek at legislative business. That peek finally came in the late 1940s as Congress opened its committee proceedings—not its floor proceedings—to television. Senate Crime Committee hearings in 1951 caused a sensation when committee chairman Estes Kefauver (D-TN) opened them to television cameras. Equally sensational were telecasts of the Army-McCarthy hearings in 1954. In addition to giving such hearings far greater exposure than they likely would have otherwise received, television also boosted the celebrity of hearing participants. Estes Kefauver, for instance, rose from committee chair to presidential contender in 1952.

As successful as committee hearings were in publicizing specific issues, Congress began to fall behind the executive branch during the 1960s and 1970s in using television to address the public on important issues. Presidents Kennedy, Johnson, and Nixon were particularly astute at using television to speak directly to the American people.

Congress responded to this institutional imbalance in 1973 by establishing the Joint Committee on Congressional Operations, which, among other things, began a serious investigation of implementing televised coverage of House and Senate chamber proceedings. The committee found little reason to continue barring television cameras from congressional chambers and, as a result, the U.S. House voted in 1977 to allow such access. Not until March 1979, however, would live televised coverage begin.

The U.S. Senate was not as quick as the House to televise its floor debate. One reason was a feeling shared by several Senate veterans that their chamber's procedural rules might create a negative public image of the body. For instance, senators are free to speak for as long as they desire, on whatever topic they choose. And senators who engaged in the traditional filibuster as a means of blocking legislation had been known to read entire books aloud in order not to relinquish the floor to their opponents.

Senators Howard Baker (R-TN) and Robert Byrd (D-WV) argued that, procedural issues aside, the Senate stood to gain far more than it would lose by televising its proceedings. The arguments proved convincing, and Senate television began in 1986. Television feeds from both the Senate and House were made available to any television station or network wishing to carry them. In addition, the cable-TV industry created a unique program service called the Cable-Satellite Public Affairs Network (C-SPAN) to carry live congressional debates to cable households.

Broadcasters and cable-TV systems wishing to use the C-SPAN feeds or otherwise to carry direct feeds from the Senate and House floors must agree not to edit any portion of the coverage. Rules committees in both the Senate and House have formalized such editing prohibitions in order to guard against the "filtering" influence of news reporters, editors, and producers. Members of Congress themselves are prohibited from using any video and audio originating from official House or Senate activities for political or commercial purposes. It should be added that all congressional committees devise their own rules for audio and video coverage of hearings or deliberative activities. Generally, these rules are meant to minimize disruption and to maintain decorum.

Keeping in Touch: The Individual

One reason that members of Congress agreed to television coverage of their proceedings was to improve the institution's public image. That has yet to happen, though, as opinion polls consistently place the institutional popularity of Congress below that of the U.S. president. Even when former president George W. Bush's public approval rating dipped to a low of 25 percent in October 2008, according to the Gallup Poll, the congressional approval rating stood at an even lower 18 percent.

A phenomenon of opinion polling is that the public traditionally thinks more highly of individual members of Congress than of the collective Congress. Part of the reason for this is that members of Congress begin, from their first arrival in Washington, to establish themselves as an independent voice. And television has assisted their efforts. Congressional hearings, as noted above, were for many years the foremost means by which senators and representatives brought attention to themselves. Reporters have long noted that committee-member attendance at hearings oftentimes coincided with the presence of television cameras.

Perhaps remembering the free time that radio networks afforded members of Congress in earlier years, Senator William Fulbright (D-AR) introduced legislation in the late 1960s that would have mandated television networks periodically to provide free time to congressional spokespersons to present House and Senate views on important public issues. The Fulbright measure met with opposition from Senate colleagues who noted the futility in supposing that one person or only a few persons could represent the collective views of Congress. More important, however, the powerful National Association of Broadcasters (NAB), representing television and radio station owners whose support members of Congress relied upon, regarded the Fulbright proposal as a First Amendment intrusion and an unnecessary invasion of broadcasters' programming prerogatives. The troublesome measure never moved beyond committee, and nothing like it has emerged from Congress since.

Failure to legislate a congressional "right of access" to television did not mean that senators and representatives lacked the resources or the creativity to achieve some degree of radio, television, and cable access. There currently are several means at their disposal for getting their voices and images to the public and, most importantly, to their constituents.

The first of these, for U.S. House members, comes courtesy of the short speeches made from the House floor either prior to or immediately following each day's legislative business. Called "one-minute speeches" at the beginning of the day or "special-order speeches" at day's end, these brief statements allow House members to address colleagues on topics ranging from the mundane to the significant. Such comments make perfect sound bites that radio or television stations may record for later airing. Special-order speeches have become particularly partisan in recent years, and House members who have used them effectively, such as former House Speaker Newt Gingrich (R-GA), have risen from obscurity to prominence.

Radio and television stations send their own reporters to Washington or rely on stringers for news about Congress, and all major broadcast networks and cable TV/DBS news and information program services have at least one congressional correspondent. These reporters have access to senators and representatives in their offices or in the small radio and television studios that are maintained by the Senate and the House Radio-Television Correspondents' Gallery. In 1994, radio talk-show hosts for the first time were provided facilities in the Capitol basement from which to originate their programs.

As just noted, the Senate and House both maintain well-appointed recording studios for their respective members to record programs and interviews that may then be provided to home radio and television stations or to any interested news service. In addition, each party caucus in the Senate maintains its own television studio and production facility. The studios may link members of Congress to local stations via satellite for live interviews.

Reaching the Voter

Members of Congress make few radio and television performance-of-duty appearances that are not infused with some degree of self-promotion. In a very real sense, elected officials nearly always are looking to the next election. And now more than ever, a candidate's success is measured by how effectively he or she uses the electronic media.

The linkage between political campaigns and the electronic media came early in this country. When radio was first used in 1922 as a campaign medium, the *New York Times* suggested that such campaigning "soon might leave the field of novelty and become a practical everyday proposition during political fights." It did that and more, of course. By the 1960s, television had displaced radio as the preferred campaign medium, and as the twentieth century drew to a close, television was considered to be "the true currency of American politics."

The efficiency and effectiveness of the electronic media as campaign tools carry a tremendous price. "You cannot run for major office nowadays," according to writer Max Frankel, "without spending millions for television commercials that spread your fame, shout your slogans, denounce your opponents, and counteract television attacks." Fundraising, then, becomes an enormous but nonetheless necessary burden that one observer has characterized as "the cornerstone of getting your message out to the right voters."

The sums of money required to finance a political campaign have become so great in recent years that illegal or questionable activities associated with fundraising have become more prevalent. And since so much campaign money is earmarked for the electronic media, reformers have begun searching for ways to reduce that expense and, thus, the fundraising burden. One obvious solution is for radio and television stations, cable-TV systems, and DBS providers to supply candidates for federal elective office free air time. But free time for congressional candidates is rare, since it would replace time that otherwise could be generating advertising revenue.

Efforts to mandate free air time for congressional candidates seemed promising in 1997, when a campaign finance reform bill sponsored by Senators John McCain (R-AZ) and Russell Feingold (D-MN) included a provision that would have provided free air time for candidates who agreed to observe certain campaign spending limits. The provision, however, was dropped after broadcasters complained that it violated the First Amendment.

Bills sponsored by several key Senate and House members in 2007 proposed, among other things, the creation of a voucher system to allocate funding to qualified U.S. House and Senate members to help subsidize the cost of purchasing television time for political campaign messages. The vouchers would have been funded by a "public interest" tax assessed upon each broadcast station licensee. Broadcasters already were required to charge the lowest unit rate for campaign messages, based on the comparable rate charged established customers for purchase of product advertising time, but the proposed bill would have added an additional discount as elections neared. But like the 1997 bill, the 2007 campaign-finance reform bill failed.

Current legal responsibilities and parameters for using radio, television, cable TV, and DBS facilities for political campaign announcements and programs are embedded in Sections 312 and 315 of the 1934 Communications

Act. The Communications Act, despite several major revisions over the years, remains the foundational law for regulating electronic media in the United States. Section 312 of the act requires that legally qualified candidates for federal elective office be provided with reasonable access to broadcast station and DBS (technically considered "over-the-air") provider facilities and that legally qualified opponents of these candidates be afforded equal opportunities in use of the same facilities. Section 315 does not require access, as does Section 312, but it does require that if a legally qualified candidate for any elective office is provided use of a broadcast station, DBS provider, and/or cable-TV facility, then any legally qualified opponent(s) of the candidate must be afforded equal opportunity in the use of these facilities. The Federal Communications Commission (FCC) has defined "legally qualified candidate" as any person who "has publicly announced his or her intention to run for nomination or office" and "is qualified under the applicable local, state, or federal law to hold the office for which he or she is a candidate."

Broadcasters, cable TV–system operators, and DBS providers also are prohibited from censoring any comments aired under Section 315's authority. Moreover, a candidate's appearance in a bona fide newscast, news interview, news documentary, or on-the-spot coverage of a bona fide news event exempts broadcasters, cable TV–system operators, and DBS providers from equal-opportunity obligations. Most important monetarily is the Section 315 requirement that candidates be charged the lowest unit rate for time purchases.

The above provisions are but the tip of the iceberg with respect to political campaign law and regulations. Persons who are serious about the subject should consult a number of excellent sources. The FCC website, fcc.gov, provides links not only to specific commission rules and regulations, but also to all relevant political campaign laws included in the *U.S. Code.* Two other valuable website sources provide more analytic information for people wishing to bypass the FCC's legalese: the "Political Broadcast Manual" produced by the Womble Carlyle Sandridge & Rice law firm's Telecommunications Group (wcsr.com/resources/pdfs/politicalbroadcastmanual.pdf) and the Campaign Legal Center's "The Campaign Media Guide 2004" (campaignlegalcenter.org/attachments/1121.pdf). "The Campaign Media Guide" is somewhat dated, but its easy-to-understand explanations of various arcane laws and regulations continue to make it a valuable source of information for anyone involved in political campaigns.

Last but not least is the NAB's *Political Broadcast Catechism.* This very detailed and frequently updated guide was in its 16th edition as of 2008 and is available for purchase online (nab.org). The publication was prepared originally to assist broadcasters and their attorneys in dealing with the specific application of political campaign law and regulations. As such applications have become more diverse and more intricate over the years, the *Political Broadcast Catechism* has undergone considerable revision and expansion.

However capable a candidate for public office may be in using the electronic media to reach voters, a campaign's message—whether by radio, television, cable TV, or DBS—is under the control of a gatekeeper. Reporters who cover campaigns and report about them to voters play the most active gatekeeping role. Their reports can assist candidates when they include positive messages about a political campaign. In addition, the news reports are free, and they reach a substantial number of voters. Media consultants work hard to solicit such attention.

Candidates for congressional office as well as sitting members of Congress may be either the victims or the beneficiaries of advertising by political activists. Such advertising ranges from directly supporting or attacking an individual to directly supporting or attacking issues closely identified with an individual. Both kinds of ads usually are the handiwork of political action committees (PACs). The particular slant of PAC ads has to do with tax exemption and financial requirements established by the Internal Revenue Code. Section 527 of the code pertains to PACs (commonly referred to as "527s") that are required to disclose their donor lists to the IRS but who otherwise can produce ads attacking or supporting an individual or issues related to the individual. Section 501c4 pertains to PACs that are not required to disclose their donor lists to the IRS but who otherwise are limited to producing what are called "issue ads" or engaging in "advocacy advertising." These ads promote certain social or policy agendas and are presented in the context of political-campaign advertising. The ads do not explicitly recommend that viewers or listeners vote for or against a particular candidate; rather, they recommend that voters contact the candidate and express an opinion regarding a particular issue.

Both kinds of appeals are protected by the First Amendment. What's more, groups and organizations producing ads that make such appeals, whether at the 527 or the 501c4 level, are clearly within their right indirectly but forcefully to enter a political campaign and spend whatever amount of money they choose on air-time purchases.

New Platform Services

The Internet has revolutionized the electronic communication process. Web-based platforms now perform interactive functions that immediately connect the institutional Congress and its many committees and offices, as well as individual members of Congress, with every person who has access to the Internet. A recent Congressional Research Service report noted that offices of each member of Congress, as well as committee offices, are wired into a variety of electronic networks and databases for quick access to a range of information sources.

It is rare to find a member of Congress or a congressional committee that does not maintain its own website. These websites provide constituents information about pending legislation; they may also serve as an interactive platform to gather constituent feedback and in some cases to allow participation in actual hearings. Then-House Speaker Nancy Pelosi began urging House committees in 2007 to webcast their hearings as one more step toward making what they do more available to the general public.

Of course, public-interest and activist groups also use the Internet for their own purposes: to inform about legislative matters, to support or oppose legislation, or to support or oppose a congressional candidacy.

Use of web-based platforms by activist or constituent groups and by Congress itself raises an important question about the relationship between these sophisticated platforms and what some refer to as "MSMs" or members of the "mainstream media." Do the web-based tools expand the capabilities of the MSMs, or do they simply compete with them? More important, how is the relationship between web-based platforms and MSMs evolving?

Online access to Congress was greatly facilitated in 1995 when the U.S. House inaugurated its THOMAS Web site [thomas.loc.gov] as a portal not only to various congressional offices, but also to the vast amount of information and documents either produced daily by the institution or otherwise archived there. In addition, a number of new tools such as blogging, podcasting, and YouTube postings have joined an expanding family of existing or emerging web-based technologies that connect information originators with information consumers.

Much of that information relates to congressional activities and personnel. Michael Scherer has observed, for instance, "Every day at personal computers across the nation, people are speaking back to their politicians—posting essays and videos that will be seen by thousands, organizing their neighbors and delving deep into the issues they care about on their own terms."

Blogging has become a particularly potent political tool. Blogs appeared first in the late 1990s, and by 2006 the so-called "blogosphere" consisted of over 40 million dedicated "blogophiles." Blogs have been characterized as the foundation of a new "information ecosystem" that "is changing politics, business and popular culture for the better by reducing the influence of elites and institutions and allowing for wider public participation." Bloggers represent "trade associations, watchdog groups, and special interests," whose objectives range from informing and persuading members of Congress on a variety of issues to the ultimate political act of helping either to re-elect or unseat these same members.

The Congressional Research Service report noted earlier concluded that the "Internet's impact on the legislative branch is extensive because it influences nearly everything that Congress does, from policymaking to representation to Member office operations." The Internet has greatly increased congressional transparency by providing access to legislative documents, as well as to the legislative role-players and to the very process of legislation. Internet-based e-mail has improved the ability of members of Congress to both send and receive information. And the Internet has created a new kind of electronic forum with the potential to allow more Americans than ever before to share in the democratic process.

The availability of web-based technology does not guarantee its use or its effectiveness. Senior members of Congress who are unfamiliar or uncomfortable with the more sophisticated communication tools have been slow to adjust. They tend to see their jobs at a more personal level, engaging colleague and constituent alike on a person-to-person basis whenever possible. Younger members of Congress, in contrast, more accustomed to using the new communication technologies, can easily adapt to them and are much more amenable to their use in the legislative process.

Electronic Media Audience

The Pew Research Center's Project for Excellence in Journalism issues an annual report titled the "State of the News Media." Regarding the role of new platform media, the Pew Center's 2008 report observed, "Audiences are moving toward information on demand, to media platforms and outlets that can tell them what they want to know when they want to know it."

Two of the study's findings suggested that the manner by which citizens utilize traditional or "legacy" electronic media as well as the new web-based platform services may push Congress to reassess how best to communicate with Americans. The first finding was that the electronic-media audience is splintering or fragmenting. Part of the split is generational. Older viewers remain satisfied with and loyal to the news programs that legacy network television provides. Younger viewers, however, reflect a more technology-savvy inclination to seek out new ways of accessing electronic news and to do so on their own terms. To them, network television news is outdated and stodgy.

The second finding, flowing naturally from the first, was that the electronic-media audience is shrinking. Audience numbers for local and network television news and information programming have been trending downward for several years. The cable TV–news networks also have not been immune to that trend, but they seem better positioned than the broadcast networks to experiment with ways of regaining lost viewers. What's more, viewer migration to cable TV networks that represent a particular ideological slant have pushed those networks to respond by scheduling more and more opinion programs with an ideological emphasis.

Radio is faring much better. According to Arbitron, "Traditional radio commanded a weekly audience of 93.3% of the population 12 and older as of the spring of 2007. . . . This translates into nearly 233 million people over age 12 who tuned into the AM/FM dial at least once during an average week." But the sparsity of radio stations that provide any news programming at all means that listeners must seek out the stations in their market that provide a talk/news/information format. And like the cable TV–news networks, radio stations that specialize in such a format have gradually been fashioning that content to reflect a particular political—usually conservative—ideology.

Audience drop-off or not, most Americans still depend heavily on traditional electronic-media news sources. According to a Pew Research Center survey released in the summer of 2008, roughly 46 percent of the public falls into what Pew called the "Traditionalists," who rely on legacy electronic media for their news. People who rely primarily on a web-based news source, called "Net-Newsers" by Pew, comprise only 13 percent of the public. About 14 percent of the population cares little about the news and falls into Pew's "Disengaged" category. The big story, however, is found in what Pew calls the "Integrators." The roughly 23 percent of the public who falls into this category are avid news consumers and continue to rely on network television as a main source for their news, but they also rely on web-based news for frequent updates throughout the day. Also interesting is the demographic similarity between the Integrators and the Net-Newsers. While Integrators tend to be older, persons in both groups are affluent and highly educated. Moreover, since 72 percent of adult Americans were found to be regular Internet users as of early 2008 (according to the Pew Internet and American Life Project), chances are that the number of persons populating both the Integrator and Net-Newser categories is on an upward trajectory.

Conclusion

A question that remains is whether the growing array of electronic media technologies and delivery systems will make Congress a body that is more effective and more responsive to the needs of U.S. citizens. This and similar questions were considered during a 1996 House hearing entitled "21st Century Congress." Peering into the century that was fast approaching, hearing participants were less than optimistic about how well Congress might utilize electronic media or, more importantly, how Congress might be changed by these media. Problems foreseen were not ones of ineffectiveness, as might be expected, but rather ones of overabundance. Hearing participants concluded that the electronic mass media were evolving in such ways, and so quickly, that their utilization, unless carefully and thoughtfully planned and managed, could well transform the U.S. Capitol of the twenty-first century into a modern-day Tower of Babel.

At the end of the new century's first decade, there is insufficient evidence to judge how insightful the 1996 panelists happened to be. What is obvious, however, is that electronic media have widened opportunities for two-way communication between the public and members of the U.S. Senate and U.S. House of Representatives in ways that were hardly imagined in the last decade of the twentieth century. What is also certain is that advances in electronic communication will continue to be rapid and revolutionary, and that Congress will have little choice but to incorporate such advances into the manner by which the institution and its members do business.

SUGGESTED READINGS

Chester, Edward W. *Radio, Television, and American Politics*. New York: Sheed and Ward, 1969.

Frankel, Max. "Money: Hard, Soft, and Dirty." *New York Times Magazine*, October 26, 1997.

Frantzick, Stephen E. *The C-SPAN Revolution*. Norman: University of Oklahoma Press, 1996.

Garay, Ronald. "Broadcasting of Congressional Proceedings." In Donald C. Bacon et al., eds., *The Encyclopedia of the United States Congress*, vol. 1. New York: Simon & Schuster, 1995.

Garay, Ronald. *Congressional Television: A Legislative History*. Westport, Conn.: Greenwood Press, 1984.

Hess, Stephen. *Live from Capitol Hill!: Studies of Congress and the Media*. Washington, D.C.: The Brookings Institution, 1991.

Mann, Thomas E., and Norman J. Ornstein, eds. *Congress, the Press, and the Public*. Washington, D.C.: American Enterprise Institute and the Brookings Institution, 1994.

Nielsen Media Research. Online at: nielsenmedia.com.

Pew Research Center Project for Excellence in Journalism. *The State of the News Media 2008: An Annual Report on American Journalism*. Online at: stateofthenewsmedia.org.

Scherer, Michael. "You Have the Power." *Parade*, November 18, 2007.

6

The States and Campaign Finance Laws

DAVID SCHULTZ

During the 2002 and 2004 election cycles, the national association of the 21st Century Democrats made numerous contributions to its Minnesota affiliate in order to help the latter influence state legislative elections. These contributions, totaling nearly $300,000, were instrumental in the Minnesota Democratic Farmer Labor (DFL) Party picking up numerous legislative seats, coming within two victories of switching partisan control of the state's House of Representatives.

While the affiliate organization of the 21st Century Democrats was registered with the Minnesota Campaign Finance and Public Disclosure Board, as required by state law, the national organization was not. According to Minnesota law, it is illegal for an unregistered political association to contribute in excess of $100 to a registered political organization. In seeking to defend its actions, the attorney for the national organization declared that it operated in many states and that it sought to conform to national law and not necessarily to that of individual states. The 21st Century Democrats were eventually found to be in violation of the law and fined nearly $300,000—an amount equal to their contributions—for their transgression.

The moral of the story is that political organizations and associations often forget that there is not one but fifty-one sets of laws governing the financing of campaigns and elections in the United States. One set of laws controls federal elections for Congress and the President. But there are also fifty separate bodies of laws controlling state and local elections across the country. Often these laws impose a different set of rules than those found at the federal level, and in some cases they also impact congressional and presidential races. Ignoring this fact is something for only the most foolish of candidates, consultants, or campaign managers.

If states are, as Justice Louis Brandeis once remarked, laboratories of democracy, they have definitely proved to be so when it comes to regulation of money in politics. While some states, such as Texas and Illinois, have placed minimal limits on political contributions and expenditures, others—including Vermont, Maine, Arizona, and Minnesota—significantly regulate them, either through direct mandated limits or by way of providing voluntary partial (Minnesota or Vermont) or total public (Maine and Arizona) financing for all or some of their state races. Even some municipalities, such as New York City, regulate money in politics and provide public funding to candidates for office.

While no brief discussion can fully describe the plethora of state regulations, this chapter examines the legal basis for this regulation of campaign financing across the fifty states.

The Constitution and State Campaign-Finance Regulation

In general, states cannot regulate the conduct of federal elections when it comes to political contributions and expenditures in terms of who may give or spend or how much. States may regulate some aspects of federal races when it comes to disclosure and registration; more importantly, they have significant authority to legislate when it comes to their own campaigns and elections. The U.S. Supreme Court has outlined a complex framework of constitutional law that describes what states can do when it comes to the regulation of money in politics in their own elections. Any discussion of campaign financing must begin with *Buckley v. Valeo*, 424 U.S. 1 (1976).

Buckley raised several challenges to the 1974 amendments to the Federal Election Campaign Act (FECA), which mandated disclosure of political contributions and expenditures, and limited to $1,000 political contributions by individuals or groups and to $5,000 by political action committees and party organizations to candidates for federal elective office per election cycle, with a cap of $25,000 by an individual per election cycle. In addition, individuals and groups were limited to $1,000 as the amount they could expend per election on a clearly identified candidate. There were other restrictions on how much of one's personal wealth could be spent, as well as overall campaign expenditure limits. In its decision, the Supreme Court defined the constitutional law of campaign finance–reform law that remains in effect to this day.

In examining limits on contributions and expenditures in a *per curiam* opinion, the Court applied very different lines of constitutional analysis. First, the Court noted that Congress had broad power to regulate federal elections, yet the question in this case was whether the contribution and expenditure limitations violated the First Amendment free speech clause. The court of appeals, in upholding the FECA contribution and expenditure limitations, held that the restrictions were directed towards conduct and not speech and that, accordingly, the frame of analysis as dictated by *United States v. O'Brien*, 391 U.S. 367 (1968) should apply. The court rejected the assertion that contribution and expenditure limits were conduct and not speech, stating that the giving or expending of money for political purposes raised First Amendment free speech concerns.

In regard to campaign contributions, the Court ruled that preventing corruption was a sufficiently compelling reason to justify restrictions. In addition to recognizing the abating of corruption as a compelling governmental interest, preventing its appearance was also accepted by the Court as a legitimate reason to limit contributions. Thus, preventing corruption or its appearance was enough to uphold the $1,000 limit on individual contributions. By the same logic, the Court upheld the $5,000 contribution limit on political committees and the overall $25,000 contribution limit during any calendar year.

Yet while preventing corruption or its appearance was compelling enough to restrict contributions to candidates, these two justifications were not sufficiently compelling in terms of limiting independent expenditures that were not made in coordination with a candidate. The Court said that independent expenditures not tied to candidates or coordinated with them posed no danger of quid pro quo corruption or its appearance. The independent expenditure ceiling thus failed to serve any substantial governmental interest and was therefore unconstitutional in terms of its application to individual expenditures, expenditures by candidates from personal or family resources, and total campaign expenditures.

In addition to its rulings on contribution and expenditure limits, the Court upheld the FECA disclosure for contributions above $200 and for expenditure and reporting requirements. Second, the Court made a crucial distinction between what has come to be referred to as express advocacy versus issue advocacy. If a political message specifically referred to a candidate for office and urged her election or defeat, it would be considered express advocacy; communications that did not expressly advocate a candidate's election or defeat would be a form of issue advocacy. The test for distinguishing between the two forms of communication was articulated in footnote 52 of the *Buckley* opinion, in which the Court stated that: "Communications contain . . . express words of advocacy of election or defeat, such as 'vote for,' 'elect,' 'support,' 'cast your ballot for,' 'Smith for Congress,' 'vote against,' 'defeat,' 'reject.'" Often referred to as the "magic words" test, the importance of this distinction is multifold. First, issue advocacy was clearly a form of protected First Amendment speech that cannot be limited or regulated (at least according to the *Buckley* Court), whereas in some circumstances express advocacy can be subject to contribution limits. In addition, specific agents can be denied the ability to engage in express advocacy. For example, labor unions and corporations cannot spend funds to directly influence a federal election through expressly advocating for or against the election of a candidate. (Many states have similar laws that apply to their own elections.) However, they may engage in issue advocacy and participate in discussions of issues that are important to them. Thus, depending on how the political communication is classified—as express advocacy or issue advocacy—the speech of a union or a corporation may or may not be subject to regulation.

One final legal legacy of *Buckley* is that while the Court struck down mandatory expenditure or spending limits, it did rule that voluntary limits were permissible. Under a voluntary public-financing schema, Congress and the states can impose a variety of conditions upon candidates running for office. These conditions could include spending caps and limits on how much a candidate may contribute to one's own campaign, among other stipulations.

Overall, the constitutional legacy of *Buckley* was to place the expenditure of money for political purposes under the protection of the First Amendment. In *Buckley*, the Court stated that it would uphold contribution limits if one could show that they corrupt or lead to the appearance of corruption. The Court also declared that limits on expenditures were effectively unconstitutional. It held that disclosure was permitted in some circumstances, that there were a difference between express and issue advocacy, and that independent expenditures effectively could not be banned. Yet a voluntary public-financing system would permit Congress and the states to impose additional limits or regulations upon candidates as a condition of their receiving public financing.

In addition to *Buckley*, in *Nixon v. Shrink Missouri Government PAC*, 528 U.S. 377 (2000), the Court ruled that state contribution limits set lower than those upheld in *Buckley* were constitutional (in this case, some limits were as low as $250). In upholding the limits, the Court appeared to rethink some of its *Buckley* assumptions, specifically what standard of proof was necessary to demonstrate corruption or its appearance. According to the Court:

> While *Buckley's* evidentiary showing exemplifies a sufficient justification for contribution limits, it does not speak to what may be necessary as a minimum. As to that, respondents are wrong in arguing that in the years since *Buckley* came down we have "supplemented" its holding with a new requirement that governments enacting contribution limits must "demonstrate that the recited harms are real, not merely conjectural," a contention for which respondents rely principally on. We have never accepted mere conjecture as adequate to carry a First Amendment burden.

The Court appeared to make it easier to enact some forms of contribution limits, opening up the use of public-opinion polls and other sources of data that could constitute evidence of corruption or its appearance. Yet the Court did impose some outer limit on how low contribution limits could be, stating they would be unconstitutional if the "limits were so low as to impede the ability of candidates" to "amas[s] the resources necessary for effective advocacy" (393). Thus, so long as candidates were not impeded in their ability to acquire the resources they needed to mount an effective campaign, it appeared that the Court was willing to let states set contribution limits lower than the $1,000 *Buckley* amount.

However, in *Randall v. Sorrell*, 126 S.Ct. 2479 (2006) the Court appeared to clarify the outer limits on campaign contributions. At issue was a Vermont law referred to as Act 64, which imposed contribution limits as low as $200 for state offices such as representative and $400 for statewide positions such as governor. It also enacted expenditure limits for campaigns, with, for example, the governor capped at $300,000 for a two-year election cycle. Justice Stephen Breyer, joined by John Roberts and Samuel Alito, used the *Buckley* framework to strike down both the contribution and expenditure limits.

In first examining the expenditure limits, Breyer stated that *Buckley* and subsequent decisions had found no government interest to be compelling enough to justify them. This was again true here.

Turning to contribution limits, the Court relied on *Buckley* and *Shrink,* asking if the caps were so low that they made it difficult to amass the resources necessary for effective advocacy. They concluded that they were beyond this minimum threshold, in fact, lower than ever approved by the Court, at least in comparison to the limits permitted in *Buckley*, and therefore were unconstitutional. Thus, because of *Sorrell*, states cannot constitutionally enact mandatory expenditure limits, and contribution limits as low as Vermont's are unconstitutional.

Another pair of issues that the Supreme Court has addressed are soft-money contributions and independent expenditures. Soft money is a type of contribution to political parties for the purposes of party building, get-out-the-vote (GOTV) efforts, and voting registration. At the state and federal level, these contributions were generally unlimited. Independent expenditures are expenses made by third-party groups (other than candidates and often not political parties) during campaigns. *Buckley* ruled that limits on independent expenditures were unconstitutional, but the problem with these expenditures is twofold. First, often these expenditures finance attack or negative ads against candidates. Second, under the *Buckley* framework, as long as these ads did not expressly refer to a candidate they were considered issue advocacy. If so categorized, even corporations and labor unions—both barred under federal and many state laws from expending money to influence an election—would be permitted under the First Amendment to engage in issue advocacy. Thus, soft money, independent expenditures, and issue advocacy represented for many, such as Senators John McCain and Russ Feingold, significant campaign finance–reform holes.

The Bipartisan Campaign Reform Act of 2002 ("BCRA" or "McCain-Feingold") sought to fill in these holes. While both BCRA and challenges to it contained many different components, Title I of the act prohibited national political party committees and their agents from soliciting, receiving, directing, or spending any soft money. It also prohibited state and local party committees from using soft money to engage in "federal election activity" (subject to a minor exception that allows the use of "Levin" money to finance some limited state activities). "Federal election activity" referred to voter registration activity 120 days before a federal election; or to voter identification, GOTV efforts, and generic campaign activity conducted during an election in which a federal candidate appears on the ballot; or to any public communication that referred to a clearly identified federal candidate who appears on ballot and that promotes, supports, attacks, or opposes the candidate.

In addition, BCRA sought to close the issue-advocacy loophole from *Buckley* by defining a new category of speech called "electioneering communications." Any reference to a clearly identified federal candidate 30 days before a primary or 60 days before a general election would be presumed to be express advocacy. This provision in the law was meant to limit the ability of some groups, such as corporations and unions, to get around campaign-finance restrictions. Finally, other provisions of BCRA barred state and local officeholders and candidates from soliciting soft money to influence federal elections, redefined and limited issue advocacy, and mandated that candidates for federal office authorize political communications with statements such as, "I am Jane Doe and I approve of this ad."

In *McConnell v. Federal Election Commission,* 540 U.S. 93 (2003), the Supreme Court upheld all of these requirements. The ruling appeared to free up states to enact their own bans on soft money or unlimited contributions to political parties and require more disclosure of candidates and political organizations seeking to influence elections. It also placed some limits on the ability of individuals and organizations to circumvent campaign-finance laws by using issue advocacy as a mask for express advocacy. However, while *McConnell* signaled broad authority for the federal and state governments to regulate money and mandate disclosure, there appears to be limits to that authority.

First, in *McIntyre v. Ohio,* 514 U.S. 334 (1995), the Court struck down an Ohio law that prohibited the distribution of anonymous political speech. Elsewhere, in *Watchtower Bible and Tract Society of New York v. Village of Stratton,* 536 U.S. 150 (2002), the Court invalidated a local law requiring individuals to possess a displayed permit to go door-to-door for political purposes. In *NAACP v. Alabama,* 357 U.S. 449 (1958), it also held that the First Amendment bars compelled disclosure of membership lists of organizations. While *Buckley* and *McConnell* support broad authority of states to mandate disclosure, there may be some limits to that authority, especially when it comes to enacting some disclaimers on political ads. Second, in *Federal Election Commission v. Wisconsin Right-to-Life, Inc.,* 127 S.Ct. 2652 (2007), the Court struck down as an applied challenge some of the BCRA provisions as they related to federal electioneering communications. This decision leaves in doubt regulations that would appear to limit the ability of individuals and political organizations to restrict so-called issue advocacy, even if they refer to identifiable candidates. Then in *Davis v. Federal Election Commission,* 128 S.Ct. 2759 (2008), the Court declared unconstitutional another provision of BCRA known as the "millionaire's amendment." This amendment sought to raise contribution limits for candidates facing rich opponents who self-financed their campaign beyond a certain dollar amount.

Thus, the constitutional framework that states face is that mandatory expenditure limits by candidates, parties, or independent groups are unconstitutional. These limits will be upheld if tied into a voluntary public-financing system. Contribution limits are permitted to abate corruption or its appearance, as long as the limits are not too low. Most disclosure laws will be upheld, but there are some problems requiring individuals to comply if they are engaged in *de minimas* political activity. Limits or bans on soft money, corporate, and union express advocacy are permitted; even some limits or bans on PACs or target contributions by specific groups, such as lobbyists, may be upheld. States cannot limit negative attack ads or independent expenditures, but they can raise candidate spending (if they participate in a voluntary public-financing system) to offset them.

In the last three presidential election cycles, two other issues have emerged that test the limits of state regulatory activity. In an effort to circumvent disclosure and other campaign finance laws, nonprofits and 527 organizations are increasingly being created by groups to raise and spend money for political purposes. Under IRS regulations, 501(c)(3) organizations are barred from engaging in partisan activity, but they may engage in some limited grassroots lobbying and advocacy. In contrast, 501(c)(4) entities can engage in more political activities and endorse candidates. Contributions to these entities are unlimited and subject to minimal disclosure. Under IRS rules, 527 entities are generally not required to file with the Federal Election Commission. Contributions to them are generally unlimited, and disclosure is minimal. While 527s and nonprofits have generally been used more at the federal level, increasingly they are becoming major players in state races. While states are generally limited in their ability to regulate (being preempted by federal law), they can mandate 527s that operate within their jurisdiction to register and comply with state disclosure laws. States can also mandate that nonprofits register and comply with state charity laws.

The Variety of State Regulatory Activity

An exhaustive review of state laws and regulatory activity cannot be provided here. In addition, one can debate the merits and efficacy of the different regulations in terms of promoting party competition, reducing incumbency advantages, lowering the cost of elections, or reducing some of the other problems many allege. Earlier studies by this author in 2002 and 2005 offer some assessments. Additionally, the Center for Governmental Studies offers outstanding details on the many specifics of state campaign-finance regulatory laws. However, a few brief words on state laws are still in order.

First, it is literally true that while regulations vary by state, there are common patterns and themes. For example, many states—such as Texas, Idaho, Alabama, Nebraska, and Utah—impose no contribution limits. Other states had imposed some limits on who can give. Minnesota, for example, has a bar on direct corporate contributions to political candidates. Twenty-two and 14 states respectively bar corporate and union contributions to candidates. Colorado, Connecticut, Iowa, and Massachusetts, for example, prohibit corporate contributions, while Ohio, Pennsylvania, Texas, and Wisconsin do the same for unions. However, in *Citizens United v. Federal Election Commission* (2010), the United States Supreme Court struck down the federal ban on corporate and union independent expenditures on behalf of candidates. North Carolina prohibits lobbyist contributions; Louisiana does not permit contributions from the gaming industry. Other states—such as Hawaii, Michigan, Vermont, and Oklahoma—impose different limits for statewide versus legislative races. Other states—such as Massachusetts, Ohio, and Maryland—mandate either overall aggregate contribution limits or different limits depending on whether one is an individual, candidate, party, or PAC.

Second, disclosure laws also vary by state. Federal law requires individual disclosure once one has given more than $200 to a specific candidate or party. This disclosure includes the contribution amount, donor name, employer, and occupation. Some states, such as Minnesota, have $100 disclosure thresholds, while other states have higher or different requirements. Candidate committee, party, and PAC disclosure and reporting requirements (amounts, timing, etc.) often also differ from what is found at the federal level. Some states allow for electronic disclosure; others still rely on hard-copy reporting and filing.

Third, states demonstrate wide variance in how they fund elections. Most states have no public-financing system in place, but 16 do provide for some public funding in the form of either tax credits or subsidies. These systems include partial public financing in Minnesota, Wisconsin, and Vermont, as well as total "clean money" systems in Maine and Arizona.

Finally, many local governments have their own campaign-finance regulations that often mirror state or federal laws in terms of disclosure, public support, or contribution limits. New York City, Los Angeles, Miami-Dade County, Boulder, Colorado, Austin, Texas, and Tucson, Arizona, for example, have different systems that regulate how money may be spent to influence their elections.

Conclusion

States and their local governments are laboratories of democracy when it comes to the regulation of money meant to influence their campaigns and elections. Often, these laws are very different from one another or the rules that govern federal races for Congress and the presidency. Candidates, parties, consultants, and others who wish to participate in these races need to know and understand these laws in order to comply with applicable regulations and avoid the pitfalls that the 21st Century Democrats faced.

SUGGESTED READINGS

Center for Governmental Studies. *State Public Financing Laws.* Los Angeles, Calif.: Center for Governmental Studies, 2005.

Center for Governmental Studies. *State Public Financing Charts.* Los Angeles, Calif.: Center for Governmental Studies, 2007.

Gross, Donald A., and Robert K. Goidel. *The States of Campaign Finance Reform.* Columbus: Ohio State University Press, 2002.

Michaelson, Ronald D. "Campaign Finance Activity in the States: Where the Action Is." *Public Integrity* 3:1 (Winter 2001): 33–51.

Schultz, David. "Disclosure Is Not Enough: Empirical Lessons from State Experiences." *Election Law Journal* 4 (2005): 349–70.

Schultz, David, ed. *Money, Politics, and Campaign Finance Reform Law in the States.* Durham, N.C.: Carolina Academic Press, 2002.

Thompson, Joel A., and Gary F. Moncrief. *Campaign Finance in State Legislative Elections.* Washington, D.C.: Congressional Quarterly, 1998.

Techniques and Types

7

Television Ads and Video

DANE STROTHER

I'm to write about TV commercials. But what is TV? We have Apple video boxes that allow us to buy what we want when we want it, Web TV shows, pay per view, podcasts, and soon wireless spots available on our cell phones. It's impossible to write about TV commercials in 2011 without a discussion of the many platforms available for political commercials. Writing about broadcast commercials alone is like explaining cell phones features with no mention of texting or discussing the Internet without mentioning e-mail.

Video communication has changed more in the past four years than at any time since the advent of cable television. When I make television commercials today, they are for YouTube.com, cable, broadcast, and e-mails. More people saw an attack ad targeting Hillary Clinton on YouTube in the 2008 presidential race then ever saw a Hillary Clinton ad.

We are creating ads for YouTube that can be as long necessary; the 30-second confines of broadcast are irrelevant to the Internet. We create ads for e-mail distribution that we fire off simultaneously with the broadcast version.

As recently as the 2004 presidential election, there was no YouTube and TV spots were never e-mailed. We don't know how exactly we will communicate with voters four years from now. But we do know that if we operate off today's playbook, we will not be effective.

The names, techniques, and approaches will most certainly be different the next time there is an open presidential seat. The stars of tomorrow are tinkering with an offbeat idea today.

Indeed, NBC's new star political commentator and White House correspondent, Chuck Todd, began his improbable climb to the top of the network tree with a lowly web TV show for a very D.C.-insider publication called the *Political Hotline.*

This is not a Nietzschean statement—TV is not dead. But it's different.

Broadcast TV

Broadcast TV is still the largest piece of the campaign communication's puzzle. A television spot is usually created to solve a problem for a campaign or to create a problem for the opposing campaign. Even seemingly innocuous spots lay groundwork for a future attack or response. Every spot is different, and each campaign requires a unique approach. Consultants who use cookie-cutter ads and simply plug one candidate into another candidate's spots will eventually fail.

Candidates should be wary if a consultant assures him or her that "this script always works." For whom, where, how? During the 2008 election cycle, a firm insisted on making a "Veterans" spot in a California race even though the economy was melting down. That firm already had the Veterans spot written and much of the b-roll shot. It was a convenient short-cut, and it failed.

Television still matters disproportionably because as much as people claim they aren't affected by television ads, they're wrong. Video can make a hero look like a villain, stir anger, seize hearts, capture minds, affect change, and leave a lasting impression.

Costs

Professional television is expensive to create, deploy, and maintain. There was a time when only major political races had the luxury of TV ads, but the Internet and YouTube have evened the playing field a bit. There is so much money in politics today that even state senate candidates manage to get on TV, while candidates who can't afford to place broadcast spots can make video for websites and the Internet. Technological advances in cameras and production gear have made it possible to create a broadcast-quality video for a fraction of what it once cost. Today, cameras are thousands instead of tens of thousands of dollars. But television technology is advancing as well. The newest product is high-definition television, and the cameras for it are vastly more expensive. So while someone with a business card and $5,000 can make a political TV spot, only those with resources, know-how, and the proper lenses can make a high-end spot using HDTV.

Once the spot is created, a long-time concern of political consulting becomes paramount: buying air time. In many parts of the country, it costs an enormous amount to air a spot in the major metropolitan areas. The ability to buy broadcast is most problematic in the biggest media markets, such as New York, Los Angeles, and Chicago. Moreover, the cost of placement in any media market is volatile. Radio and television rates reflect the number of people who see or hear the spots, so it's much less expensive to buy television in Des Moines than in New York. One buys television not by the number of spots but by the gross rating point (GRP). Arbitron, a rating service, determines how many people watch a certain show in a certain market. For example, we know that a major prime-time show can have a rating of 32. That means that 32 percent of viewers who are camped in front of their TVs are watching that specific show. It should be noted that no cable show has a rating of even a 2.

So buying an ad in prime time will cost considerably more than buying a show during late-night, which may have a rating of 6 or so. Television-placement purchase rates are set at a cost per point. A purchase of 100 points means that everyone in the market ideally will see a spot once. A purchase of 1,000 points means that the average viewer will see a spot an average of 10 times. The cost per point is set for each of the 211 markets in America, and every market has a slightly different cost. For example, the cost per point in Baton Rouge is roughly $40, while the cost in Atlanta is $350.

Politicians, as always, have taken care of themselves and, by law, they have guaranteed they get lowest unit rate. This means that a political campaign can pay less than commercial advertisers if the spots run within 90 days of Election Day, which is called the political window. But political rates are still expensive.

Buying television time is a science. It's not enough simply to produce a spot and throw it on the air. The key is determining what TV shows a campaign's targets are watching and ensuring that the spots run during those shows. Saturday morning cartoons are out because children can't vote. But if the target audience for a campaign is working-class women over the age of fifty who have little formal education, then soap operas are prime buys.

Regardless of when it runs, no ad stands alone. The office seekers of October have to compete not just with AT&T, Coors, and the local Buick dealer, but also with hundreds of other candidates for all sorts of races. The explosion of advertising clutter means that a spot must be hammered home over and over before the message is retained. Whereas a campaign might have once run a spot for 600 points, today 1,200 or 1,300 points are necessary. While we who make political ads try to distinguish ours from the pack, in the end it's understandable that voters might disconnect from so many similar messages, staging, and plotlines. The result is ever-increasing expense to distribute less information, and with diminishing returns.

Accordingly, the goal for a political producer is to make a spot that has the production values and quality to stand up to the national ads that often bookend it, all without costing a fortune. Political producers are exceedingly adroit at making television spots quickly and inexpensively.

A well-run campaign spends 80 percent of its war chest communicating with voters. The idea is to keep overhead—salaries, candidate travel, and re-search costs—low so that the bulk of the money can be directed at the voter. In essence, a campaign is nothing more than a vehicle to deliver a message to voters; that message is a candidate's sales pitch. Giving voters a reason to support a candidacy is the only way to win a political campaign. And the more times voters hear a candidate's message—assuming it's a message they are open to hearing and that it's well-delivered—the more likely those voters are going to remember it.

Included in the 80 percent of campaign expenditures earmarked for com-munication is the cost of production. Television production costs roughly 10 percent of the actual time buy. This varies according to the producers' ego and ability to keep costs down. Political advertising differs greatly from com-mercial advertising in the directness and cost of the production. Political producers are always looking for ways to keep production costs to a minimum. It is unusual for a political television commercial to cost more than $10,000, which is about a tenth or less of what a consumer ad costs to make.

Positive, Contrastive, and Negative Ads

There are basically three different types of political television commercials: positive, contrastive, and negative. The mix and use of these three genres seems to change virtually every election cycle: no lessons are permanent.

All three ad types are essentially used to define both the candidates in a race. The idea is to paint a beautiful picture of one's client and a less-than-flattering view of the opponent. Polls are used to determine what aspects of a candidate's life or views are best received by voters. For example, if the fact that a candidate is a self-made success moves undecided voters to him, then the television ad shows and tells that story. "John Doe is an up-by-the-boot-straps American success story. He's turned his life from challenge to fortune by believing he could, working hard, being honest, and standing up through tough times that would knock down most people."

Positive ads seldom, if ever, mention the opponent. Rather, they offer an introduction to a candidate and his family, testimonials from people he has helped, or an explanation of what he hopes to do if elected. Each political-consulting firm has a different philosophy about positive ads, but increasingly we are using them, packed with more information, than we once did because they are more compelling and because we need to provide a lot of information in a short time. Yet the directly opposite approach worked in the 2008 election cycle, when a congressman named Charlie Dent from Allentown, Pennsylvania, ran a great deal of TV and not a single positive ad. He hit his opponent, never made his case for himself, and won by a large margin. Incumbents are better able to run a larger mix of negative ads because they are known in the community and don't have the burden of introducing themselves on TV. Challengers, however, must introduce themselves *and* make the case for firing the incumbent.

But generally, positive ads are the backbone of a good political campaign. A good positive ad begins to set up a contrast with the opponent without being obvious about it. In that sense, a positive ad can contain implied critiques of the opposition. This is because, ultimately, campaigns are about differences. Voters have to reach for one lever or another in the voting booth, and they usually know little more than they have gleaned from television ads, the Internet, or from neighbors or friends, who also got their information from the public domain. A campaign must give voters a reason to support a certain candidate while at the same time providing a reason not to support the opponent.

Nevertheless, the rules on negativity are changing. We are increasingly seeing that harsh negative ads are backfiring. For two decades, the pundits and national press corps have complained that campaigns were little more than intellectual mud wrestling. Year after year, however, political professionals would use negative information about their opponent and see a positive effect. It seemed a textbook truism that "attacks work."

But a funny thing happened on the way to victory. Voters finally decided that they had had enough of the malicious tactics; they seemed to be genuinely tiring of slashing, demeaning ads, and they reacted by tuning out the message and turning against the messenger. Today a smart political professional uses a scalpel—not a chainsaw—to dismember an opponent's campaign. For example, spots we produced for Louisiana senator Mary Landrieu in her initial race for Congress in 1996 were slash-and-burn attacks, with ominous music, dark pictures, and a sneering announcer. Those spots worked then but would be the cause of shaking heads today. When we once tossed up unsubstantiated attacks and let the opponents respond as best they could, today we must have third-party validation. And we know that when we go too far, the blogosphere and the press will team up to harm the campaign. This new oversight and accountability is good for the political process.

There will always be several roads to the truth in television ads. People vote for and against bills for a bevy of reasons, and sometimes a good idea is killed because it abuts a bad idea in a bill. Political pros will always be looking for the twist and the turn as a way to spin, but that's what we're paid to do. And quite honestly, a candidate's true leanings and beliefs can be ferreted out by the bills he or she supports or opposes over a number of years. The truth is that some Republicans do believe the Department of Education should be abolished, but they would never say so publicly. It's up to their opponents to give voters a true sense of their views.

The switch from harsh negatives began just over a decade ago, in Georgia. In the 1998 governor's race, Guy Millner spent hundreds of thousands of dollars attacking his Democratic opponent, Roy Barnes, even before Barnes became the official nominee. Millner tried to demonize dozens of votes that Barnes had cast as a member of the state legislature. For four months, Milner aired one negative ad after another. According to the old manual, this was good politics: define your opponent before he gets a chance to define himself.

For the most part, the attacks were factual, but they were out of context. Barnes had cast more than fifty thousand votes in the legislature and each of them for a good reason. To the voters' credit, they understood that. Millner's tactless campaign was defeated by 10 percentage points. Millner was done in because he did not notice that the electorate was changing.

More recently, we saw the same problem in Arizona senator John McCain's 2008 presidential campaign. McCain's people tried to tie then-Senator Obama to a washed-up former "terrorist," and voters were simply not going to accept such a stretch. A negative ad today must pass not just a truth test but a "smell" test: Does it feel right to voters? Again, there are no absolutes in political advertising, but there are general truths. Watching the electorate closely and gauging what does or does not move voters is the key to staying relevant and successful.

There will never be an end to negative ads by any means. But the question now is: What is a negative ad? Is it negative to point out that an opponent truly wants to abolish Head Start? Or to explain to voters that school vouchers could mean less money for public schools? Is it negative to explain that a candidate's plans to "redistribute the wealth" could mean less money for your family?

Today's voter is increasingly more responsive to what are called comparative ads. Eschewing screaming or name-calling, the best of the comparative ads simply put both candidates side by side and measure their records. Since today's wily voter refuses to believe any unsubstantiated charge, it's imperative that media consultants support all statements with documentation on the screen. Focus groups have taught us that using a headline from a newspaper makes an ad more believable, and using the banner from the newspaper makes it more believable yet. Interestingly, the federal requirement forcing candidates verbally to approve an ad at its beginning or end has made political advertising even more believable. The more information, the better.

It's worth noting that one venue where disclaimers and accountability are not legally required is the Internet. We can put any video online and not be forced to state who paid to produce it. That's a loophole Congress may want to close, as the Internet and television are quickly merging into the same box.

A final thought on negative ads is about how the issue of gender has changed. Not too long ago, it was believed that a male candidate had to be exceedingly careful in attacking a female opponent. Those days are over. Today voters view men and women as equals on the campaign battlefield, and the discussions about whether to go "softer" or not are over. Nancy Pelosi, Sarah Palin, and Hillary Clinton are prime examples of women leveling the playing field in terms of gender. The Obama campaign attacked Hillary Clinton in many states. In South Carolina, Obama's team questioned her commitment to African Americans. All candidates, regardless of gender, are becoming fair game.

The Research Imperative

Once upon a time, consultants created television ads with little more direction than a gut feeling or an idea from a friend or campaign employee. The lore of spots being written on the back of cocktail napkins is widespread. Single-malt whiskey often served as a muse, and a campaign's strategy could change with the moon. Those days are done.

If a modern consultant tells a candidate he or she has a "hunch," the candidate should start looking for a new consultant. Creating television commercials has become as much science as art. Tens of thousands of dollars are spent on research before writing the first draft of a script, much less the permanent stump speech.

First, there is an extensive interview of a candidate by a consultant. Who is he or she? What makes her tick? What is he truly passionate about? Often this interview is videotaped and held for future reference. Indeed, a solid answer eventually could be cut for a video segment of a website. Once personality questions are exhausted, then issues are hashed out. Some candidates are willing to switch from unpopular positions, such as partial birth abortion. Others are resolute in their core beliefs and intransigent despite the risk of espousing an unpopular stance. Depending on the issue, such intransigence can cost a candidate a race. In a representative democracy, it is imperative that a candidate share the views of the voters. But candidates have every right to stick by their positions, especially when those views are of moral import. How a consultant explains an unpopular position is what separates a winning consultant from an also-ran.

Following the interview, a media consultant will travel with a candidate to see how he or she interacts with people and whether the campaign work is relished or endured. Speech patterns, intensity, delivery, and style are studied for days. The reason is simple: ultimately, a consultant must capture a candidate's entire being on film. If a candidate is vigorous or contemplative or brilliant, these traits must be evident in the paid media. And that's no easy task, because people rarely play themselves well on television. For example, one of the most dynamic people I've worked for is Mayor Shirley Franklin in Atlanta. Shirley is a dynamo, and I had to capture that intensity of spirit and never-ending energy. So I produced spots that had her walking in one side of the frame and out of the other. It was as if the viewer was walking at a brisk pace with Shirley.

Once the "getting to know you" stage is over, it's time to have opposition research conducted on the client as well as on the opponents. Never trust a client who promises to tell you all the problems and confess all the warts. They seldom, if ever, remember everything or provide all the necessary information. I once had a candidate running for mayor of Denver who was the city auditor. Our message was about doing more with less, cutting the budget, streamlining, and cleaning up corruption. My client refused to pay the $10,000 to have himself researched. Four days before Election Day, the paper broke a story that my client had used public money for private uses. It wasn't much, and debatably was improper, but it contradicted our message. Instead of charging ahead, we merely limped into the runoff.

Following the opposition research, a poll questionnaire is developed. This is often done with the help of all the consultants in a campaign. It takes three to six days to conduct a poll and another week or so for a pollster to write a report. This accomplished, the campaign's message is determined, and a media consultant begins thinking about the direction the campaign's communications should take. Candidates and consultants alike must recognize this truth: polls should drive the content of television ads, as well as all video and audio communication. No candidate should forsake his or her core beliefs to satisfy a consultant or completely bend to a poll. But the language tested in a poll should be the language used in communication. A good poll will help candidates best discuss not only popular beliefs but also controversial ones. And if a candidate follows a poll but tries to be something he or she is not, the voters ultimately figure it out. For example, John Edwards ran an entire campaign on the "two Americas." The problem was that he lived at the very, very top of the most affluent America. And voters ultimately saw through his shtick.

Television and the Real World

The decision-making processes in a political campaign do not exist in a vacuum: real-life campaigning is often a series of compromises with reality, especially when dealing with the monetary drain of television. Two races in Oklahoma well exemplify the difficulties of real-life campaigns and all of the roadblocks, diversions, and drama associated with taking on candidates (and their friends and family) and winning elections.

The first case is a 2006 race for mayor of Tulsa, in which Democratic challenger Kathy Taylor opposed the Republican incumbent, Bill LaFortune. Taylor had never run for office. She was an enormously successful businesswoman and had been Oklahoma's Secretary of Commerce. The political climate in Tulsa was tough; it is the home of conservative U.S. Senator Jim Inhofe and in 2004 voted more than 65 percent for President George W. Bush. LaFortune was a moderately successful mayor whose father had been a famous and beloved mayor of Tulsa. There are parks in the city named for the LaFortune family.

Taylor ran a primary race against a former city councilman and successful businessman who spent more than $1 million of his own money in the small Tulsa media market. He ran the ultimate "locals" campaign, with local consultants and a new message every week. He had many spots, all of which looked completely different from one another. There was no consistency, no common thread, no backbone holding it all together. Taylor won handily. It was time to oppose the current mayor.

We researched LaFortune, polled the findings, and determined several angles of attack. The most damning angle was simply that the people of Tulsa feared its best days were behind it. There was great anger at the widespread graffiti and boarded-up buildings.

Taylor proved to be an incredibly quick study. She mastered the issues, and in a series of midnight e-mail exchanges we honed the message of "bringing a business outlook to running Tulsa." Our first few spots featured Taylor speaking into camera, introducing herself for the general election. There was little contention about the scripts for the spots. Taylor applied her personal touch, which often works well with smart candidates. But then we hit a snag.

We were behind in the polls and decided we had to attack LaFortune. We made a spot that showed Tulsa in a poor light and promised to clean up the mess. And that's when the textbook approach was thrown off track. Taylor refused to go negative or show the city in a poor light. "I'd rather lose than do that," she said in a Sunday afternoon conference call. She loves Tulsa and refused to denigrate the city in any way.

So we pressed on with more positive ads highlighting Taylor's business background, which LaFortune could not match because he had never run a business. We created subtle differences. And we switched from having Taylor talk into the camera, instead featuring third-party validators who spoke about how well and frugally Taylor managed her businesses.

The message was not what the consultants would have advised, but that's the real world in campaigns. There is always a candidate, best friend, local consultant, or spouse who throws rocks on the tracks. Taylor won by five points and went on to be a great mayor. She's positioned to be governor or senator if that's her inclination. But in the same state there is another woman I worked for who won in a race that was completely different from Taylor's campaign.

Kim Holland was running for reelection as Oklahoma's insurance commissioner. She had previously been appointed to that position by the wildly popular governor Brad Henry to fill the term of the elected insurance commissioner, who had been sent to prison for accepting kickbacks. Our challenge in the campaign was explaining to Oklahomans that Holland had nothing to do with the previous commissioner. Our polling was conducted by legendary consultant Celinda Lake. Polling indicated that there was great voter mistrust of anyone who served as insurance commissioner and absolutely no understanding that Henry had appointed Holland to clean up the office.

We also had a cash problem in the campaign. Holland did her part, but raising money in a down-ballot race is difficult and advertising statewide is expensive. We didn't have the money to run many TV spots spelling out her entire story. So I created a political format called 15–15. The basics are simple. When a candidate buys 30 seconds of TV, there is no requirement that the 30 seconds run at once. So we made two 15-second ads for a commercial break. The goal was to have stations run one of the 15-second ads at the head of the commercial break and the second 15-second ad at the end of the break. This meant for the price of one 30-second spot, we managed to get two messages to voters. The key was making both spots look and sound alike so that viewers put the two together. A greater challenge was limiting the script copy so that it neatly fit into 15 seconds. A 30-second ad is basically 65 words, so a 15-second spot had to be 32 or 33 words. That's not a lot of time to say anything. So we wrote scripts and then whittled them down again and again.

Once the scripts were approved, we put Holland on a white sound stage, which means she was standing with nothing but white all around her. She was the only object for the camera—and, by extension, the viewer—to focus on. Holland nailed the scripts to camera. In the first spot we had the camera on a crane, and when the shot pulled back Holland was standing just in front of a black line that said "Starting Line." She held up a dollar bill to make the point that she was saving taxpayers money and said, "We've recovered more than a thousand of these babies and we're just getting started."

In the second 15-second spot, we explained that Governor Henry had appointed Holland to clean up the office of insurance commissioner. She delivered her lines to the camera holding a bottle of Windex and a rag. Near the end of her script, she sprayed the lens, wiped it off, and said, "Governor Henry appointed me to clean up this office. Well, we are [spray and wipe] squeaky clean."

The spots were a huge hit. Two years later, people were still telling Holland to "clean up that office—squeaky clean." A phrase was coined

Then the curveball dropped into the race. A wealthy Texan who believed his insurance company was improperly maligned by Holland's department spent hundreds of thousands of dollars on television in an independent expenditure against her. Her two 15-second spots had not run long enough to pull them, and there was not money for a parallel track of TV. So we were faced with the tough choice of switching TV ads to answer the attacks or fighting back in the free press and forging ahead with our strategy. That's where experience in hundreds of campaigns made the difference. Rather than risk losing the messages we were pushing by switching tracks, we stayed the course and held our breath. Kim Holland won her race. She has a bright future because she had the nerve and instincts to follow sound advice and make good decisions. The way we communicate in political campaigns has changed more in recent years than at any time since the advent of television. Technology allows campaigns on Facebook; it enables political Twittering and texting. But one thing has not changed, and that's the need for a good candidate and a solid campaign plan.

8

Newspaper Advertising

THOMAS N. EDMONDS AND JOHN E. KIMBALL

While the much-maligned daily newspaper industry is painted as a dying breed, when it comes to political and issue advertising, nothing could be further from the truth. In fact, "Newspapers are back." That's what political consultant Cathy Allen told the *Wall Street Journal* in late July 2007. Under the headline, "Political Ads Stage a Comeback in Newspapers," the *Journal* feature article went on to document the major turnaround that the medium had staged in garnering increased political ad revenue. In fact, the turnaround is so dramatic that starting after the 2000 elections, the newspaper industry has not only been substantially increasing its political ad revenue every two years, but also increasing its share of total media dollars. But its reality, like its perception, has not always been so rosy.

Newspapers

Before radio and television, newspapers were the dominate communications medium and virtually the only place where voters could get information about elections and campaigns. So it wasn't surprising that, with no competition, newspapers set the rules for political advertising—rules that were frequently not accommodating to the needs of campaigns. The landscape began to change in the 1930s, when Franklin Roosevelt used radio to break the newspapers' monopoly on mass communication. Despite the competition from radio, however, the print medium steadfastly adhered to its old ways. Even with the arrival of television in the 1950s, newspapers could not be prodded into being more accommodating and competitive in the ever-growing political advertising arena.

Newspaper Industry Political Ad Revenue

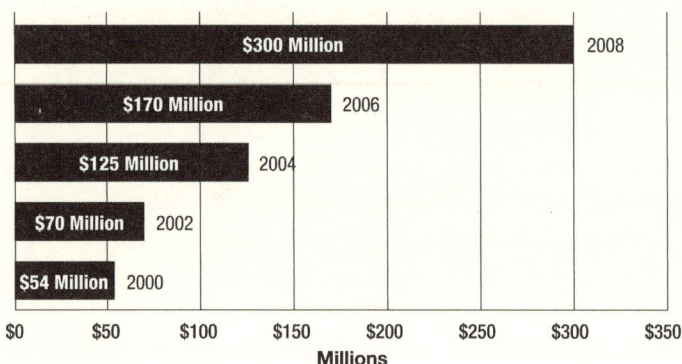

$300 Million 2008
$170 Million 2006
$125 Million 2004
$70 Million 2002
$54 Million 2000

$0 $50 $100 $150 $200 $250 $300 $350

Millions

Source: Newspaper Association of America

Whether real or perceived, there were many common criticisms of newspapers in the political community:

- Newspapers cost too much.
- Newspapers' salespeople aren't receptive to the needs of campaigns.
- Newspapers turn down ads that conflict with their endorsements.
- Newspapers' extensive campaign coverage means readers get the message without anyone having to buy advertising.
- Newspapers can't respond quickly enough in the heat of the campaign.
- Newspapers lack the impact of television and radio messages.
- Newspapers can't be targeted to specific voters.

As the twentieth century was nearing its close, newspapers' share of the political ad dollar had fallen to an all-time low (about 2–3 percent). Meanwhile, the amount of money spent on elections and issue-advocacy campaigns had continued to skyrocket, becoming a multibillion dollar industry. Then revolution joined with evolution and the newspaper trend line began to bend upwards. First and foremost was the maturation of the Internet and the advent of cable, which eroded the dominance and allure of broadcast television. Add DVR technology to the mix, making it more difficult to get advertising messages across to a public more empowered to avoid them, and the foundations were laid for significant marketing changes in all advertising. At that juncture, the newspaper industry finally began to reinvent itself, addressing not only legitimate criticisms but changes in the marketplace that had been fueled by new technology. Newspaper websites began to dominate their markets as the most visited local sites, offering readers and users a 24/7 information experience online to match the tactile print experience that continues to attract readers and advertisers. Online video found its way to newspaper websites. The print product began to match the innovation shown on the digital side, with great color, superior targeting for regular in-paper ads and inserts, front page Post-It notes, plastic carrier poly-bags, and superior freestanding inserts. In short, what was old became new again.

In areas where such changes have been implemented, political advertising in newspapers has increased. Many consultants are discovering the distinct advantages of newspapers and the benefits of using the powerful combination of print and online editions to complement their broadcast buys.

Advantages of Newspaper

Jordan Lieberman, immediate past president and publisher of *Campaigns & Elections* magazine, says that a growing number of political consultants feel that today's newspapers offer distinct advantages over television and other media. According to Lieberman, "Newspapers have credibility and an engaged audience that other media can only hope for." While Lieberman was speaking specifically about daily newspapers, local weekly newspapers also carry a high degree of audience engagement and credibility, as they are often the primary source of very local community news. As such, their audience is also highly valued and sought after by political campaigns.

Starting after the 2000 elections, the newspaper industry, through its trade association, the Newspaper Association of America, began an aggressive marketing campaign aimed at the political community, proclaiming the advantages that newspapers offer candidates and other political advertisers. Using proprietary polls and data from a variety of independent surveys of voters and their media habits, the print industry regained its footing and realized that it had numerous advantages to offer campaigns and their consultants. Among them:

1. *Newspaper readers are voters*
   No medium has a higher correlation with voting than newspaper. In

the 2004 presidential election, 9 out of 10 newspaper readers cast a ballot. In the 2006 midterm elections, when voting is typically much lighter, newspaper readers still delivered the vote, with more than 8 out of 10 newspaper readers going to the polls. In both the 2008 primaries and the general election, Barack Obama, Hillary Clinton, and John Mc-Cain all realized that the voters they needed to attract were newspaper readers—both print and online. In a number of instances, the major presidential campaigns actually cancelled broadcast schedules and shifted the funds to newspaper advertising.

2. *Newspapers are credible*

Results from several national surveys show that voters from all demographic groups find political newspaper ads more credible than political ads on television, radio, direct mail, or even the Internet.

3. *Newspapers consistently reach voters*

Voters consistently look to newspapers to help make up their minds about how they will vote. In spite of the explosion of other media options, this remains a universal political truth. While the perceived usefulness of other media rises and falls as a campaign progresses, newspapers maintain their strength for influencing voter opinion. Voters count on newspapers to deliver the whole story about the candidates and issues, from the earliest moments of the campaign right up until Election Day.

4. *Newspapers reach crucial undecided voters*

Conventional wisdom among consultants indicates that only 5 to 10 percent of the electorate is typically up for grabs at the end of any campaign. However, these late-deciding voters almost always provide the margin of victory. Here again, research shows that the audience coming to critical campaign information through the newspapers' print and website products has the highest concentration of this crucial target audience, with no fewer than 3 out of 4 undecided voters identifying themselves as "regular newspaper readers."

5. *Newspaper readers look at advertising differently*

People don't DVR a newspaper ad or read a newspaper to escape from reality. Newspapers epitomize "permission advertising" because readers accept the ads on their own terms, deciding when and where to read them, and actually considering them to be an integral part of the media. A 2009 survey from MORI Research found that newspaper advertising remains the leading advertising medium cited by consumers in planning, shopping, and making purchasing decisions. The study, part of a series entitled "American Consumer Insights," also found that 82 percent of adults said they "took action" as a result of newspaper advertising. Today, in a world where people routinely opt out of advertising, newspaper readers choose to "opt in" to the advertising—in fact, they view it as content.

6. *Newspapers have improved targeting*

The degree to which newspapers can be targeted is not something that many political campaigns or their consultants know about. Most newspapers have gone beyond merely establishing geographic zones. Now, they can target preprinted fliers or brochures for insertion and delivery within a specific zip code; many can target delivery down to the census tract, block, or even house. Similar targeting is being done with Post-It notes placed on the front page, or even on the delivery bag in which the newspaper arrives. Many newspapers can demographically target these options as well. The bottom line is that the newspaper you receive may be different from the one your neighbor does. Obviously, newspaper websites, which are dominant in most media markets, have all of the targeting capabilities that are inherent in new media.

7. *Newspapers can provide more information to voters*

Less is more only when you have nothing to say. The entire content of a network evening news broadcast would not fill the front page of a major newspaper. Unlike a 30-second television or 60-second radio spot, a newspaper ad can deliver a longer message and provide greater detail and documentation in an environment where the reader is not only tolerant, but is expecting a fuller picture of the issues. This is just one of the many reasons that candidates and issue advertisers so covet the endorsement of their local newspaper and its editorial board.

8. *It's easier to advertise in newspapers*

The newspaper industry has made great strides in accommodating political advertisers. Replacing the need to contact each newspaper individually for placement in its print or website vehicles are network ad placement organizations. Typically a media buy can be completed with a single order and one check, regardless if the buy is for one newspaper, every newspaper in a state or newspapers in several states. Special political rate cards, trained political-sales staff, quicker closing dates, and electronic submission of ads for next-day publication have all made the medium more competitive and advertiser-friendly.

9. *All politics is local*

In nearly every market in the United States, the best-known local brand belongs to the newspaper and its companion website. Newspapers continue to be the place where voters to go to find out what's going on in their communities. This kind of local environment offers valuable competitive advantages for political advertisers.

10. *Newspapers dominate on the Internet, too*

As the Internet continues to grow and mature, at one point or another between a third and half of all voters turn to it for expanded election news. And when they do, according to surveys, they are three times more likely to go to a trusted newspaper website than any other site, including their local TV or radio stations, social-networking sites, or blogs. According to a June 2009 Nielsen survey, in a single month, newspaper websites attracted more than 70.3 million unique visitors, a figure amounting to nearly 36 percent of all U.S. Internet users. The size of this web audience, along with newspapers' reputation for thorough and credible reporting, helps extend brand loyalty and trust to newspaper websites as well. People tend to trust brands they know well.

Newspapers and the Internet

In this age of evolving media platforms, it is becoming more and more difficult to neatly categorize any medium. For instance, a news channel such as CNN or FoxNews can be available via cable, satellite, podcast, or on its own website. Newspapers are no strangers to this evolving technology; indeed, they have been quick to see its advantages. The Internet has allowed newspapers to go from single-platform, static information-delivery vehicles to multiple-platform media companies offering true 24/7 publishing options. As ink on paper continues to be just one of a newspaper's brands, the local media market increasingly consists of a dominant newspaper with many brand extensions. Certainly the cornerstone of a newspaper brand remains its print edition. But its websites, blogs, social-networking sites, and alliances with other media have created an expansive and powerful portfolio that savvy political consultants can use to their competitive advantage. A survey commissioned by Google in 2007 found that newspaper print ads do drive consumers to the web, heightening the importance of newspaper websites and the growing need for them to be integrated with other types of offline media. Use a search engine on the Internet and, more often than not, the news content you find is generated by a newspaper. Newspapers and their newsrooms spend billions of dollars each year in the gathering and editing of news and information that other media simply cannot afford. The Internet has also allowed major national newspapers to become local, so that, for example, a campaign can advertise in the WashingtonPost.com just in the state of Texas. Recognizing that there is less resistance among political advertisers to the Internet, most newspapers sell advertising packages that offer both print and online versions in a powerful combination. Software that converts campaign television commercials to online video on newspaper websites has opened the door to new revenue streams as well.

Magazines

By definition, any discussion of political print advertising would have to include magazines as well as daily newspapers. However, for a variety of reasons, magazines do not lend themselves well to political advertising. In today's 24-hour news cycle, a medium that only changes weekly or monthly (and requires even more lead time than that) is not well suited for a political message. Exceptions might be magazines with a specific target audience within a candidate's jurisdiction—for example, a statewide business journal, hunting publication, or other trade publication. Like daily newspapers, news magazines are being forced to reinvent themselves. Many have done so by changing the content and format of their print publications, as well as by increasing their presence on the Internet. For instance, *Time* and *Newsweek* have abandoned their old template and opted for in-depth reporting on a few select topics rather than a comprehensive review of the previous week's news. Magazine websites do offer political and issue advertisers an audience that can be a valuable part of a campaign's media mix.

Summary

While not without its challenges, the newspaper industry is surprisingly well-positioned for the future. More and more campaigns recognize the necessity and value of including newspaper-branded media in their campaign media plans. That's why newspapers will likely continue to increase their share of the political ad dollar as they evolve and refine their brands and product lines based on a newfound respect for political ad revenue.

Newspapers will also benefit from an electorate that increasingly demands substance over sound bites and that is turned off by the theatrics, redundancy, and polarization of broadcast and cable news programs.

The bottom line is that the total audience for news and information developed and delivered under the local newspaper brand is growing, not shrinking.

Note: Statistics based on nationwide surveys of voters and the media, including joint Cromer Group (Washington, D.C.–based Democratic firm) and Moore Information (Portland, Oregon, Republican firm) poll (Aug. 2003); Pew Internet and American Life Project (Jan. 2007); American Voter Media Use Study conducted by Costas Panagopoulos, Yale University (Jan. 2008); and Moore Information (Mar. 2008).

For More Information
Newspaper Association of America
4401 Wilson Blvd. Suite 900
Arlington, Va. 22203
naa.org

Magazine Publishers of America
810 Seventh Avenue, 24th Floor
New York, N.Y. 10019
magazine.org

9
Radio Advertising
BILL FLETCHER

Television is the dominant medium in America, and that includes politics at virtually every level. But in spite of the power, growth, and reach of television, radio remains a dynamic medium for modern politics. It is on the radio where democracy and commerce collide. Radio offers politicians and political groups a relatively captive audience twice each day, on voters' morning drive to work and their afternoon drive home. Radio is also the most imaginative medium: one can suggest in a few reasonably priced words and sound effects what would take millions of dollars to visualize on a television screen.

Because radio deals in sounds and impressions, it is a much less forgiving medium than film or television. If you throw enough money at any film script, it can look slick in spite of ridiculous situations and inane dialogue. But you can't hide bad writing in a radio commercial.

There have been dramatic improvements in audio technology in recent years. In the not-too-distant past, radio commercials were recorded on quarter-inch analog tape and literally edited with a razor blade and tape. Today, most radio commercials are recorded on digital systems with electronic storage and then delivered to the radio stations via an MP3 file, with not a piece of tape (audio or sticky) in sight.

Good radio, however, is more dependent on talent than technology. The talent is expressed in the voices, the script (writing, plot, and ideas), direction (managing voice, words, and action), and, equally important, the media buy (when and where to place the spot).

Voice

The voice is the heart and soul of a good radio commercial. That is why political professionals use voice actors, not radio personalities. Most radio announcers are ill-suited to voice a political commercial. They usually have one gear for their voice, and they stay in it all the time. A great voice actor can shift tone and diction with ease to connect with the listener on an emotional level. A great voice actor can add emotion and pathos to a well-written script.

Political professionals often develop creative partnerships with voice actors. Often when I'm writing a spot for television or radio, I will hear in my head the voice of the actor I plan to use. These professional relationships are a "value added" benefit that political professionals bring to the table. We know the voice actors who have the range and acting ability to pull off a soft biographical spot, a hard sell, an attack, or an explanation.

Script

The most common error in radio scripting is overlong or overripe writing. Freed from the limitation of 30-second television spots, many consultants try to jam too many ideas, words, and concepts into a 60-second radio commercial. Then they compound the error by forcing the voice actor to rip through the spot, rushing past the natural breaks, until the entire commercial takes on the semblance of a legal disclaimer for a car dealer.

The best way to make sure you haven't tried to cram too much into a radio spot is to read it aloud and time yourself. Be careful to enunciate each word clearly so as not to cheat the time. With the legally required disclaimer detailing who paid for and authorized the ad, this leaves about 55 seconds. Allowing for time to establish music and for any sound effects, the voice actor's script should be between 50 and 55 seconds long.

The first sentence of a radio commercial is the most crucial. In most cases, it should be simple, declarative, and designed to invite the listener to tarry for a moment. The opening of a radio spot is also a good place to trot out those quotes and other bon mots you've been saving in your filing system since college.

Below are some examples of good opening lines for a radio spot:

• "Once in a very great while . . . someone moves us, changes us, gives us hope. This year that extraordinary person is congressional candidate Jane Doe."

- "You can tell a lot about a man by what he does when he thinks no one is watching."
- "There once was a man who took from the poor and gave to the rich. His name is John Smith, the Reverse Robin Hood." [Delivered in a Monty Python–like British accent.]
- "The year was 1985, and somewhere a child was crying. And not just one child . . . hundreds. John Smith heard the children and became their champion."
- "'They're counting on you. In the corridors of political power . . . they are counting on you . . . not to vote."
- "Everybody knows a man like John Smith . . . up with the sun, loving his family, working on his farm, serving his community."

By design, none of these openings sound particularly political. The only way to hold the modern, cynical audience and to communicate a political message is to begin with an emotional connection or an intellectual challenge.

Following are a few bad ways to start a political radio commercial:

- "This is State Representative Bubba Gump and I want to ask for your vote."
- "John Smith is a liar and I'm here to set the record straight."
- "The election is just a few days away. . . ."

Start a radio commercial like that and the next sound you will hear is hundreds of thousands of people changing the radio station to try to find a traffic report.

In *A Moveable Feast,* Ernest Hemingway wrote of a technique he used in his short stories. He wrote in the cafes of Paris and then set his work aside for a few days or weeks. When he returned to his manuscript, he would read it until he found the first "true" thought; then he would discard everything else and begin again from that point.

The brevity and emotional understatement present in Hemingway's work is a great tutorial for radio writers. Write down your thoughts, then comb through them looking for the truth—the essence of what you're trying to communicate. Then jettison the chaff and commence with that thought.

Direction

Even the best voice actors need direction when voicing a political commercial. They need to know the tone of the commercial and the context of the spot in the overall campaign. Voice actors with whom I've worked for years have often complained to me about producers and directors who simply don't know what they want.

When directing a radio commercial, it's not enough to tell the actor, "Just read it." For example, let's assume you are producing a political commercial for a congressional candidate. The first third of the spot is biographical, the middle third touches on the major issues of the campaign, and the final third is an appeal for support and votes. You might say something like this to the voice actor: "Perform the first two paragraphs in a soft, languid, nostalgic style. Then shift to a tougher, faster, news read and punch the first two words as you come to each major issue such as Social Security, the environment, health care. Then, for the close, shift back to the original tone and tempo but read with great authority and confidence."

Another common mistake is for directors to allow voice actors to read in a full, loud voice as if they are trying to be heard over the roar of traffic. When I'm looking for a softer read I will often direct voice actors to read as if there is a sleeping baby in the next room they are trying not to awaken.

Typically, the voice actor will make notes and marks on the script to indicate your direction. After the first read, offer comment and criticism and let the actor read the script again. Usually, you'll get the read you're looking for in five or six attempts. If you get the first half of the spot down just the way you want it, don't make the actor read that part over and over again. Spend your time on getting the second half right and let your audio engineer edit the reads together.

Buying Radio Time

Radio is a tough medium to buy for political campaigns. Stations are constantly changing formats, which means the station that was rock and roll last week might be gospel today. Also, there is a widely held misconception that radio is cheap. The only cheap radio is on small stations with tiny audiences. In some markets, commercials on large, major-market stations are often nearly as expensive as television commercials. The campaign should employ the services of a professional media buyer who is either familiar with the market or who can research the market and identify where the voters congregate.

In general, people listen consistently to one format: country music, talk shows, oldies, urban contemporary, light rock, or (unfortunately for media buyers) public radio. Alternative and modern rock stations usually don't have significant numbers of voters. There are exceptions in every market, of course, which is why a professional media buyer is critical.

Radio listeners also divide themselves along race, sex, age, and other demographic lines. Women, Latinos, African Americans, angry white men, conservatives, Christians, and many other subsets of the general electorate congregate at stations that cater to their music, culture, and ideas.

One efficient way to buy radio time is through radio news service networks, which are typically organized by state. They gather groups of stations together and make it relatively easy to buy time on dozens of radio stations using one central contact.

The various ratings services offer valuable information to media buyers on the demographics and listening habits of radio audiences. Keep in mind that these ratings measure listenership every quarter-hour: this short span is necessary because people tend to jump from one radio station to another as they drive. Most political buys are placed on the top four to seven radio stations in a market to make sure to reach all the voters who are jumping from station to station. Your best political buys are during the morning and evening commuting times on weekdays.

Sample Radio Scripts

For almost any member of Congress, letting the folks back home know that he or she is staying in touch is critical. We developed this script for Congressman Bart Gordon, chairman of the House Science and Technology Committee, to drive home the point that he is listening to their voices.

"Letters from Home"
Radio: 60—Bart Gordon for Congress
Fletcher Rowley Riddle, Inc.

Bart Gordon stays in touch in a lot of different ways. He has regular open meetings here, and he's a familiar face on special days in our community.

But there's another way Congressman Bart Gordon stays in touch. Every morning, no matter if here at home or in his office in Washington, Bart begins his day by reading personal letters from people like you and me.

For Bart, it's another way of staying in touch. For us, it's a way to let him know when we have a problem, an idea, or a concern.

And because Bart Gordon stays in touch, he's made a difference on things that matter to us, the same things we write about in our letters.

Things like protecting Social Security, cleaning up waste and fraud in the federal government, and keeping Tennessee from becoming a dump for nuclear waste.

Bart doesn't just come around at election time asking for our votes. He's here all the time, listening to us, standing up for us, and, every morning, reading our letters.

Bart Gordon. In touch.

In keeping with Hemingway's admonition to search for the "first true thing," the inspiration for this radio spot came from a conversation with Congressman Gordon in which he told me that he has his staff put any real, handwritten letters into a folder for his review each morning. He didn't tell me this in the context of a commercial, but the image of him sitting quietly in his office in Washington and reading letters from home stuck with me and was later developed into this radio spot.

Gordon's staff reported that after the commercial ran, they had an increase in the number of real letters that he received. This dramatically demonstrates the power of a well-conceived radio commercial. Apparently, some people heard the spot and understood, perhaps for the first time, that they could sit down and draft a letter to their congressman and it would end up in his hands within just a few days.

Radio is also an excellent medium for attacks and counterattacks or to explain a complicated issue in more depth than is sometimes possible on television.

When state senate candidate Charlie Justice was attacked by his opponent in Florida in 2006, we needed to explain the context of the attack and rebut it, so we produced this ad.

"Straight Justice"
Radio: 60—Charlie Justice for State Senate
Fletcher Rowley Riddle, Inc.

Sometimes elections get confusing. . . . That's why it is so important to know what the *St. Petersburg Times* had to say about the race between

Charlie Justice and Kim Berfield.

The newspaper said Kim Berfield's harsh, negative campaign against Charlie Justice is "bizarre."

The newspaper said Berfield, an advertising consultant, even accused Justice of being against children . . . which must have come as a surprise to Charlie's wife and his two young daughters.

The *Times* said Berfield "failed miserably" as a legislator and became a "pawn" and "legislator of the year" for the insurance industry that rewarded her with $125,000 for her campaign.

The *Times* summed it up by saying: Kim Berfield had her chance and failed. Charlie Justice voted against the insurance rate increases that Kim Berfield pushed through the legislature.

The *St. Petersburg Times* endorsed Charlie Justice and his plan to cut the cost of homeowner's insurance.

Here's the bottom line . . . if you want real change and a chance for your homeowner's insurance to go down instead of up . . . then Charlie Justice is the clear choice.

Charlie Justice for State Senate. The next best thing to voting for yourself.

Paid for by Charlie Justice for State Senate.

By using quotes from the local newspaper, we were able to bring a credible third party into the conversation surrounding the campaign and to dismiss the attacks of Justice's opponent. In spite of being outspent by a three-to-one margin, Justice prevailed.

In 2008, we effectively used radio to win a race in Mississippi that the late Tim Russert described as "seismic." Travis Childers ran for and won a congressional seat in the 1st District of Mississippi that had been in Republican hands for more than two decades. Childers's primary election fell on the same day as the historic battle between Barack Obama and Hillary Clinton, and emotions ran high within the Democratic electorate. We produced this radio ad to promote Childers's candidacy without getting tangled up in the presidential primary. We used four voice actors in a rapid-fire delivery to create a spot that could hold the interest of busy commuters.

"Change Radio"
Radio: 60—Childers for Congress
Fletcher Rowley Riddle, Inc.

(Music up)

Voice Actor #1: Times are tough.

Voice Actor #2: Tough.

Voice Actor #3: We need a congressman who understands

Voice Actor #4: about working hard, needing a job

Voice Actor #2: . . . concerned about health care.

Voice Actor #1: That's Travis Childers.

Voice Actor #4: Democrat Travis Childers.

Voice Actor #1: As a teenager, Travis Childers father died.

Voice Actor #2: He worked full-time . . . eight-hour shifts to help support his family.

Voice Actor #3: An economic development leader, Travis Childers helped create over one thousand jobs.

All Actors: Jobs.

Voice Actor #4: One thousand jobs.

Voice Actor #4: Childers will work to bring more jobs to north Mississippi

Voice Actor #1: and oppose trade deals . . . that cost us jobs.

Voice Actor #2: Childers is committed to affordable health care,

Voice Actor #3: protecting Social Security,

Voice Actor #4: and providing in-home health care for seniors.

Voice Actor #2: Childers.

Voice Actor #3: Democrat Travis Childers.

Voice Actor #4: Remember, Election Day is March 11.

Voice Actor #1: Whether you vote for Hillary,

Voice Actor #2: Obama,

Voice Actor #1: Hillary,

Voice Actor #2: Obama,

Voice Actor #1: Either way, vote Childers. Write it down.

Voice Actor #2: Tuesday,

Voice Actor #3: March 11.

Voice Actor #1: Don't forget.

Voice Actor #4: March 11.

Travis Childers: I'm Travis Childers and I approved this message.

Voice Actors: So did we.

Voice Actor #1: Paid for and approved by Childers for Congress.

The radio spot became a bit of a sensation. Childers reported that people would meet him on the street and sing out, "Obama! Hillary! Obama! Hillary!"

Video Didn't Kill Radio

Television is, and will remain for the foreseeable future, the dominant medium for political communication. Even the advent of the Internet has failed to dent the power of video, as the ability to stream television commercials and long-form videos via broadband connections has extended the reach of this powerful medium.

There remains, however, a simple power in the use of radio for political communication. I like to imagine a commuter driving toward work or home listening to his favorite radio station when one of our radio commercials comes on. It's a great opportunity to engage the commuter in the theater of the mind. It is an opportunity to force him to think, to transport him to another time or place, to explain a complex subject, or, in some cases, simply to make him summon the image of his congressman sitting at his desk reading handwritten letters from his neighbors.

The first music video played on MTV in North America was "Video Killed the Radio Star" by the Buggles. At least for the purposes of political communication, the Buggles were wrong.

10

Outdoor Advertising

SEAN REILLY

In his 1983 rematch with incumbent Louisiana Republican governor Dave Treen, former governor Edwin Edwards set the tone early. Though Treen was personally popular and respected, his administration was laboring under a sputtering economy. There was a sense among the electorate that times weren't as good as when the "crafty Cajun" Edwards occupied the governor's mansion. So, a year before Election Day, billboards went up all over the state saying simply, "Hang on Louisiana, Edwin's coming!" The short and pointed message was executed in the familiar blue-and-yellow graphics of the Edwards campaign, and it hit every motorist in the state right through the windshield for six months. Down the stretch, those boards would reinforce television ads, delivering the same message as Edwards's 30-second spots, which carried the same tagline. They both depicted the Louisiana ship of state as the *Titanic* going down.

This creative use of outdoor advertising to establish a campaign theme early on represented the use of billboards at their best. The graphics were simple and the copy was short. But most importantly, the content had wit and bite. In combination, these qualities projected a message that could be instantly understood by an audience driving by at high speed. In addition, as with other well-executed political billboards, the "Hang On" campaign caught the eye of the other media, garnering extensive free coverage by television and newspapers.

Another example of effective outdoor advertising from Louisiana political lore is the independent expenditure campaign that erected a billboard for Edwards's fourth race for governor, this one against former Ku Klux Klansman David Duke in 1991. Here the graphics were stark and insistent. The billboard simply spelled out "DUKE," followed by a huge swastika with a superimposed slashed red circle. This message was certainly not subtle, but it was effective. Pictures of that billboard showed up in television newscasts and newspaper layouts across the state. Indeed, news coverage extended nationwide as wire services from across the country picked up the story. The advocacy group People for the Ethical Treatment of Animals (PETA) provides another example of the use of outdoor advertising for shock value and the extra media coverage it can create.

Where the Audience Is

Americans are spending more and more time out of the home. In fact, mobility has increased 143 percent over the past 40 years. Americans are also taking control of their advertising environment. With the help of technology, they are becoming increasingly resourceful when it comes to avoiding various types of media. As media become narrower and narrower, the ability to reach a larger audience is also narrowing. Out-of-home advertising is the only true mass medium left, and it continues to gain exposure time with consumers.

Outdoor advertising has long been used to build candidate name recognition, and this remains the primary reason candidates buy outdoor media early in a campaign cycle. Also, outdoor advertising can be more cost-effective than other media because of its relatively low cost per thousand impressions and the opportunity it provides a candidate to target his or her message to specific voters in the district.

In statewide races, outdoor advertising's cost-effectiveness allows a candidate to save much-needed resources for the home stretch. In terms of value, it can't be beat. You can't zap it, put it aside, turn the page, toss it out, or turn it off. The cost per thousand impressions is typically one-third that of radio and magazines, and one-seventh to one-tenth that of network television. This means that a campaign's budget will not be blown too early on the simple function of name identification. There is added value in getting the candidate's graphics, name, and picture across the state a full year to nine months before the election. This makes the candidate a player in the eyes of the voters so that as the campaign unfolds, other media appearances and speeches resonate to a greater degree. This is the "name in lights" effect: from our film-going experience, we think of people whose names are biggest as the stars.

In non-statewide elections where the district consists of a portion of a major media market, billboards can be targeted at voters in certain neighbor-hoods. The use of costly television and newspaper ads for the simple function of introducing the candidate to the voters in a small district race would be an imprudent use of funds. Outdoor media, in contrast, can be highly targeted so that advertising dollars aren't spent on those who don't live in the district. With outdoor advertising, a campaign can position its message in locations that reach everyone coming into or leaving a specific market area. Advance-ments in technology, such as GPS tracking, have benefited the out-of-home advertising industry in terms of demographic mapping capabilities and the ability to target a specific audience. Online Geographic Information Systems are now the core of how outdoor advertising media is selected, reported, and tracked. The ability to deliver messages within specific geographic areas allows a campaign to buy media where the candidate needs it most and not pay for unnecessary coverage.

In 2008 the Traffic Audit Bureau for Media Measurement (TAB), with the support of the outdoor advertising industry, introduced the Eyes-On study, a new form of audience measurement. Eyes-on impressions, or EOIs, will be the new audience-measurement currency for buying and selling out-of-home media in the U.S. market, replacing daily effective circulations, or DECs, as the core metric. Historically, the industry has used traffic counts to deter-mine audience size. Traffic counts determine how many people are exposed to or have an opportunity to see an outdoor display. DECs have long been the standard by which media buyers determine the relative merits of each display. However, ad buyers consider DECs to be too large and not comparable to other measured media, which makes the metric a lesser-valued currency. As a result, outdoor media typically has only been involved in the ad-buying process, not the ad-planning process. EOIs represent the average number of persons who are likely to notice an ad viewed on an outdoor display. This advancement will greatly enhance outdoor advertising's accountability and measurability.

Let's Get Creative

Production for a name-recognition message has simple ground rules. The tech-nology of digital printing on vinyl has made it possible to create outstanding, magazine-quality graphics, so a flattering photograph of the candidate works best. The graphics and colors should be clean and simple, the copy short and uncluttered. Voters have four to five seconds to see a billboard, on average, so a campaign must determine the most important message about its candidate and say it in seven words or less.

Whether the message is name recognition or something with a little more substance, there are some standard guidelines to follow:

First, type and lettering should be clear and easy to read. Words made up entirely of capital letters are usually not as legible as words in both upper and lower cases. Care should be taken with spacing between letters and words. Letters with too little spacing tend to merge when viewed from a distance. Avoid overly bold or thin lettering. Heavy typefaces tend to blur at long distances, while fine typefaces tend to fade or break up visually. Simple, sans serif typefaces work best in outdoor advertising; ornate serif and script do not. Typefaces with excessive contrast between thick and thin elements greatly reduce legibility.

Second, when choosing colors for outdoor advertising, the designer should use those with high contrast in both hue and value. Hue is the identity of the color, such as red, green, or yellow; value is a measure of the color's lightness or darkness. Contrasting colors work best when viewed from a distance. Colors without contrast blend together and obscure the message. Hence, reversing white out of any dark-value color enhances visibility by providing a strong and effective contrast.

Technically Speaking

Digital displays are outdoor media's most flexible type of advertising. Utilizing the newest technology, digital displays are computer-controlled electronic billboards. They transmit light through Light Emitting Diode Display (LED) technology. The board holds a message for up to 10 seconds before the next message is displayed. For the first time, the advertiser is in complete control of his or her advertising. Never before have advertisers had the flexibility to change a message as often as they like. Putting a message out or changing it is as easy as sending an e-mail; it can be changed weekly, daily, or even hourly. With no production costs, digital displays save time, money, and the hassle of a production and installation schedule.

Digital displays offer an important advertising component for political campaigns because of their ability to reach many people in a timely manner. The displays can be networked to each other in any way that the advertiser needs, so candidates can post their message in a certain zip code for smaller elections or statewide and even nationwide for larger elections. The information is uploaded onto the display digitally, so candidates can change their message as often as they like and can immediately respond to breaking news or election results.

The world of political campaigning has seen several exciting and innovative uses of digital and traditional billboard technology to provide valuable public service. The eyes of the nation were on Iowa on January 3, 2008, when the caucuses there reshaped the 2008 presidential race. The eyes of Iowa drivers were on digital billboards across their state. Outdoor-advertising operators in Iowa teamed up to provide real-time caucus results on digital billboards in four outdoor markets (Des Moines, Cedar Rapids, Dubuque, and Waterloo). Teaser creative spots ran the day of the caucus, telling drivers to watch during the evening for live results. The digital billboards went live shortly after the caucuses opened and were updated every 7 to 10 minutes until the winners were declared, when the boards switched to a winner graphic. Press coverage of the event was substantial and uniformly positive. Operators reported getting calls from as far away as New York, asking about using digital billboard technology to advertise.

The 2008 presidential election showcased the nimble capabilities of high-tech outdoor formats. A blockbuster news story, the election highlighted the growing awareness by other media of the benefits and creative uses of outdoor advertising. For example, the ABC-TV affiliate in Milwaukee, Wisconsin, posted election results on digital billboards after the polls closed. Nationally, MSNBC election results were displayed on Clear Channel digital billboards in 20 markets, digital taxi tops in New York City and Boston, and digital signage in Westgate City Center in Arizona. As polls closed across the country, the digital displays were constantly updated with real-time election results, right up until winners were announced.

Lagniappe

Outdoor advertising can be a critical component of a political campaign. In spite of being the oldest medium around (it was first practiced by the ancient Egyptians), it has embraced the newest technology, and this has given it some unique advantages in the world of campaigns. In summary, the same elements that work for Madison Avenue when convincing people what to buy also work in elections when convincing people how to vote. Keep the message simple, keep the graphics interesting, and keep the copy short. If the goal is to attract the attention of other media, produce an ad with a witty or even somewhat controversial tone. If executed early and well, a billboard can become a political landmark.

11

Earned Media

BUD JACKSON

Back in the old days, news deadlines for airing or printing stories were, for the most part, once per day. Newspapers came out daily and network television news aired once per night, while local television news aired around dinnertime and just before bedtime, with morning news reporting what had happened the day before. The "hole" to fill for news content was restricted by the medium and the technological capability to deliver content.

Fast forward to today, and deadlines for stories are increasingly irrelevant. An explosion of news programming has created a bottomless hole for news that seemingly can't ever be filled to the top. Suddenly, media are less restrictive with the advent of 24-hour cable news networks and the emergence of the Internet. Technology has made it easier and cheaper to file stories and to deliver video to news consumers. Where newspapers' content was restricted to the paper it was printed on, and television and radio news stories restricted by available airtime, now media organizations enjoy a new content delivery portal—a website—to complement their traditional news-distribution medium. The Internet provides media organizations with a relatively inexpensive way to post nearly limitless news stories where word counts aren't as important as they once were and where, in theory, reporting can be more comprehensive. Broadcast journalists can now publish long written essays, and print publications can produce stories with video. With more freedom, lines are blurring. Now there are even web-based "news" providers who have no traditional journalism training and who are intent on promoting "news" with an agenda—or by another name, propaganda.

The evolution and expansion of news reporting has made "earned media" an even more crucial element for any political campaign or organization with a communications strategy to execute. Earned media is the art of generating or shaping favorable or tactically advantageous publicity by using some or all available platforms. Once known as free media, the new term reflects its growing importance; earned media is not free for the taking but is achieved only with a substantial amount of time and effort. And in today's new media world, earned media is more important than ever.

The proliferation of news content and delivery portals also means there are more resources at one's disposal to utilize when executing a communications plan. Different media organizations, websites, news shows, blogs, podcasts, and columnists means more tactical opportunities available to help achieve strategic goals. A communication plan is no longer just about how to generate publicity; it's about tactically using all the earned media tools available to achieve specific goals and maximize message effectiveness.

So let's address some fundamental steps needed to develop a successful earned media strategy and some of the tactics that can make that strategy a success.

Research for an Earned-Media Plan

Before formulating a comprehensive earned-media plan, a campaign must first study the media outlets that could potentially cover a campaign. These are essentially the resources available for a campaign's plan. This is not just a matter of accumulating an email list; the researcher must profile and qualitatively assess each potential contact, as described below.

Develop a media list of all traditional newspaper, radio, and television outlets that could apply to a campaign. Further research the programming they offer their audience, noting the shows that might be useful avenues for exploitation. What content do they offer and via what portals? For example, does a newspaper media outlet also offer content on a website? Media lists should include the contact persons' names, media deadlines, and phone and e-mail addresses.

Identify which reporters will be covering the race. If unsure, a polite introductory call should be made to the media outlet's editor or news director. Determine if the reporter has additional content avenues to consider in a strategy, such as a blog or online or in-print column.

Study each media outlet's ideological leanings and get a sense of its general attitude toward politics. Past editorials and news stories are the best guide for potential future slant and interests. Who have they endorsed? Who have they reviled? Do they favor liberals more than conservatives? Do they approve of or oppose courses of action on issues relevant to a campaign? Have they written past stories on the candidate or the opponent(s)?

Become acquainted with the reporters, editors, columnists, talk-show hosts, and the bloggers who will be covering your campaign. Research their past stories, columns, and shows to understand their individual biases and points of view. Make an effort to establish a positive working relationship. Oftentimes an off-the-record lunch, dinner, or happy hour can go a long way toward cultivating a positive working relationship.

Research "vertical" media outlets, such as non-traditional blogs, websites, or trade publications. This includes specialty publications, such as newsletters or e-mail newsletters that cater to specific groups, like senior citizens or veterans; it also includes like-minded organizations, from gun owners to environmental protection groups. News stories in these outlets are generally easier to place and are more likely to be written in a manner desirable for a campaign. Some may even allow you to write your own article.

Implementation

Several methods can be used for enacting an earned-media strategy. Some consist of constructive activities, and some are to be avoided. Understanding how and when to use these methods will maximize favorable coverage and will also minimize embarrassing mix-ups.

Press Releases, Video News Releases, Radio Actuality

To do:

- Send out an occasional press release. Press releases tailored to specific media outlets and their individual audiences will likely generate more stories. Develop a local angle or "hook" to entice journalistic interest. For example, if doing a news release about senior citizens who face rising prescription-drug costs while living on fixed incomes, put the issue in the context of local senior citizens.
- When appropriate, submit video clips to news stations with a news release explaining the footage. Television news operations are limited by the number of cameras they have to cover a day's events. Some-

times they will use footage provided by a campaign to do a story. Higher-profile campaigns may even warrant an interview of a candidate or spokesperson from a satellite center, making it that much easier for a television news operation to cover a candidate or issue.

- Use your own website to post positive video and news stories.
- When you have video you would like voters to see and the traditional broadcast new media refuse to cover it, post it yourself to a site like YouTube or your own site and draw attention to it, forcing the traditional press to cover the issue.
- Offer actuality clips to radio stations. A radio actuality consists of a 30- to 60-second audio clip of a candidate or spokesperson talking about a relevant issue. Typically, there is a brief introduction at the beginning of the clip stating who is speaking, what the topic is, how long the clip is, and then a 3-second countdown to the start of the candidate or spokesperson speaking. These audio clips can be e-mailed, along with a news release, to most radio stations as .wav or .mp3 files. The clips are typically included in radio news programs.
- Follow up with the appropriate people to make sure they have received the news release, clip, and so on.
- Hold an announcement event or send an announcement news release. Most media outlets offer every candidate or cause this introductory story. Post video and audio of the event to your own website and offer a link to it in your news release e-mail.

To avoid:
- Do not send out a news release every single day. A constant dribble of news releases without any substantive news will damage the campaign's credibility among the media.
- Do not send a news release to the wrong audience. For example, a news release touting cuts in veterans' benefits should not be sent to a publication for veterans.
- Do not badger or anger reporters and editors for not doing a story based on a news release. Also avoid picking needless fights with the media. They have barrels of ink and hours of airtime to get in the last word.
- Do not call a reporter or editor minutes before deadline unless they have asked for a call.

News Conferences, One-on-One Interviews, and Photo Opportunities

To do:

- Hold a news conference, providing there is a compelling reason to draw reporters to cover the news event.
- When possible, hold a news conference at a location that is relevant to a topic at hand. A news conference could also become a photo opportunity if conducted at a visually stimulating or issue-relevant location.
- Send out a media advisory alerting the media of an event. Follow up with phone calls.
- Have a campaign take its own photos and video of candidate appearances and submit them to the media with press releases and captions, or include a link to where you have the content posted on your website.
- Generate one-on-one interviews when it makes tactical sense. Perhaps it's an interview in the candidate's home to showcase his family; or maybe it's to address a controversial topic without exposing the candidate to a potentially dangerous news conference.
- Always be prepared. Always strategize all the questions that a media member could potentially ask and know what your answer will be, in advance, to prevent being caught off-guard and to avoid making a message mistake.

To avoid:

- Do not hold a news conference if you are trying to avoid or reduce exposure to risk or trying to maintain control of your message. News conferences afford reporters the opportunity to ask any question they want on any topic and can place the candidate in an adversarial environment, which exposes them to greater risk of making a mistake and going off-message.
- Do not hold news conferences or events that are in a remote location, too far away from the media covering the race.
- Do not plan to do many news conferences on local and district levels, unless the candidate and campaign staff want to be all alone at the conference.
- Do not plan a news conference or photo opportunity that is too close to important press deadlines.

- Do not plan marginally important news conferences on potentially busy news days. The press will be even less likely to attend.
- Be mindful of what could go wrong or be embarrassing, which could include everything from being caught in bad weather to creating a traffic jam or anything else that could make the candidate look foolish.

Special Events and Speeches

To do:
- Have the candidate speak at special events, such as public-service club meetings, when appropriate. Make sure the remarks take the audience into consideration and that they will be warmly received in order to avoid public embarrassment—unless the point is to spark controversy by challenging the sponsoring organization.
- Invite the local media with media advisories from a campaign or group sponsoring the event.

To avoid:
- Do not hold or attend a special event or speech every week and expect to receive coverage each time. This applies even more to lower-level local and state legislative races.
- If the press attends, do not take questions after the speech unless the candidate is prepared potentially to take a story's focus away from what he said in his speech. Alternatively, if questions are taken, be prepared to pivot away from off-topic questions with answers that return the focus back to the desired messaging.

Editorial-Board Meetings

To do:
- Request to meet with editorial boards. Use previous research to prepare and to understand their ideological leanings and positions on relevant issues before attending the meeting. Answer their questions and soften criticism by taking their biases into consideration.
- Bring a press kit with favorable clips, speeches, and campaign literature so boards can better understand what a candidate or campaign

has been doing. The content should be compiled with consideration of the individual media outlet's perceived biases.

To avoid:

- Do not get angry if an editorial board refuses to meet with a candidate or campaign. Simply send a press kit and a request for an endorsement if they choose not to have a meeting with a candidate or campaign.
- Do not go into an editorial-board meeting until a candidate and campaign are knowledgeable enough about their own positions and relevant campaign issues to answer questions comfortably and in-depth

Talk Shows: Radio, TV, Internet

To do:

- Understand the format and subject material, host biases, and program audiences for all local radio, television/cable, and Internet talk shows that are relevant to a campaign. Know their show days and times.
- If the show is appropriate, ask producers or hosts if a candidate or spokesperson can be a guest.
- Have people—but not paid campaign staff—prepared to call in to say positive things and ask easy questions, if calls are taken.
- Know the issues; put off a guest appearance until a candidate or campaign is comfortable with them.
- Instruct a candidate or spokesperson to expect the unexpected and to not become unraveled when challenged by inhospitable hosts, panelists, or callers.

To avoid:

- Do not go on a show that has no tactical benefit or whose host(s) will probably try to embarrass or ambush a candidate or spokesperson.

Maintaining Relationships with the Media

To do:

- Have an early conversation with the journalists covering your race that establishes clear working guidelines on what each expects from the other, particularly when it comes to issues that are important to maintaining a trusting working relationship. A discussion about going "off the record" or talking "on background" and what those terms mean to both you and the reporter will help avoid future confusion or situations in which one party feels as if the other was unfair or unprofessional.

- In general, information given off the record is meant to help guide a reporter, but the information being provided cannot be quoted or attributed in any way to the reporter's source. "On background" can be potentially problematic if people aren't clear. On background (also referred to as "not for attribution") typically means that a reporter can quote you but cannot directly identify you by name. He or she can identify you in general terms, such as a "source close to the candidate" or a "campaign staffer." You should have an explicit conversation about how you will be identified, even in these general terms. Rather than just saying "on background," it will be better for you to avoid a misunderstanding by laying out your expectations in as much detail as possible. For example, "On background and not for direct attribution, but you can refer to me as a top campaign staffer" leaves less room for misunderstanding than simply saying to a reporter, "On background."

- Tell all candidates that there is no such thing as speaking off "the record" or "on background." They must abide by a higher standard and the expectation that they are always on the record and could be quoted at any time. Subscribe to this philosophy to avoid risk as much as possible; otherwise, your candidate will be taking his or her chances by playing with fire. There's no reason why a campaign staffer can't deliver the same information and thereby remove the candidate from potential risk exposure.

- If there is a media outlet of particular importance, offer it a potentially newsworthy exclusive—with the up-front understanding that it will, in fact, do a complete story. Generally, a campaign staffer, not the candidate, should contact the outlet. Candidates trying to cut public-relations deals are in a position of greater risk, which could have been avoided, and which also tends to make reporters and their editors uneasy because it opens them up to greater risk as well. Silly as it sounds, dealing with a staffer gives a journalist at least one degree more of separation from any potential appearance of impropriety or of being in direct cahoots with a candidate.

- Offer exclusives only infrequently and only after carefully weighing the advantages and possible pitfalls of shutting out other members of the media.
- Have a good working relationship with the media outlet about to be propositioned. You need to trust them to do a fair job.
- Keep in regular touch with columnists, talk-show hosts, bloggers, and producers who might be useful or supportive in the future.
- If there is an established, trusting relationship with a media person, pass along truthful deep-background information about the opposition that calls into question its credibility and deserves to be investigated further. Voters have a right to know some matters about which the opposition might not want them to be aware.
- Offer a story or column idea, even if it is not a political topic or related to your campaign at all. The gesture will ultimately garner future goodwill from a grateful member of the media.

To avoid:
- Do not jeopardize the bond of trust you have cultivated with reporters, show hosts, editors, and the like by passing on false information or by failing to keep promised commitments.
- Do not assume bloggers and non-journalists who run websites share the same ethical and professional standards as professionally trained journalists.
- Do not ask to be "off the record" or "on background" after you have already said something.

Third-Party Endorsements

To do:
- Seek third-party endorsements that benefit a candidate or cause.
- Allow a third party to send out a news release, on its own letterhead, with glowing quotes about a candidate or issue campaign. That person could also hold a news conference, stage an event, appear on talk shows, and so on. Endorsements from a person or group not directly affiliated with a candidate or campaign carry greater credibility.
- Make an attempt to collaborate with a third party about the message. A unified effort means more effective publicity.

• As a group endorsing a candidate or cause to e-mail or direct-mail their membership a letter announcing the endorsement and also to post it on their website. Ask them to release the letter to the press at an advantageous moment.

To avoid:

• Do not actively seek or encourage publicity about endorsements that do not benefit the campaign. For example, if a candidate supports the death penalty but is running in a very liberal anti–death penalty district, do not publicize pro–death penalty organization endorsements.

Op-Ed Pieces

To do:

• Submit occasional opinion pieces to be printed opposite newspapers' editorial pages.
• Pick a relevant campaign topic and consider how the piece could be used to achieve a tactical political objective.

To avoid:

• Do not annoy editorial-page editors with several e-mails or phone calls when they've turned down a piece for publication. They won't change their mind.
• Do not write anything that can be used against the candidate or campaign in the future. The piece is, after all, a public document.

Letters to the Editor

To do:

• Organize an effort to have people in the community send or e-mail letters to the editors of newspapers supporting a candidate or cause or criticizing the opposition.
• Help letter-writers tailor their message in conjunction with what a campaign desires.
• Actually write the letters for willing supporters who agree with the letter's content.

To avoid:

- Do not have people send in form letters or letters so similar in wording that it is obvious a campaign is orchestrating the effort. Editors will be even less likely to publish the letters.
- Do not encourage people to write letters who are considered strange or extremist or who are not well-liked in the community.

Reader or Viewer Feedback, E-Mail, and Phone-In Opportunities

To do:

- Have people e-mail and call in to reader or viewer feedback phone lines and e-mail boxes, whose numbers and e-mail addresses are often printed in the paper or played on-air.

Monitoring/Using the Media and Independent Websites and Blogs

To do:

- Always monitor what is being written about your candidate, especially on websites and blogs. Sometimes news will appear there first and will then jump to more traditional news outlets, such as a newspaper or television station. By monitoring, you will sometimes get a head-start on planning your response or strategy to the mainstream media questions that will soon follow. Take advantage of companies that offer (some for free) alerts each time a keyword—for example, your candidate's name or the names of opponents—is mentioned in a news story or website that is tracked by their service. Google's News Alerts is perhaps the most widely known Internet-based service that does this for free, but there are many others, including for-a-fee subscriber services that even track and capture video when triggered by a keyword.

The Brave New World of Social Media and the Blogosphere

One of the more recent phenomena associated with the rise of the Internet has been the rise of blogs. Reporters are blogging in addition to their official work responsibilities, candidates are blogging, special interests are blogging, and somewhere in your own neighborhood regular Joes or Jills are blogging.

This is one of the newer, Wild West regions of politics, and it deserves a moment of discussion.

For the media, blogs afford reporters another avenue to get out information, often immediately, and with more ability to inject personal opinion with their stories, which are referred to as "posts" on their blog. At best, blogs allow reporters to get out more information in real time rather than the next time their publication is printed or their broadcast aired. At worst, blogs almost allow reporters to moonlight as columnists and opine their beliefs on the people and topics that they cover as reporters. Blogs also allow columnists to write multiple opinion pieces per day on multiple topics in addition to the columns they traditionally write or broadcast for their media outlet. The ability of reporters to blog blurs the line between acting as a neutral reporter and expressing opinions. This is a debate on journalistic ethics that we cannot solve here, but we must at least be aware of the new tool available to reporters and columnists, for better or worse.

Additionally, the rise of blogs has created portals that act or appear as credible, non-biased media outlets. The danger here—or the opportunity, depending on your perspective—is that these blogs can be created and used as propaganda organs dressed up to look like credible media outlets. Their biases can be hidden and their writing published as if their words were written by an independent and fair-minded person. Their stories can be written in a slanted way or without an opposing point of view specifically to promote their own agenda. Bloggers for these sites can post comments about people— even outright lies—that would have never made it into the mainstream media because they lacked credibility or relevance and out of fear of being sued for defamation of character.

We must always remember that bloggers, whether from your neighborhood or writing on a well-known national blog, are often not trained journalists and need not adhere to most widely accepted journalistic ethics. On blogs, there often is no editor demanding sources or documentation to back up assertions of fact. There often isn't balance given to a blog post. So when viewing a blog, reader beware. Always take into consideration the person doing the blog, as well as the content of the blog itself, to determine the credibility and balance of the information you are viewing.

To do:
  • Monitor blog posts and the comments often found at the end of the

posts: sometimes overeager supporters of an opponent will leak out what will soon be coming down the pike as an attack on your candidate. Reading what has been written as rumor can afford you an invaluable opportunity to get the real story and to prepare a course of action should the attack arrive. Whereas the mainstream media may not have enough information to print a story, a blog may print it anyway.

- There may be times when you have information about an opponent that isn't substantial enough to generate a mainstream media story, or information that you simply don't even know is truthful. Sometimes, by anonymously posting this information, you can learn new information from other posters whose comments respond to what you have written. Such a post may also draw more mainstream media attention and encourage a reporter to research the issue more thoroughly or to call an opponent about the information.

To avoid:
- Do not assume that "anonymous" postings are anonymous. They can often be traced back to your computer.
- With that in mind, do not allow the candidate to post to websites or blog items unless he or she understands that his or her name will or could be attributed to the posting.
- Do not post anonymous items from campaign computers or well-known campaign supporters, such as other public officials or the candidate's family members.

Earned Media in Today's Campaign Environment

Two phenomena of the modern media age make earned media an increasingly valuable campaign tool. First, we live in an era of public cynicism about paid political information. People are conditioned to be skeptical of political, partisan-paid ads, spots, and other promotional items. In such a climate, earned media can be an important tool to create credibility for a campaign's message. A campaign's message is more likely to be believed when it is part of a news story, written by someone outside the campaign, or delivered by a radio or television talk-show host. Endorsements, headlines, and quotes from the media add legitimacy to a paid media program and reinforce the campaign's overall message when included in television spots, radio ads, e-mails, websites, direct-mail pieces, and other available media.

Second, there is the problem of overload. The expanding number of media outlets—from all-news stations to radio talk shows to Internet websites—has changed the traditional news environment. People now get their news from more sources than the network television news and the daily papers. News cycles that were once easily measurable are now far less obvious, and news is now being delivered virtually real-time into people's homes through computers and satellites. Consequently, campaigns have more media targets to reach, each with their own audiences and some with deadlines that are not daily but instantaneous.

It is increasingly obvious that a crucial step on the path to public persuasion—and victory—is establishing a comprehensive earned-media strategy that explores all available tactics and integrates them into the overall strategic goals of the campaign.

12

Speechwriting

TREVOR PARRY-GILES

Before polling, before direct mail and focus groups, before 30-second spots and voter targeting, politicians were giving speeches and hiring experts to write them. The first known speechwriters were Corax and Tisias, two resourceful fifth-century B.C. Athenians who recognized the opportunities before them as the art of oratory was taking hold in ancient Greece. As humans began to give speeches—at ceremonies, in deliberative bodies, in the courts—the need arose for speechwriters. Prospective orators realized they lacked either the time or the ability to formulate a good speech, so they hired skilled practitioners and teachers to write their speeches for them.

Ancient speechwriters were called "sophists," a word that means "wisdom-bearer" in Greek, though its original meaning has changed considerably. Sophists soon began teaching their craft—the art of rhetoric—to future citizens and public leaders. Speechwriting and oratory came to dominate public life in ancient Greece and Rome.

In America, speechwriting is a time-honored art and science that remains in high demand in a political climate increasingly dominated by television and other mass media. Yet whatever its form, whoever does the writing or the speaking, or wherever it is practiced, speechwriting has certain basic principles that can be culled from historical precedent and applied to modern considerations.

Smart and Wise

Many Greeks and Romans believed that speechmaking was an indispensable practice for a community to perform in order to survive. Rhetoric was essential in their societies—it was a central feature in government, law, and social occasions. But the ancients also feared that rhetoric could be manipulated and misused—hence Plato's castigation of sophists as eloquent deceivers. They believed that the way to prevent demagogues and liars from damaging the polity was to ensure that speechmaking and speechwriting were performed by learned, ethical people. This requirement survives to this day.

A good speechwriter is broadly trained. It is not enough to know how to craft speeches, to be trained simply in technique and skill. Narrowly educated, technically trained people lack the expansive knowledge and understanding required to create truly eloquent oratory. Unfortunately, college and university programs in public relations and journalism are insufficient in training effective speechwriters. Speechwriters write speeches that are about something—the economy, public-policy issues, foreign affairs—and it's useful for the speechwriter to know something about these subjects. As such, the good speechwriter is someone who is well-read, who has a deep understanding of philosophy, history, literature, economics, psychology, and art. This person understands and appreciates the power of language and the influence that eloquent uses of language can have on audiences. This individual values and appreciates the oratory of both Abraham Lincoln and Malcolm X. The good speechwriter recognizes just how Ronald Reagan and Barbara Jordan were able to use language and rhetoric masterfully and artistically to convince audiences of radically different ideas. And the good speechwriter treats the spoken language with respect and understands the ethical limits to which the power of oratory should be used.

Limited Forums and Genres

As they examined where and when speeches took place, the ancients realized that political speeches generally occur in three forums. Ceremonial speeches are the first type of speeches that politicians are asked to give. A second type of speech is a deliberative speech. The final type of speech is a forensic speech, such as is given in courtrooms and other legal settings. Generally, these same categories exist today, and for political speechwriting, the deliberative and ceremonial settings are the most common. Deliberative speeches include speeches to constituents, floor speeches, and committee statements; they are usually about major public-policy issues. Ceremonial speeches are typically those speeches that might be given at funerals or award ceremonies. Ribbon-cuttings or the dedications of monuments, buildings, schools, and the like may all require some comment from a political leader.

A good speechwriter recognizes the differences between types of speeches. This awareness comes from effectively analyzing the situation facing the orator. Good speechwriters also have a keen awareness of previous examples of oratory in different settings. Speechwriters are students of public address— they've read the classic orations of our culture, which include many more speeches than just John F. Kennedy's inaugural address and Martin Luther King, Jr.'s, "I Have a Dream" speech. They have also read the orations that aren't classics, the ones that are given every day by political leaders across the country, to audiences composed of many different types of people. The sample speech provided, for example, is one presented by President Barack Obama to celebrate the Pittsburgh Penguins and their winning of the Stanley Cup. A very typical, formalized speech, this sample is like the hundreds of speeches speechwriters are asked to craft. Learning how previous orators and speechwriters have handled different speech situations, both the great and the mundane, is a good way to discover the best ways to address a contemporaneous speech situation.

The Steps of Speechwriting

The first speechwriters realized quickly that all speechwriting involves specific steps or procedures, and they labeled these the five canons of rhetoric. These steps are still relevant today.

Step One: Invention. This step involves discerning the message, arguments, evidence: indeed, the very content of the speech.

First, get as much information as you can about the speech setting itself. Where will it be delivered? What time of day? Will your speaker be the only speaker at the event or one of several? What will be the layout of the speaking situation?

Second, learn as much as you can about the audience. Who are these people? What demographic characteristics do they possess? How do they feel about the speaker? How do they feel about the topic of the speech? Have they heard from the speaker on previous occasions? There are several sources for information about the audience. Important sources include the organizers of the event itself—event planners, advance people, campaign staffers. Polling data may also be quite helpful in identifying the attitudinal profile of the audience. Consulting with local media outlets—newspapers or television stations—can offer insights as to what is important and pressing for a given audience. Notice how the sample speech recognizes various people in the audience. Read the speech and identify specific ways in which you believe the speechwriter researched the audience and the occasion.

Third, figure out what the predominant theme, argument, message, or idea of the speech will be. Consult with the speaker, if possible, or with his or her surrogates concerning the speech and its message. What is the main idea that must be communicated? Is that idea likely to be received favorably by the audience? Can it be easily and clearly understood? Is the central theme capable of sustaining a full speech, or is it so complex that it can't possibly be discussed in a brief oration? And is the core message of the speech consistent with the overall communication strategy or narrative arc of the campaign? What is the central idea of President Obama's speech for the Penguins? How do the president's speechwriters construct a larger lesson or central idea from a rather typical celebration speech for a world champion hockey team?

Fourth, gather evidence and information for the speech. Find compelling statistics, funny jokes, dramatic stories, and authoritative studies that will support the main idea you want to communicate to the audience. In the sample speech, notice how President Obama employs different facts and anecdotes about the various Penguin coaches and players to make this speech more interesting and personal. Ask members of the staff, local experts, media sources, and other knowledgeable people for information. And remember, it is always better to have too much information than not to have enough.

Step Two: Organization. Audiences generally are not very good at listening—especially to political speeches. One way to maximize the listening capacity of an audience is to structure clearly the speaker's message. Make certain that transitions are clear, structure is apparent, and repetition is frequent. A good outline is essential for a well-organized speech.

First, the introduction of the speech must be compelling and complete; it should make appropriate acknowledgments and seek to secure the audience's attention. This may involve a joke, a meaningful narrative, a quotation, or a startling statistic. Whatever is used, the introduction must command attention from the audience—if not, you can forget about the rest of the speech. The sample speech contains an introduction that involves the audience, highlights the speaker's credibility, and makes clear the central idea of the speech.

Second, offer the audience a well-defined sense of the purpose of the speech. Indicate what the core idea of the speech is, and demonstrate why the speaker is qualified to discuss this topic. Even the most comatose member of the audience ought to know and remember what a speech is about.

Third, structure the main points of the speech clearly. Each of the main points should relate back to the central idea of the discourse and should be well-supported with evidence, a story, or statistics. Each of the main points should also relate to the audience. And there ought to be evident transitions from one point to the next, to help the audience to follow the progression of the ideas.

Fourth, develop a conclusion that "makes the sale." Reiterate the main points of the speech and make the case for why the audience should accept the argument and should vote for or support the speaker. Leave the audience with something meaningful, humorous, dramatic, or otherwise substantial; do not throw away the ending of speech. As they say, first and final impressions are the most lasting.

Step Three: Language. The language used to express the ideas of a speech is critical. Unfortunately, speechwriters are often more skilled at a written style of language than they are with a spoken style of language. Spoken language is clear, more concrete than abstract, more specific than general, shorter rather than longer, and more attuned to the ear rather than the eye. Capturing this difference is crucial if a speech is to be successful with an audience. President Obama's speech contains illustrations of spoken language and language style that are useful for political speechwriting. Examine the speech for how the president uses shorter sentences and concrete examples, how the speech is clearly written to be heard rather than read.

Imagine if John F. Kennedy had said, "And so, my fellow Americans, I encourage you to ponder and inquire of yourself what you might do for your nation—don't simply demand to understand what the government can provide to you." Or if Ann Richards had said, "Poor George Bush. We must forgive him his inability to understand working Americans because he was born wealthy and never wanted for any need or requirement," rather than "Poor George Bush. He can't help it. He was born with a silver foot in his mouth." Would we remember Ronald Reagan's challenge to Mikhail Gorbachev to "tear down this wall" if he had said, "Mr. Gorbachev, the time has come to remove this wall from our midst and allow peace and democratic freedoms to reign once again throughout the European continent?" Kennedy, Richards, and Reagan (and their speechwriters) were effective precisely because they understood the difference between language written to be heard and language written to be read.

Steps Four and Five: Memory and Delivery. Good speechwriters understand their speaker—they know how he or she speaks, what he or she can remember, the hard-to-pronounce words the preferred cadences. When writing a speech, the speechwriter should always try to write for the speaker in a way that will maximize not only the ideas he or she is communicating, but also the manner in which those ideas are uttered. For instance, a speaker without a strong sense of cadence should not be given a speech that includes a great deal of repetition or parallelism. The connection between the crafting or wording of a speech and its delivery before an audience must be foremost in the speechwriter's mind.

The Role of Media

The rules and principles about public oratory from ancient civilizations are still relevant today. But our earliest speechwriters could never have envisioned a time when speeches would be broadcast to millions over radio and television or when oratory would be available simultaneously all over the world via telephone lines and the Internet, on blogs and forever captured on YouTube. Thus we need to adapt and alter our understanding of rhetoric and speechwriting for political life in the contemporary, mediated age.

Contemporary speechwriters must recognize that the speeches they write may appear on television. So while the speechwriter tries to account for the specific audience gathered to hear the speech, he or she also has to think in terms of sound bites and the larger voting audience at home. This situation creates new demands and conditions in the speechwriting process. Most important, as New York University professor Mitchell Stephens concludes, we live in a time in which the image is overtaking the word. Speechwriters, who deal almost exclusively in words, need to consider the power of images and the place and fit of their words in those images that define their candidate. The language of a speech is not separate from the image of the candidate as she or he delivers that speech. Bill Clinton's finger-wagging denial of an affair with "that woman, Miss Lewinsky" or George W. Bush's 2001 bravado with a bullhorn at the Ground Zero site in New York City, for example, will forever be etched in the public consciousness, as much because of the pictorial images of these presidents as for the words they uttered.

The rise of mass media and television has also made the public speech of even greater importance in a campaign and in political life. One slip, one gaffe, and a candidate will forever face commercials with the mistake and news footage of the error. Dan Quayle spelling "potato(e)" and Gerald Ford's assertions about Eastern Europe are just two examples. This is why political leaders and candidates take so much time to make certain that the speech is just right. Of course, the offshoot of that attention is that speechwriters must be able to take criticism—to leave their egos at the door and adapt what might be fine oratory to the needs of the client. Arguably, this is one of the hardest aspects of speechwriting. The speechwriter will believe in the speech and the ideas it expresses, only to be told to do it again by a fussy client or officeholder who is not quite able to articulate his or her complaints about the speech. Taking and adapting to criticism is a central requirement for an effective speechwriter.

The mass media also contribute to a punditocracy in which speechwriters lose their anonymity and invisibility. We've gone from the time of the obscure and unknown Judson Welliver (the first known White House speechwriter, hired during the Harding administration), to the era of the late Tony Snow and Peggy Noonan, where a stint as a speechwriter in the White House is but a stepping-stone toward future public and journalistic success as a public commentator. President George W. Bush's chief speechwriter, Michael Gerson, went from his job in the White House to a position as a regular featured columnist in the *Washington Post*. Another Bush speechwriter, David Frum, has penned a book and regularly appears on news programs as a political commentator. Interestingly, it was Frum who achieved some notoriety when his spouse e-mailed friends and colleagues claiming that her husband wrote the phrase "axis of evil" after President Bush used it in his 2002 State of the Union address.

This shifting in roles requires some potentially complicated ethical and philosophical juggling by the speechwriter. Do you protect the myth that effective oratory is merely an extension of the speaker with no credit due the speechwriter? Do you, like President Kennedy's speechwriters, refuse to take credit for effective, enduring language and lofty ideas? Or do you capitalize on your fame and write books or go on television to talk about the intricacies of the speechwriting process? Do you exploit your proximity to power and celebrity to enhance your own status? These questions reflect the dilemma, and are just a few of the challenges, facing speechwriters in the contemporary political age, dominated as it is by the mass media and 24-hour-a-day television.

Among all the activities of the contemporary political operative, none has a longer history than speechwriting. For centuries, humans have sought to persuade and inform, inspire and motivate with the spoken word. And now, with television and the Internet, the reach and power of those words is even greater. Adapting ancient practices to contemporary circumstances, under-standing audiences and appreciating occasions, knowing much about many things—these are the skills of the successful speechwriter and the basis of a strong and effective speech.

Appendix

President Barack Obama Welcomes the Pittsburgh Penguins to the White House

September 10, 2009

THE PRESIDENT: Thank you. Thank you. Please, everybody have a seat.

First of all, I'm sorry to keep you guys waiting—I have all these things I've got to do—(laughter)—as President. This is by far the most fun thing that I'm doing today. So welcome to the White House. We are extraordinarily pleased to have the world-champion Pittsburgh Penguins—(applause)—with their third Stanley Cup. (Applause.)

Just a couple of acknowledgments in the house: Pittsburgh Mayor Luke Ravenstahl—where's Luke? Where's the mayor—I thought he was around here. Well, he should be. (Laughter.)

Senator Bob Casey—is he around? (Applause.) Come on, Bob Casey. (Applause.) Senator Arlen Specter in the house. (Applause.) Repre-sentative Mike Doyle. (Applause.) I know he's a fan. Representative Jason Altmire. (Applause.) Representative Chris Carney. (Applause.) Representative Tim Murphy. (Applause.) And Representative Glenn Thompson. (Applause.) And even though he's from Iowa, this guy grew up in Pittsburgh, is still a fanatic, and that is Secretary Tom Vilsack, Agricultural Secretary. (Applause.)

I have to say all of you look pretty good without your playoff beards. They're pretty good-looking guys without all that. (Laughter.) I want to congratulate all the fans back home who made Mellon Arena such a tough place for visiting teams this year. With the Steelers and the Pen-guins I guess it's a good time to be a sports fan in Pittsburgh. (Applause.)

I was complaining about this—it's been a while since Chicago won anything, Coach. (Laughter.) And I'm not happy about that. But as many of you know, I have a special place in my heart for Pittsburgh and so if it can't be the Blackhawks, then the Penguins aren't a bad choice.

The last time this team was here was during the playoffs against the

Washington Capitals. It was a hard-fought series, but it showed everybody how enthusiastic our hockey fans are also here in the nation's capital.

I want to thank Coach Dan for being here. Not only did Dan win the Stanley Cup in his first season as head coach—that does not happen very often—but he also brought a new sense of purpose and excitement to the team—and made sure his players had a little fun along the way.

Having Mario Lemieux here is a pretty big deal. (Applause.) He won a couple of these trophies as a player, but this is his first as an owner—and he's still got a big smile on his face, so I guess it feels pretty good this way too.

I want to thank Willie O'Ree for joining us. Willie is a hockey pioneer in his own right, who has worked tirelessly to make sure kids from every background can learn the lessons that hockey has to offer. So we are grateful to you, sir—please give him a big round of applause. (Applause.)

And this team would not be here without two of its youngest members. So first of all, I want to congratulate Sidney Crosby on becoming the youngest captain in history to win the Stanley Cup. (Applause.) And Evgeni Malkin for being the third-youngest player ever to be named playoff MVP. (Applause.)

You know, we've had a lot of championship teams visit the White House—I've seen a lot of trophies—there is something special about the Stanley Cup, other than it just being really big. (Laughter.) Winning this trophy takes a whole new level of sacrifice. It takes a group of players who can persevere through injuries and pain and setbacks and seven-game series. Above all, it takes a team that is willing to stick together, because nobody wins the Stanley Cup on their own.

And that's why after the last buzzer sounded back in June, these players took the Cup on the road to say thank you to all the people who helped get them here. They took it on fishing trips and stopped by neighborhood barbeques; they visited elementary schools, and brightened the days of children recovering in the hospital. I think this Cup has even held a baby or two. So this is a team that understands that being a champion doesn't end when you step off the ice.

Service is a way of life for these players back in Pittsburgh. Earlier today, Willie and the guys put on a clinic for kids here at Fort Dupont as part of our United We Serve summer of service. And besides teaching the kids a few moves, they stressed the importance of staying in school and leading active and healthy lifestyles. (Applause.) I understand we've got some of those young players from Washington, D.C., and Pittsburgh here with us—go ahead and wave, guys. There you go. (Applause.)

That's what the Stanley Cup is all about—not just having your names engraved alongside the best players in history, but also giving back to others along the way. And this spirit of service helps to strengthen our communities, it strengthens our country—and I know this team gets a lot in return for it as well.

So I want to again just say congratulations for your outstanding season, for not just your athleticism, but also your sportsmanship. Coach, we're very proud of you. Thank you very much. (Applause.)

SUGGESTED READINGS

Benson, Thomas W. *Writing JFK: Presidential Rhetoric and the Press in the Bay of Pigs Crisis.* College Station: Texas A&M University Press, 2003.

Gelderman, Carol. *All the President's Words: The Bully Pulpit and the Creation of the Virtual Presidency.* New York: Walker, 1997.

Jamieson, Kathleen Hall. *Eloquence in an Electronic Age: The Transformation of Political Speechmaking.* New York: Oxford University Press, 1988.

Max, D. T. "The Making of the Speech." *New York Times Magazine,* October 7, 2001, 32.

Noonan, Peggy. *What I Saw at the Revolution: A Political Life in the Reagan Era.* New York: Random House, 1990.

Ritter, Kurt, and Martin J. Medhurst, eds. *Presidential Speech-Writing: From the New Deal to the Reagan Revolution and Beyond.* College Station: Texas A&M University Press, 2003.

Schlesinger, Robert. *White House Ghosts: Presidents and Their Speechwriters.* New York: Simon & Schuster, 2008.

Scully, Matthew. "Present at the Creation." *Atlantic Monthly,* September 2007, 76–88.

Stephens, Mitchell. *The Rise of the Image, the Fall of the Word.* New York: Oxford University Press, 1998.

Waldman, Michael. *POTUS Speaks: Finding the Words that Defined the Clinton Presidency.* New York: Simon & Schuster, 2000.

13

Modern Campaign Polling

ROBERT K. GOIDEL

Public-opinion polls are a valued tool in the arsenal of any serious political candidate. They help candidates set their campaign agendas, craft messages, and otherwise communicate with the public. One can argue that public-opinion polls improve the electoral process by giving candidates a better understanding of the public they hope to serve and a more effective mechanism for mobilizing supporters while persuading undecided or weak partisans. Effective use of polling helps candidates better identify the targets of campaign messages, construct more effective messages, and evaluate the effectiveness of communications. Campaigning in the absence of good poll data is like shooting at shadows in the dark. You may hit something, but it is difficult to discern what you were shooting at, what you hit, or what to aim at next.

At the beginning of the campaign season, candidates often commission *benchmark surveys*. Benchmark surveys tend to be fairly long (15–20 minutes) and are designed to capture the general political mood, the most important issues, and perceptions of candidate favorability. Benchmark surveys often test political messages to see which messages will be most effective. These questions are generally stated as follows: "Would you be more or less likely to vote for Candidate X if you knew . . . ?" Because benchmark surveys test negative messages, they are often confused with push polls. Push polls are only used to spread misinformation and are not part of systematic data collection and analysis. Message testing in benchmark surveys is used explicitly to develop campaign communications. It is not uncommon for candidates to drop out of a race after a benchmark survey indicates their favorability ratings or name recognition are too low or that the political mood is unfavorable. Political parties have used benchmark surveys to discourage intra-party competition in districts where they know that one candidate clearly more viable than another.

Benchmark surveys are often followed by shorter (5–10 minute) *trend or brushfire surveys* to track the progress of the campaign or address issues that emerge during the election. The format is similar, and campaigns use the polling numbers to understand if the public mood is shifting or if events have affected voter concerns or candidate evaluations. These should not be confused with tracking surveys, which contain only a few questions centered on hypothetical ballots and a limited set of demographics or political orientations. In tracking surveys, polling occurs continuously and data are aggregated over a 4–5 day period to provide a rolling average of candidate support.

Tracking surveys are designed to give pollsters an idea of the campaign's direction and to help decide whether to adjust messages or strategy. Candidates may decide to "go negative" in the final days of campaign if their tracking numbers are showing declining support or if they have failed to gain ground. While voters often express dismay about the level of negativity in political campaigns, negativity persists because consultants know from tracking-poll experience that negative messages are much more likely to move favorability ratings.

The Uses of Polling

Despite the important role polls play in elections, the use of polls is frequently misunderstood. According to a common misperception, candidates blindly follow polls, switching from one position on an issue to another in an unprincipled effort to win election. Once elected, officials use polls as part of their governing strategy, carefully testing the political winds before making decisions. It is worth noting the paradox of this criticism. Citizens rarely want leaders who ignore public opinion; they just prefer candidates who intuit public preferences rather than systematically measure them.

This criticism is caricaturized in perceptions of the Clinton administration. Every decision was thought to be calculated to bolster approval ratings, and Clinton was misperceived as lacking real convictions. Disdain for polls was frequently expressed by the Bush administration. As Bush stated in his 2004 reelection effort, the public knows "I'm not going to shift principles or shift positions based upon polls or focus groups." In an interview with Martha Radditz of ABC News, Vice President Dick Cheney declared, "You cannot be blown off course by the fluctuations in the public opinion polls." The public impression was that the Bush administration ignored the polls and dug in their heels as the war in Iraq grew unpopular.

Both of these caricatures are decidedly misleading. To take the least obvious example, the Bush administration relied heavily on polling to shape its message on Iraq—particularly Bush's resolute support for the war and his emphasis on victory. The Bush administration example is instructive, as candidates generally use polling not to follow public opinion but to lead it. "The politics at the White House is less about how does this impact us politically," Bush strategist Karl Rove explained, "and more about how do you go about politically, go out here and make a case for this and who do you make the case to?" Political considerations were rarely absent from Bush administration policy decisions. As explained by Bush pollster Jan Van Lohuizen, polling on Social Security reform was directed at understanding "how do we sell it and what are the words and what is the language?" The Obama administration has followed suit, selling the 2009 economic stimulus package as economic recovery (as opposed to recession) and investment (as opposed to infrastructure). As these examples illustrate, politicians use polling to construct arguments and communicate in language that provides the highest probability of political success.

If the notion that politicians blindly follow polls is unfair to candidates, it also reflects a fundamental misunderstanding of the nature of public opinion. Public opinion is often contradictory, reveals considerable ambivalence (as opposed to certainty), and—at least when it comes to the level of specificity on issues and candidate preferences—is fluid rather than static. Core values and political orientations remain more stable, but even more deeply rooted orientations can change over time. This is not to suggest that public opinion is easily manipulated or that it is subject to the whims of news media coverage or political spin. The idea of a highly malleable public was discarded with the earliest studies of American voting behavior. Citizens actively filter campaign messages through partisan and ideological lenses.

But if moving public opinion is no simple task, it is hardly impossible. First, campaigns tend to revolve around a limited set of issues at the expense of other issues or considerations. This campaign agenda is set in part by the context, but it is also the result of the interplay between campaigns, the news media, and the voting public. The 2008 presidential election, for example, focused on the economy to the advantage of Barack Obama and the disadvantage of John

McCain. The Obama campaign was assisted by the economic collapse of the financial sector in September 2008; but even before the collapse, Obama was better positioned on economic issues and the economy topped voter concerns.

Carefully constructed public-opinion polls can inform campaigns about the importance of various issues and the degree to which they are advantaged by a particular set of issues. Campaigns use this information to focus their communications on favorable issues and by narrowing partisan gaps on unfavorable issues. In 1992, candidate Bill Clinton reduced a partisan gap on crime-related issues that heavily favored the Republican Party with "tough on crime" rhetoric and support for the death penalty. In 2000, George W. Bush reduced a partisan gap favoring the Democratic Party on education by advocating for an expanded federal role in education. And in 2008, Barack Obama all but erased John McCain's advantage in perceptions that McCain was better equipped to deal with an unexpected crisis.

Second, political campaigns can influence the framing of individual issues as well as the overall campaign narrative. On a number of issues, the public is ambivalent or holds contradictory opinions. For example, the public is supportive of health-care reform but concerned that changes in the system might adversely affect the quality of care they receive. In 1994, Bill Clinton's effort to reform health care failed not because he misread public opinion but because he could not alleviate concerns about how reform would impact individual care. On budgetary matters, public opinion is liberal when it comes to spending but conservative when it comes to taxes. How these issues are framed— what considerations are emphasized as important—has a profound impact on public opinion.

Framing of issues does not just happen but is the result of framing contests, in which campaigns, outside groups, and the news media negotiate the meaning of political issues. Republican efforts to repeal the estate tax, for example, were assisted by renaming it the "death tax." Likewise, Democratic spending proposals are perceived more favorably when they are referred to as "investment" or "stimulus" as opposed to "tax and spend" or "redistribution of wealth."

A similar logic applies to candidate image. In competitive elections, candidates are advantaged relative to the opposition on some traits but disadvantaged on others. The challenge resides in defining your candidate in favorable terms and the opposition in unfavorable terms. Efforts to define a candidate's image—particularly for better-known candidates—cannot be made up out of whole cloth but must be based on existing public perceptions. In 2004, John Kerry was portrayed as someone who straddled both sides of the fence on contentious issues. The Bush team used Kerry's own statements ("I actually voted for the $87 billion before I voted against it") and imagery (John Kerry windsurfing) to help drive the Bush message home. In 1992, Bill Clinton was able successfully to emphasize his compassion for voters facing economic uncertainty while portraying George H. W. Bush as out of touch.

On those occasions where candidates do shift positions because of polling, it is either on issues they do not care deeply about or else are critical to winning election. Mitt Romney was pro-choice when he was governor of liberal Massachusetts but switched to being pro-life in his bid to win the Republican presidential nomination. Had he not switched his position, it is unlikely that he would have been able to mount a serious campaign. Equally important, had he won the nomination and been elected, it is likely that he would have pursued pro-life judicial nominations.

Interpreting Public Opinion

While polling provides candidates with valuable information, it is no magic bullet. Perhaps the most important limitation is that the data do not speak for themselves. Data must be interpreted, preferably by analysts who understand the ambivalence, contradictions, and uncertainty that underlies contemporary public opinion. Take, for example, an issue like climate change. Most citizens lack the detailed knowledge required to have an informed opinion on the science of climate change. Many citizens are simultaneously concerned about the problem and uncertain about policy solutions. To treat a single survey response or a single survey as definitive would be decidedly misleading.

On many issues, citizens are not well enough informed to have a preexisting opinion and are, in fact, making up their responses as the questions are being asked. As a result, public opinion is highly sensitive to the wording of questions; it also demonstrates considerable instability over time and a lack of constraint across opinions. Critics take this sensitivity as evidence that poll results are meaningless or subject to manipulation. The mistake is to believe that variations across questions or contexts are not revealing of underlying values and sentiments. Some of the more interesting survey results reside within the details of how language affects survey response and how citizens respond differently to different issue contexts or frames.

Likewise, it is a mistake to assume that the politically meaningful dimensions of public opinion can be captured by examining only the direction of opinion on a given issue. Intensity (how strong is the opinion) and salience (how important is the opinion relative to other opinions) matter as well. There are countless examples of an intense minority winning against a less committed majority. On gun control, for example, polls routinely show broad support for restrictions on gun ownership but gun-rights supporters are more intense and more likely to be single-issue voters.

In the 2008 Democratic nomination, Barack Obama was able to capitalize on the intensity of his support in the early caucus states, especially the highly influential Iowa caucus. During the general election, polls routinely revealed an enthusiasm gap between highly energized Obama supporters and more reluctant McCain supporters. Democrats, for their part, were on the losing side of an enthusiasm gap in the 2004 election between George W. Bush and John Kerry.

Candidates are well advised to understand the distribution of opinion. The conventional wisdom is that candidates run to their base during nomination campaigns (Democrats to the left and Republicans to the right) and to the center during the general election. But much depends on the distribution of public opinion around the campaign's most pressing issues. If opinion is distributed in a normal distribution, with the average voter falling in the middle, moderating an issue position is an effective course of action. On a bimodal distribution, where voters fall mostly into one or two camps, such a strategy would not only be unproductive, it might prove harmful.

Public opinion changes as citizens learn more about issues and candidates. For candidates, the challenge is to understand how public opinion might move over the election. Proponents of deliberative opinion polling argue that traditional polling captures on-the-spot reactions to political issues rather than the opinion that would emerge from informed discussion. Recognizing this, political campaigns often supplement polling with focus groups—small group discussions of 10–12 participants, purposively selected to represent key demographic groups or voting blocs—to provide depth and context to poll results.

Finally, it is important to understand opinion among key subgroups. This comes through an examination of the crosstabs by key demographics and orientations to target potential supporters. In the 2008, for example, Barack Obama began the campaign running behind Hillary Clinton among African Americans. Early on, there were questions about whether Obama—whose father was Kenyan and mother was white—was "black enough" to appeal to

African Americans. The attention garnered by his early victories—as well as an ill-timed comment by former president Bill Clinton—moved African Americans solidly into the Obama camp. Overall, interpreting public opinion requires understanding a given set of poll results, as well as an ability to place them in context and to understand what—within the numbers—will remain the same and what is possible to change.

The Challenges of Contemporary Polling

Mark Blumenthal of Pollster.com called the 2008 election the "perfect storm" in that it combined an increasingly cell phone--only population, an African American candidate as a major party nominee and looming questions about a potential "Bradley effect," and a highly mobilized electorate. Add in a long-term trend of declining response rates to polls, and the polling industry looked to be confronting what might have been another "Dewey Wins!" catastrophe.

The relative success of the polls in 2008 does not mitigate the broader challenges confronting the polling industry. First, response rates to surveys have declined significantly over the past several decades and will likely continue to decline into the foreseeable future. In the 1970s, response rates to telephone surveys were often 70 percent or better. Today, response rates frequently fall below 25 percent and are often in the single digits. Notably, response rates are, by themselves, not problematic if differences between nonrespondents and respondents are small. Studies to date indicate that declining response rates are less of a problem in practice. Difficult-to-reach respondents are similar to respondents interviewed after one or two attempts. The challenge for survey research is that we rarely know whether response bias is affecting a given set of results.

Second, the 2008 election raised questions about whether surveys would accurately reflect white support for an African American candidate. Previous statewide elections in California (Tom Bradley) and Virginia (Douglas Wilder) illustrated a tendency for minority candidates to perform better in the polls than at the ballot box. Obama's victory in 2008 would appear to put the so-called Bradley effect to rest. All polls, however, have to deal with questions about the accuracy and honesty of survey responses. Particularly problematic are questions where there is a strong social-desirability effect. For example, more survey respondents report that they will (or have) voted than actually vote. Questions of race remain difficult, despite the Obama victory, as prevailing social norms make overt expressions of racism unacceptable and difficult to capture in telephone interviews.

Third, substantial proportions of the public are increasingly outside of the sampling frame of landline surveys. As of June 2008, approximately 2.5 percent of the population had no telephone service at all and 17.5 percent of the population was wireless only. The degree to which this affects survey results depends on whether the cell-phone-only population is significantly different than the landline population. In terms of demographics, the cell-phone-only population is younger, poorer, and more African American and Hispanic. Until quite recently, post-stratification weighting adjustments effectively minimized any bias due to missing the cell-only population. Evidence from Scott Keeter at the Pew Research Center for the People & the Press indicates small but significant differences in 2008 survey estimates of the presidential vote. Adding further concern is research indicating that 13.3 percent of households can now be classified as cell phone mostly, meaning that while they have a landline phone they almost never answer it. In total, nearly a third of the population may be outside of the reach of landline surveys, and this population is growing.

Finally, election surveys not only have to correctly predict candidate support, but they also have to predict voter turnout. Notably, there is no standard methodology for determining likely voters, and different survey organizations generate decidedly different numbers. This problem was brought to light during the 2008 election amidst concerns that the normal likely voter models might miss Obama's highly organized mobilization efforts. In response, Gallup developed two sets of likely voter models for the 2008 campaign: (1) A traditional likely voter model based on past voting behavior and current intentions; and (2) An expanded likely voter model based on current intentions.

At the end of the 2008, public-opinion professionals could breathe a collective sigh of relief. The "perfect storm" of low response rates, a growing cell-phone-only population, a potential Bradley effect, and a highly mobilized electorate had not materialized into an election-night disaster. The issues confronting public-opinion polling that made surveying during the 2008 election cycle a risky proposition, however, continue to grow. To continue to reflect public sentiments, pollsters will likely need to supplement traditional landline surveys with other modes of data collection. As a result, the costs of interviewing survey respondents will increase substantially. Despite the challenges confronting pollsters, the value of high-quality data on public opinion data is unlikely to diminish over time, and the polling industry will adapt to fill this need.

SUGGESTED READINGS

Baker, Peter, and Dan Balz. "Bush Words Reflect Public Opinion Strategy." *Washington Post,* June 20, 2005.

Blumenthal, Mark. "Pollster's Facing Election's Perfect Storm." *National Journal,* Oct. 8, 2008. Online at: www.msnbc.msn.com/id/27084438/.

Gallup. "How Do Gallup's Likely Voter Models Work?" Online at: www.gallup.com/poll/111268/How-Gallups-likely-voter-models-work.aspx.

Keeter, Scott, Michael Dimock, and Leah Christian. "Cell Phones and the 2008 Vote: An Update." Pew Center for the People & the Press. Online at: pewresearch.org/pubs/964.

14

Focus Groups

MALCOLM P. EHRHARDT

During the first decade of the twenty-first century, focus groups during major candidate debates became a form of instant gratification for the media in presidential campaigns. Nationally prominent researchers gathered demographically balanced groups of undecided voters and outfitted them with electronic devices that monitored their responses to candidates during the debates, thus providing real-time indications about the perceived winners and losers. Networks dueled with their individual instant-response dial sessions, which illustrated voter reactions to candidates' comments as the debates progressed. By the end of the third Obama-McCain debate in 2008, for instance, it became apparent that undecided voters in key battleground states were breaking in large numbers for Obama as measured by the reactions of groups that were carefully selected by focus-group organizers and sponsored by the networks. These groups were microcosms of a national movement in response to issues and perceptions about how the candidates were handling their campaigns.

Focus groups are one of the best ways to use qualitative research in political campaigns because they reveal the attitudes of voters about candidates and issues, as well as the underlying reasons behind those attitudes. Away from the national TV studio arena, focus groups are typically set in facilities that allow sessions to be viewed by campaign managers and candidates through a two-way mirror. Most focus groups are 90-minute to 2-hour discussions among 10 to 12 registered voters who are carefully selected for their demographic diversity. Focus groups often reveal opinions about local, statewide, or national issues, and test reactions to candidates and their campaign messages, especially television commercials, before they are released to the general public. Frequently, these groups uncover important sentiments behind attitudes that can be used to build or restore support for one's candidate or to exploit opponent weaknesses.

Focus groups serve many purposes. Most important, they are opportunities to hear from voters and to better understand their thinking. After all, the voters decide the fate of candidates, who commit their resources, reputations, and possibly their careers when they run for office.

Survey Research and Focus Groups

The focus group is a popular form of qualitative research that complements quantitative survey research in political campaigns. Traditionally, benchmark surveys of 600 to 1,200 registered voters, usually conducted by telephone, are used to establish priorities for political campaigns. These initial surveys are important because they are statistically significant, usually with a slim margin of error (plus or minus 4 or 5 percentage points). Their results provide information on how important demographic groups perceive issues and give campaigns strategic direction on how to build upon their existing base of support and how to best approach swing voters. These polls ask voters a series of 25 to 35 predetermined questions that have been vetted by the research organization and the campaign. Because of time limitations, most—if not all—of the questions are fixed responses or multiple choices, with few, if any, open-ended answers.

Benchmark polls provide candidates and campaign managers with aggregate data and breakdowns of voter sentiment on key issues and voter identification and awareness versus other candidates—the first "horse race" data. Because campaigns are like athletic contests, with candidates running against each other and the clock, these surveys provide the initial glimpse of the race as it kicks off. Astute campaign managers will map out media and grassroots strategies based on the findings of the initial surveys, focusing on enhancing existing strengths and targeting areas where new support may be found.

Sophisticated campaigns use focus groups in conjunction with benchmark polls at the outset of the election cycle because of focus groups' ability to penetrate demographic groups, particularly those on the margins. In a racially diverse congressional district, for instance, it is important for a candidate to understand how he or she is perceived on issues—such as health care, crime, and education—that are important to members of another race. Unlike a telephone poll, in which responses are fixed, focus groups allow for deeper and more nuanced reactions that provide indications about how and when to move the campaign in a particular direction to reach targeted voters. While survey research provides valuable data for the road-map strategy, focus-group results generate the scenic view.

As a major campaign evolves, candidates and managers like to know if their strategies are working, so they usually build in more telephone surveys and at least one set of focus groups. Strategically timed focus groups during the middle and latter stages of the campaign can detect emerging themes and trend lines that can be useful in determining mid-course grassroots or media messaging strategies. The late polling tactics, commonly referred to as tracking polls, provide nightly indications on how the campaign is moving as the election approaches.

The advantages of survey research in campaigns are that telephone polls are comprehensive in reach, identify voter issues, determine public awareness and inclinations about candidates, and leave little margin for error. A recently discovered disadvantage of the traditional telephone poll is the growing use of cell phones, since the primary sources of demographic data are registered voter rolls with home phone numbers. Since the number of cell-phone users is increasing and many consumers are opting out of phone usage at home, it is increasingly more difficult to capture all demographic groups—especially younger voters—during the screening process. In the 2008 presidential campaign, some pollsters conducted surveys using cell phones exclusively, and although they claimed that the results mirrored those with home phone numbers, this practice could present problems in the future for researchers. In subsequent elections, cell-phone users have been included in surveys, assuring effective reach into demographic voter groups, such as younger voters, who might not have been reached through home telephone numbers.

Survey research is also expensive. Telephone interviews for voter samples of 600 to 1,000 people, consisting of 25 questions conducted over one week, can cost $30,000 to $50,000. Conducting tracking surveys during the last two weeks of a campaign, when 300 voters are called each night, can make the final days of a campaign costly, even while they are providing timely and useful information.

Focus Groups Offer Unique Advantages

Focus groups have several advantages over telephone surveys. They are less expensive to execute; in many cases they can be turned around and furnish actionable results in a matter of days; and they provide in-depth thought and insight through open-ended questions and the probing of responses. While survey research can detect the *what* of campaigns and candidate status, focus groups provide the *why*—the reasons that the public has formed a collective opinion about issues, personalities, or campaign developments.

Consider this situation. In a local race for district attorney in a majority African American county, there were three candidates, one African American and two Caucasians. Survey research conducted through telephone polls consistently ranked crime as the number-one issue on the minds of voters. People were displeased with the performance of the current district attorney, who was not seeking reelection, and all demographic groups were eager for improvements in the criminal-justice system. All three of the candidates had experience as prosecutors, and early polls indicated that the race would be very close. The African American candidate was eliminated in the first primary, leaving two white former assistant district attorneys in the runoff. Although their backgrounds and experiences were similar, a series of focus groups detected an undercurrent within the African American community about one of the candidates, who was a defense attorney at the time of the election. Several years earlier, he had represented three nightclub bouncers who had attacked and killed an African American patron. In the time between the original polls and the runoff election, word about the case and its gory details spread through the black community, quickly changing attitudes about the defense attorney. Even though he initially picked up the support of the defeated African American candidate, by the time of the election, black opinions were fixed. He was handily defeated.

How Focus Groups Work

The integrity of the focus-group process as a meaningful form of qualitative research rests in its organization and execution, particularly regarding the screening of participants and the types of questions that are used to detect voters' attitudes and opinions and the reasons behind them.

Research Purpose and Research Questions

At the outset of political campaigns, a range of research questions are developed regarding key issues and personalities, as well as perceived challenges and opportunities facing communities, with the goal of discovering how registered voters feel about the issues. The research questions are aimed at discovering voter impressions about whether the district, state, or nation is on the right track. They also include questions about various approaches to fixing problems and the types of candidates who might be capable of solving them.

Scheduling the Sessions

To address the research purpose and questions, a series of focus-group sessions are scheduled, preferably at a facility equipped with a two-way mirror for client viewing. The studio should also feature closed-circuit cameras and televisions, recorders, and microphones, so that sessions can be played again for campaign managers, much in the way coaches view game tapes. If professional focus-group facilities are not available, sessions are frequently conducted in hotel meeting rooms; this is especially common in small to mid-size media markets in statewide and congressional races. With side-by-side rooms, the sessions can be conducted in one room, with campaign officials and media equipment set up in the adjoining room, allowing for real-time observation on TV screens. Two-way radios allow for communication between the observers and the moderator to clarify items or to delve further into issues that arise during the sessions.

Normally, two sessions of 10 to 12 participants are scheduled in an afternoon or evening. These 90-minute sessions are spaced at least two hours apart to allow for clearing out the facilities and to avoid overlap.

The Importance of Screening Participants

Target groups almost always consist of registered voters, and usually a balance of races, gender, and ages is preferable, so that researchers can encourage interaction. Voters of different ages may have widely varying perceptions on issues such as health care and education, for instance, the face-to-face discussion in focus-group sessions can capture starkly different opinions and provide useful information to a candidate who needs to expand his or her base of support or educate new constituencies.

Focus groups also afford opportunities for sub-group sessions. To discover candid views on workforce issues, for example, it would be desirable to conduct two focus-group sessions: one with employers who are seeking to hire qualified workers, and another consisting of workers who are undergoing training for jobs. Likewise, for education issues, it is sometimes preferable to conduct separate focus groups of parents, teachers, and administrators to identify attitudes about issues such as student performance, standardized testing, or even the length of a typical school day. And sometimes candidates for political office wish to isolate the views of certain demographic groups according to race or gender, and focus groups offer that opportunity.

The most effective way to recruit participants for focus groups is to use a professional service firm that works from a list of screening questions to identify the most desirable group of participants from the entire pool. For a group of 12 participants, for example, the balance of age, gender, and races should reflect the population or voter registration at large. Alternatively, it could include a representative sample of likely voters from similar past elections.

The Moderator Does More than Spur Conversation

Moderator skill and talent can make or break focus-group sessions. As the non-threatening leader of the discussion, the moderator must be able to elicit comments from all participants and move the session along on schedule while listening carefully for the thoughts behind the expressed opinions. Once those thoughts come to the surface, he or she must be flexible enough to dig deeply and prompt more discussion—and even disagreement—without offending participants. This might seem like a tall order, but seasoned moderators understand the importance of candor and drawing out sensitivities that may uncover significant and perhaps deeply held feelings that could impact campaigns. In congressional, senatorial, and presidential races—in which issues like health care, foreign policy, an unpopular war, and immigration are important issues—a moderator must stimulate meaningful discussion and discover the true sentiments of the participants so that the campaign managers and candidates have useful information to create winning strategies.

Obviously, there are common problems that arise in focus-group sessions if moderators are not careful, or if they lose control. The first comes when the moderator allows a domineering participant to hijack the session, causing other members to lose interest or even to show contempt for the proceedings. A second, somewhat related problem occurs when a moderator simply loses control of the group through his or her own weakness. Like a teacher, a moderator must exert enough command over the situation to move systematically through the session. A third problem occurs with the reverse situation, that is, when the moderator is too stern and participants feel they must answer questions in ways that please him or her.

Developing the Questioning Route

An effective questioning route provides structure for the moderator during the session and allows the client to contribute valuable input during its development. Questioning routes almost always begin with warm-up questions that get the group comfortable with the format, the moderator, and each other. Typically, warm-up questions for political focus-group sessions include personal introductions and questions about what part of the city participants come from, what they do for a living, or how long they have been in the area. The final question of the warm-up might be an open-ended one about the general conditions of the area, something like, "What kinds of things are on the minds of people who live here?"

Following the warm-up questions, the moderator will move the group into a discussion of substantive local, state, or national issues, using high-profile events or controversial topics to gather general attitudes about the political environment and elected officials. On the subject of crime, for instance, the moderator might ask an open-ended question, such as, "Tell me about the controversy between the mayor and the police chief. What's that all about and how do you think it is affecting the city?"

The most important questions during the session, the key questions, are designed to discover the truly important attitudes of the group members and the reasons behind those attitudes. This is the most critical part of the focus group, and it is where the moderator must demonstrate a balance between control and seeking truly meaningful information. This is when surprises may occur, since the moderator uses probing questions to dig into what is really on the minds of participants. Using the crime scenario, for instance, this is where a participant might allude to the fact that there is a hint of corruption within the police department. Following up on this initial comment, the moderator will delve further, with a question or series of questions designed to discover whether this is a prevalent feeling in the group or an isolated opinion. An appropriate follow-up would be, "I think what I'm hearing is that there may be a problem within the police department that is keeping it from truly wiping out crime. Tell me more about that and what you think."

Focus groups usually end with wrap-up questions that allow participants to express any thoughts they feel were missed or not addressed during the session. At the conclusion of the session, participants are thanked for their service and rewarded for their time with an honorarium that could range from $50 to $100, depending on the locale.

Although all of the elements of focus-group methodology are important to meaningful research, the screening and recruitment of the participants—as well as the skill of the moderator—are paramount. Virtually every other facet of conducting focus groups is dependent in some way on effective recruitment and management of the sessions.

Adding Up the Costs of Focus Groups

Although focus-group research is less costly than surveys, it is not inexpensive. Costs associated with conducting focus groups can range from $4,500 to $7,500, depending primarily on recruitment and incentives (honoraria) for participants. Fixed costs include facility rental, refreshments for participants and clients, and fees for the moderator and the administrators who are responsible for the facility and video equipment. Obviously, these costs will vary depending on a number of factors, including region, screening criteria, and availability of participant pools. However, conducted properly, they are worth the investment. Ideally, many campaign managers and candidates like to use two to four groups to determine initial strategy. They should follow up with at least two sessions approximately one month from the final election to gauge the status of their strategies and campaign materials.

Focus Group Effectiveness in an Age of Interactive Technology

The interactive nature of focus groups should continue to provide advantages in exploring attitudes in an increasingly interactive society. Although television was still the major source of entertainment among three-screen (TV, Internet, and mobile devices) households through the 2008 presidential elections, much of the viewership was time-shifted. Watching video on the Internet and on mobile phones has increased dramatically, and companies are offering more programming options on mobile devices.

As a political campaign medium, the Internet has grown exponentially since its first widespread use in the 2000 presidential race, which is considered the first national online campaign. In subsequent election cycles, interactive websites have expanded the resources of campaigns and have led directly to increased voter registration, grassroots participation, and fundraising. Blogging and chat rooms expand interactivity even more, adding media richness to the Internet that invites continuous comment and opportunities for dialogue.

Focus groups will remain a viable research alternative in the future. The interpersonal experience among voters in face-to-face settings is a reliable way to discover important attitudes during critical campaign timeframes. In addition to timeliness, focus groups can be conducted in large or small markets in major statewide and national elections. They are also adaptable to emerging technologies. Today, focus groups held in one evening in Akron, Tampa, Cheyenne, and Boston can be viewed in a campaign headquarters in Austin in real time. The keys to success of this type of qualitative research will consist of the integrity of the research model, the process for participant selection, and the skill of the moderator in conducting sessions. Used properly, focus groups produce candid and useful voter responses for campaigns to observe, interpret, and convert data into meaningful strategies for winning campaigns.

SUGGESTED READINGS

Fildes, Christopher. "Ask a Focus Group the Wrong Question, and What You Get Is a Nice Answer." *Spectator*, Oct 12, 2002.

Grunig, Larissa A. "Using Focus Group Research in Public Relations." *Public Relations Review* (Summer 1990).

Hyde, A. C., and H. U Yi. "Focus Groups: It's Not Just for Social Science Research Anymore?" *The Public Manager* 29, no. 3 (Fall 2000): 57–60.

Krueger, Richard A., and Mary Anne Casey. *Focus Groups: A Practical Guide for Applied Research*. Thousand Oaks, Calif.: Sage Publications, 2000.

Stockdale, Margaret S. "Analyzing Focus Group Data with Spreadsheets." *American Journal of Health Studies* (Dec. 22, 2002).

15

Local Television News and Political Campaigns

DAVID KURPIUS

Debate over the role of local television coverage in politics is nothing new. Political campaigns and government communications staff have long viewed local television news as a good way to disseminate messages broadly. People who make a living pushing political messages know they can manipulate the medium. Their goal is to get their messages on air, intact, to large groups of people. While television audiences are in decline, news stations still draw comparatively large numbers of viewers. Local television news remains one of the most trusted sources of information for citizens, according to the Pew Research Center. However, many industry insiders and experts believe local television news and politics don't mix, complaining that stories are boring, the issues are too complex, and audiences do not care about politics. Often left out of the picture are citizens, who are treated as pawns in the political end game rather than as participants in a democratic process.

State budget crises and the excitement surrounding the 2008 presidential campaign (particularly in states where the race was competitive) led to increased interest in local newscasts' political coverage. Whether this interest was a temporary spike or a longer-term trend, as some studies suggest, may depend on what happens in television newsrooms and how campaigns approach news organizations in the future.

Inside Local Newsrooms

Recent political campaigns and economic events have elevated political reporters to rock-star status and pushed political coverage back onto the A-list. History demonstrates that this intense interest is likely to wane, returning to a more typically held view of politics as a second-rate assignment.

The best reporters add the depth, context, and relevance to a story to make it interesting to viewers. They know a good story takes a political issue and finds a character to illustrate the effects of that issue on people, making the facts more meaningful and easier to digest. This takes planning, foresight, an understanding of the issue, and a reporter who knows the community well enough to make all the relevant connections. This is Journalism 101, but it is becoming increasingly difficult to find at even the best stations.

Don't blame the reporters. It is not entirely their fault. Pressure to do more with less was growing long before the recent economic hardships forced layoffs in news departments. Few local television stations still have dedicated political reporters, favoring a general-assignment model of coverage. Even KING-TV in Seattle, with its highly regarded political reporting, had not replaced its political reporter a year after he left for a job in the Seattle mayor's office.

The time when reporters had all day to report and present one story is gone. Most reporters have long been required to do multiple live shots in the ever-growing number of newscasts aired by stations. They now must also generate web content and cover several stories in one day. Lost reporting time eats away at good contextual storytelling. It also cuts into the time needed to keep up to date on issues. News has become what one reporter calls "drive-by reporting." Quick graphics and file video, combined with a reporter live on-set or in the newsroom, suffices for coverage. The costs are extremely low and the opportunity to create other content is high.

This pressure to fill newscasts and update web content leads stations to look for news subsidies. Political freebies—such as satellite interviews with candidates and pundits, video news releases, and staged events—constitute one-stop shopping for time-starved reporters and news operations. Their overriding fear is that political content will look too canned and controlled. Reporters worry about having the opportunity to ask candidates questions, while also struggling for time to prepare for such interviews or even to be comfortable with their understanding of the issues at hand.

Fact-Checking Stories

All is not lost for political coverage on local television. People want to know the truth, and most do not have the skills or capability to dig through campaign statements to ferret it out. Some areas show promise for creating good television stories while serving citizens. Types of truth-squad reporting, from debate watches to ad watches to campaign fact-checks, are examples. This reporting has an element of "gotcha journalism" and plays a role in helping viewers cut through the clutter of campaign messages.

In the early days of ad watches, campaigns were commonly caught off-guard when a report called their ads false. Now campaigns are more savvy, providing footnotes and additional resources for their claims and preparing responses to ad-watch findings. Audiences respond well to this reporting, often commenting favorably on station feedback lines and websites. Campaigns are active participants in this game, often suggesting ad watches to stations. This style of reporting has an element of "campaign as entertainment," and campaigns expect this kind of coverage. One testament to the success of ad and debate watches is the copying of this coverage by newspapers. To take only one notable example, the *New York Times* has adopted this classic television form for their multimedia online political coverage.

Local television also contributes significantly to political coverage through polling. Often done in partnership with a polling company or newspaper, polling is a way to develop meaningful content and share costs. KING-TV, for example, often partners with Survey USA for local political contests.

Two prominent efforts to improve and increase political coverage on local television were public journalism and Best Practices 2000 (or Best Practices in Journalism). Civic or public journalism started as an effort to engage citizens in political and civic dialogue through news coverage. Although this type of coverage tended to be led by newspapers, local television news played an important role in it as well. Best Practices used less of a civic model and focused on improving the quality of coverage.

Using a project model, public journalism focused on helping journalists develop deep contextual understandings of the issues and/or communities. This usually resulted in town-hall meetings, surveys, and conferences meant to help citizens gain a better grasp of the issues and ask questions. Coverage focused on helping elected officials, citizens and community elites move toward workable solutions for civic problems, with the television station covering the process, soliciting diverse and non-traditional sources, and raising the level of coverage. While most of this type of coverage died with the loss of foundation funding, many of the tenets of this coverage still survive in daily reporting. In some places, such as Madison, Wisconsin, public journalism still thrives. A consortium of media organizations have cobbled together underwriting to support these efforts, making it the longest-running public journalism effort in the country. In 2008, the local PBS television station, public radio station, daily newspaper, and a handful of other partners used the public journalism model to cover both the national election and key state elections, including the state supreme court race.

Best Practices 2000 (BP2K) evolved from the public journalism experiment. It did not include community connections; instead, it focused on providing viewers with quality information. BP2K was funded by the Pew Charitable Trusts and the Corporation for Public Broadcasting. The model required commercial and public television stations to partner on political coverage. Newspapers were not included in this partnership model. Conferences were structured around a demonstration and sharing model, with an emphasis on building relationships and sharing ideas. Participants left meetings with a reel of good examples and an understanding of the effort needed to produce deep contextual coverage with an overlay of good storytelling. BP2K freed television to follow a story development model without the worries of covering meetings and staged events, which at times caused problems for television coverage of public journalism community work. The model still tied back to citizen voices in coverage, using citizens to make stories more relevant and drive key points home for the audience. BP2K was a strong proponent of developing ad watches and debate watches on television.

In both public journalism and BP2K, foundation support was important in funding the endeavors and in gaining buy-ins from station managers who were already seeing declining audiences and advertising revenues. For campaigns and local governments, both efforts focused on issue coverage. Serious messages, as opposed to campaign rhetoric or grandstanding, had an opportunity to earn thoughtful, well-planned coverage. Message control was limited by strong sourcing that included voters. However, good storytelling and placement on more than one station in the market (public and network-affiliated) provided greater prominence in the market. Also, in many markets, stories were reedited for use on Sunday-morning talk shows on one or both stations.

Relationships and Trust

It can be difficult to get political candidates to appear on local television because there is a perception in newsrooms that political coverage bores the audience and drives it away. There is also the problem of campaigns not understanding or missing the opportunity to make an issue local.

During the 1988 presidential campaign of Michael Dukakis, the candidate came to rural Hawkinsville, Georgia. The state Democratic leadership had touted his speech and attracted media from several state markets. It was late in the campaign, and Dukakis was trailing. Flanked by hay bales and John Deere tractors, the former Massachusetts governor delivered a speech in which he spent a fair amount of time on urban issues. The speech missed the mark—a fact that local coverage quickly pointed out.

Failure to understand the political landscape can be costly. Campaigns have to know the local issues and what people care about in a particular state and region. Media are also more wary of covering campaigns. There is a greater fear of being used. Politics is so polarized today that political stories, even balanced ones, risk a flood of partisan complaints from viewers. This is the case even if you provide context or deviate from the campaign talking points. With this in mind, there are several key points both campaigns and television news organizations should consider.

Campaigns Would Benefit From:

1. *Knowledge of media outlets*

The increasing daily pressures reporters and news managers face provide an opportunity and a challenge for campaigns. The opportunity lies in the need of the station to gather adequate content to fill its newscasts and its website. The quest for content is an insatiable beast, and development is a near-constant process. Subsidies such as satellite interviews, easy-access news conferences, video and sound bites, background information, or even verbatim transcriptions of speeches via e-mail make the journalist's job much easier. This increases the likelihood of coverage and of getting campaign messages on air or online with minimal editing. It is important to provide good quality video and sound that is credible. If campaigns lose news organizations' trust, they greatly diminish their opportunities for earned media coverage.

Building this trust requires good knowledge of the station's political coverage routines, as well as of the station staff who make coverage decisions or work as reporters in the field. This is more difficult today, as fewer stations have dedicated political reporters. Still, a careful study of the station's coverage and website can provide clues about the most likely targets. Campaigns can develop a relationship, particularly with reporters, by providing access, direct contact information, and good information.

2. *Offering interviews*

Stations remain interested in candidate interviews, with satellite and station interviews more likely to be used as they require fewer resources. A campaign should only offer interviews when it has a clear message on an issue, but it should realize that the interviewer will likely want to ask less-scripted questions. Good preparation materials should be sent directly to the interviewer as early as possible to allow time to develop questions and structure the allotted time. A recent tendency to provide pundits and endorsers for interviews is usually less successful than offering the candidate. Do not play favorites or give exclusives unless the campaign is comfortable with not having good coverage of the campaign on competing stations.

3. *Developing support materials*

Following the 2008 election, journalists and news managers noted the helpfulness of campaign materials sent to stations, such as transcripts, background information, campaign strategies, and white papers on key issues. Journalists reported that these types of materials helped them do their jobs more efficiently and increased the effectiveness of their coverage. Often these materials were simply e-mailed to key people in the newsroom. For campaigns, this action allows better message management and increases the likelihood of getting messages on air. Barack Obama used conference calls to tell stations about his campaign plans and perspectives on issues. These were often backgrounders, but they helped fulfill news organizations' need to be in the loop. Several campaigns e-mailed full-text speeches, saving transcript time and allowing reporters to work more quickly and accurately.

4. *Provide video, audio, and multimedia*

In today's world of backpack journalists, video is more likely to make it on air or on the web. Video quality standards have changed in recent years. Video that would not pass for on-air quality two years ago now regularly appears on local stations and websites. There is a developing viral nature to video, which is regularly shared on social media sites such as Facebook and Twitter. Viral video tends to have more of a home video appearance (for example, with shaky and poor lighting) and focuses on gotcha stories, political persuasion or gaffes, and humor. Viral video can often make the rounds, however, garnering enough attention to end up on broadcast news programs.

On-air use is better because the broadcast news product is perceived as more credible, according to research by the Project for Excellence in Journalism. It also creates efficiencies for journalists who increasingly are asked to multitask content gathering, formatting, and delivery. Keep in mind that some and maybe most television stations still work to maintain broadcast quality standards. Thus the better the quality of the video and audio, the more likely it is to be used by stations.

Video news releases sent to stations or made available for download are usually a combination of a written script, specific details on the sound bites, video, and natural sound. The release generally includes a completed news story with a reporter voice track on a separate audio channel, so it is easy for the journalist to edit and add a new voice track. Additional sound bites, cover video (also known as "b-roll") with natural sound, and sometimes graphics are often included. This gives the journalist options for localizing the story, editing it with a different focus, or trading out sound bites to better fit the coverage focus in the station's market area. It is important to understand that once the audio and video are made available, the station can rework or restructure a piece as it sees fit. However, given the time pressures, it is unlikely that a story will be completely reworked, and there have been cases where the story was run with only a new voice track by a station employee. Keep in mind that the station may also choose to cover the release as a story without actually running the story itself. This rarely happens, however.

Coverage likely to be used includes behind-the-scenes footage, video of campaign stops, key speeches, reactions to policy and/or campaign statements or claims, and events that are relevant to the coverage area for the station. These are just a few ideas. A good way to determine whether gathering and providing video and stories is worthwhile is to think like a journalist. What do viewers in that area want to know about the candidate or official? Why is the story newsworthy? How can it be framed to capture the attention of audience members?

What Television Can Do:

1. *Be local*

Politics is covered as if it were a sporting event on national cable channels, a strategy that doesn't serve news organizations well.

Rather, a focus on the strong local connections the station has in the community—knowing local issues and putting local concerns at the forefront of campaign and political coverage—improves content. Offer opportunities for local citizens to give feedback on coverage and join in the dialogue on websites or via e-mail. One caution: make sure the website is a safe place for civic discussion and not simply a place for ranting and attacks. Some stations now require real name registration in order to leave comments, blocking out those who fail to keep their comments civil.

2. *Assign a station campaign expert*

One key problem as news staffs decline in numbers while facing increased content demands is a lack of preparation time. Assigning a few journalists to a particular campaign—or political coverage in general—increases the chances that they will better monitor developments. It also allows for relationship-building with the campaigns, which can lead to better coverage and possibly exclusives. It also helps wrestle control back from campaigns as they work to manage messages.

3. *Create a clippings book*

Even the best-prepared stations tend to send reporters who have not closely followed a campaign out to cover that campaign. A well-maintained clippings book with newspaper and web clippings, campaign coverage notes, and other tidbits can save the day. This is best managed as an organized paper notebook because it is easy to take into the field, allowing for news preparation when computers or Internet access is not available. It also allows for notations in the margins to point out key facts or to make points important to local coverage.

4. *Look for storytelling opportunities*

"Do more with less" seems to be the mantra for today's media. This paradigm comes with a high price: the loss of contextual storytelling. Making issues and facts relevant does take longer, but it also may garner an audience following. The key is to anticipate story needs. If stations know they will cover a campaign issue or a bill at the statehouse, planning the types of sources and video needed for that story improves quality. A little planning can quickly net an additional interview and some non-event video to help in storytelling. For example, if the issue is layoffs in state government, make calls to find a state employee who might be at risk. If that person is willing to be interviewed on camera, it can help make the story come alive. This kind of planning improves context and video, which makes the story easier for the audience to relate to their lives.

5. *Seek multimedia opportunities*

The demands for multimedia continue to grow. Television stations feel pressure from owners and the audience to provide extra content on the web and on a growing collection of new media, including text messages, Twitter, and the like. Today that content is often "shovelware"—shoveling on-air pieces to the web. The better solution is original content developed for online media that fits users' needs and desires. Additional opportunities for multimedia content in order to increase coverage effectiveness include audio slideshows, video, bonus interview audio (properly edited and labeled), interactive graphics, or simply useful links.

6. *Partnerships*

Public journalism experiments left an important lesson about partnerships. Joint ventures can effectively increase coverage staff with little or no increase in cost. Partnering with newspapers on political coverage gives access to opportunities for multimedia work and allows sharing of strengths, such as newspapers' libraries and stations' video-clip files.

7. *Truth watches*

Citizens want help deciphering political communication, whether it is a debate, an advertisement, or some other form of political rhetoric. Researching issues is easier than ever before, as more libraries, public offices, and statehouses put their files online. Be careful to track down all the angles and be sure to give opportunities for a response to news reports. Also, be aware that campaigns have become more savvy in this area and will likely suggest ads to test or provide sourcing for their claims.

8. *Prepare for bias challenges*

No matter how carefully journalists work to get coverage right, it is likely that they will be challenged as biased. This may be a concerted effort by a campaign to discredit a journalist's or a station's work (whether the allegation is true or not). It also may result from audience members who don't want to see reporters deviate from campaign messages. Be prepared to answer critics. Openness is often the best remedy, though it is unlikely that news organizations can respond to every complaint to the satisfaction of the person making the charge.

Final Thoughts

Television political coverage remains a key part of both television news and campaign strategy. Using some of the techniques and ideas described in this chapter can help both campaigns and journalists provide relevant, accurate information to citizens as they work to decipher an almost-constant stream of information and make their decisions about political issues and candidates. While strategies and tactics are evolving as quickly as the media technology through which the information is delivered, the process remains an important part of the democratic process in the United States.

SUGGESTED READINGS

"Internet News Audience Highly Critical of News Organizations: Views of Press Values and Performance: 1985–2007." *The Pew Research Center for the People & the Press*, 2007. Online at: people-press.org/report/348/internet-news-audience-highly-critical-of-news-organizations.

"The State of the News Media: An Annual Report on American Journalism." *Pew Project for Excellence in Journalism*, 2009. Online at: stateofthemedia.org/2009.

16

Get Out the Vote

GERRY TYSON

Discussions about maximizing voter turnout typically revolve around technique: targeting and methodology. While these topics are critical to effective get-out-the-vote (GOTV) operations, more attention needs to be given to strategic overview in developing and executing programs that will result in maximizing the participation of a campaign's supporters. This chapter places extended emphasis on that aspect of GOTV, while also addressing tactics.

The Turnout Two-Step

Often overlooked in the effort to maximize turnout for a candidate or a cause is an important factor: voting is a two-step process. The voter first has to decide that he or she has a preference that must be expressed through voting. And then the voter has to decide that the preference is important enough actually to cast a ballot.

In most cases, voters' deliberations that lead to choosing candidates and supporting or opposing causes are straightforward. For example, although the proportion of the electorate that sees itself as not aligned with either the Republican Party or the Democratic Party continues to grow, some experts believe that the true swing vote in high-visibility partisan elections is only about 10 percent of the actual, active electorate. A significant majority of voters view their choices through their particular partisan lens, voting consistently for candidates who metaphorically wear either blue or red jerseys. It follows that strong partisan voters are more likely to turn out in elections in which the partisan choices are clear (which may include some non-partisan ballot measures). These voters dominate early and absentee voting.

In contrast, late-deciding voters—soft partisans, truly non-partisan voters, and those who tend to vote negatively ("the lesser of two evils," as it were)—are often the most difficult to deliver to the polls, not only because they have differing ways of evaluating their options and tend to await defining information, but also because of the cognitive dissonance present in such decision making, which frequently leads to non-participation.

GOTV Begins . . .

. . . not just near the finish line . . .
. . . but at the starting line.

There's a common belief that GOTV operations occur at the end of the campaign, as the last act of a mad dash toward the finish line. While eleventh-hour communications are a critical part of maximizing favorable turnout, the success or failure of a GOTV operation is as much dependent on what happens throughout the campaign as it does on what occurs in the last 72 hours before Election Day.

Targets

A successful GOTV program requires appropriate targeting of the voters who are to be urged to participate. As will be discussed later in this chapter, making certain at the beginning of the campaign that a GOTV target group will be identified during the course of the campaign is an essential step in building a winning campaign. This target group will encompass likely supporters whose tendencies to vote will vary from highly likely to not likely, and the campaign's GOTV budget will determine the extent to which supporters along this participation continuum can be included in GOTV communications efforts.

There are some voters whose support is certain from the moment that a candidate or cause gets on the ballot. Despite this certain support, however, the campaign must make targeting decisions about those who need more or less communication to reasonably assure their turnout. For example, a GOTV manager can look at voters' historic patterns of participation and isolate individuals whose frequency of voting virtually ensures that they will participate in any given election. Reliable supporters who are highly likely to vote can become a valuable resource for extending the reach of the campaign into their neighborhoods and other social networks, serving both to help deliver other supporters and to persuade the persuadable about their candidate or cause. Based upon other information, it may also be determinable whether other high-frequency voters are likely opponents or persuadable voters. Obviously, reliable opponents should be taken off the table. However, high-frequency persuadables become the prime targets of the campaign's persuasion communications.

The focus of a GOTV program will be identifiable, highly likely supporters whose infrequency of voting history over an extended period of eligibility make them targets for moderate-to-heavy communication to convince them to vote. Delivering these supporters requires a dedicated effort by the campaign to inform them, invest them in the process, and lower the barriers that keep them from being regular and reliable participants in the process. As noted, the effort required for maximizing this critical segment of the electorate must start early in the campaign if it is to be successful to any degree. It should be the goal of the campaign to turn these voters into energetic and vibrant resources well before Election Day. By achieving this goal, the campaign will not only guarantee the turnout of a large number of these supporters but will also position them as resources to register and deliver voters who were otherwise beyond the reach of the campaign. How to do this?

Talk to them. The first act of the campaign toward these infrequent voters but likely supporters should be to engage them in a conversation that confirms their support and begins the process of getting them involved early in the campaign. While determining their support may be easy, accomplishing the second objective—involvement—requires significant skill, dialogue, and persuasion by the campaign.

Reinforce them. The best kind of reinforcement comes from within the voter, when he or she decides to invest in the candidate or cause (see below). But those who are not drawn actively into the campaign must become engaged in periodic dialogue in efforts to reinforce their convictions and thereby convert passive feelings into activism. This reinforcement may take the form of repeated contacts from the campaign itself, but more effective will be communications from other supporters who reside in the passive supporters' social networks—in their neighborhoods, congregations, community groups, and so forth. Such surrogates typically have high credibility if they are also peers.

Invest them in the cause. An infrequently voting supporter who becomes active on behalf of the campaign makes an investment that transforms her or him from a passive resource to a vote-multiplier. That's because most voters who invest themselves in a cause will take steps to protect their investments and validate their decisions. For them, not voting is not an option, and their new objective is to bring others to the cause.

Communicate through them. As noted above, supporters who decide to become actively involved in achieving the campaign's objectives can turn from GOTV targets to GOTV resources. However, supporters who don't make that conversion should be told of the important role they can play by simply letting others know of their support for the campaign and asking those people to join in support. The campaign's urging of this sort can't take the usual rote approach of "Be sure to tell your friends and family," but instead should help the supporter understand and define his role among peers and in the social networks in which he resides. Properly explained, this kind of information can be empowering to the supporter and, regardless of whether she actually influences others, increases the likelihood that she will participate.

Deliver them to the polls. At the end of the campaign, some passive supporters will have made the transition to investors and activists, and their participation will be largely assured. But many will remain passive, and it is among these voters that participation hinges on the campaign's ability to allay fears and concerns about voting and to fill information gaps. It is about removing the final barriers to participation in the process.

Identifying the GOTV Targets

The discussion now turns to identifying supporters—those voters whose participation is essential to victory. While there are some voters whose support (but not necessarily their participation) comes to the campaign automatically, others must be persuaded, and the campaign has to know the difference among these voters.

The best method of building a GOTV base is through direct solicitation of support, whether by phone or door-to-door canvassing. While this is a resource-hungry approach, it is an absolutely critical ingredient in a serious campaign. However, there are methods that can narrow the universe of voters that must be canvassed for support.

A benchmark poll that identifies strong support among distinct voter subgroups may provide the campaign with guidance in building a GOTV base. Additionally, voters who have high affinity with the candidate may qualify as supporters for a GOTV program. These include voters who share a candidate's political party, ethnicity, gender, age cohort, or community. This kind of data is typically available on a voter registration file, but it should be noted that affinity in most or all of these categories is no guarantee of support, merely indicators of likelihood.

Targeting by Precinct Performance

In a partisan election, historic precinct performance can be a key ingredient in forming the GOTV base. For example, a precinct that historically delivers 70 percent or more of its vote to candidates of one party can be subjected to communications that will elevate total turnout in that precinct.

With little argument, the most powerful tool for enhancing voter participation is face-to-face communication between voters and advocates of a cause or candidate. This kind of face-to-face communication is most efficient when advocates are able to go door-to-door to virtually every voter household in a small geographic area, such as a precinct. While this kind of personal contact can increase turnout significantly, it does so without regard for the candidate preference of either the advocate or the voter. Therefore, care should be taken in such door-to-door operations that only homes highly likely to contain supporters are contacted in this manner.

Most campaigns lack the resources to operate comprehensively in all high-support precincts, so available resources must be allocated with a sound rationale. Simple indices can be generated with the following formula, which uses historic partisan performance to prioritize precinct-level allocation of resources to deliver partisan voters: Partisan performance x reciprocal of turnout = turnout priority score.

The following table shows three precincts with high average partisan performance and varying levels of average turnout. The turnout priority score calculated with the simple formula above tells a GOTV manager where to deploy limited door-to-door resources in the most efficient manner.

Average Partisan Performance	Average Voter Turnout	Reciprocal of Turnout	Turnout Priority Turnout Score
95.0%	70.0%	0.300	0.285
95.0%	60.0%	0.400	0.380
95.0%	50.0%	0.500	0.475

Put simply, although all three precincts have the same likelihood of partisan performance, there is more room for improvement in turnout in those precincts with higher turnout priority scores, and they should be given higher priority when door-to-door resources are allocated.

Targeting with Statistical Models

The use of statistical modeling to target voters is a relatively new methodology for political campaigns. Given enough quantifiable data about a large, representative number of voters in an electoral subgroup, a skilled microtargeting specialist can build statistical models that will permit the "scoring" of voters on their relative probabilities of behaving in certain ways. Such scores enable campaigns to select targets at the individual voter level, rather than at the precinct level or as one of a larger cohort (found in polling) whose members are likely supporters.

While the investment in building such models and scoring voters can be expensive, significant economies can be achieved by the application of such methodology to prioritize targets for personal communication within a large voter universe.

Types of microtargeting models commonly employed include those predicting support for a candidate or issue and reveal the probability of voting in an election. Used individually or in combination, the voter-level scores generated by these models enable campaigns to focus their scarce communications resources on targets that are highly likely to behave in a desired manner.

The data used to develop statistical models is typically drawn from voter file demographics, consumer databases, and federal census information. In addition, large-sample surveys conducted by trained interviews using appropriate sampling methods can be used to great advantage in microtargeting projects.

Communicating an Effective GOTV Message

Communication that merely reminds or urges voters to turn out on Election Day or in early voting or absentee environments overlooks the need to provide those voters with a rationale and motivation for taking time out of their busy schedules to cast their ballots.

Why vote? Voters need to believe that their participation has a realistic chance of affecting the outcome of an election. Simple homilies such as "your vote can make a difference" are overused and lack credibility. Instead, the campaign must come up with concepts that are relevant, urgent, and persuasive, crafting messages that empower the voter to help attain objectives for himself and a broader community.

Why vote for YOU? Even if a voter has been previously identified as supporting your candidate or cause, it is critical to reiterate the argument for support as part of the overall reason to vote. In this way, a GOTV message is an important part of persuasion.

Issues that have been demonstrably effective in persuading or motivating voters should be central to the GOTV message when possible and appropriate. Such issues may be chosen because they have a high profile and can move voters in the direction you prefer, such as in the case of notable public endorsements. Also, specific issues may have been identified during voter-canvassing operations as important to individual voters, and they can be used in tailored GOTV arguments.

Easing the Act of Voting

GOTV managers must understand that infrequent and first-time voters are confronted with various barriers to participation, fears, or uncertainties that they must overcome in order to decide to undertake the act of voting. These are frequently referred to as information barriers, physical barriers, and social barriers.

Overcoming information barriers. Especially with new and infrequent voters, it is important to provide basic information about the act of voting, things that regular voters take for granted but that to a neophyte may provide enough discomfort or uncertainty to prevent voting. Such information includes:

- Where to vote
- What to expect
- What the ballot looks like
- How to find YOU or YOUR CAUSE on the ballot

Campaign workers delivering GOTV messages to supporters should be trained to understand that simply providing a supporter with a place and time for voting doesn't get the job done. Telling him that Lily B. Clayton Elementary School is at 2000 Park Place may not be enough. Adding that the school is between 8th Avenue and Forest Park Boulevard helps the voter visualize the location, immediately lowering a barrier to participation. The voter can be further put at ease by knowing that there will be signs in front of the school pointing to the correct door and, once in the school, to the room where voting takes place.

The voter should be told that he and other voters will present their voting credentials to precinct officials, who will sign them in and give them ballots. Sample ballots will be posted at the voting place for examination before signing in. And precinct officials are there to answer any questions voters may have, including showing them how the ballot is laid out, where the various items to be voted on appear on the ballot, and how it is to be marked by the voter.

Overcoming physical barriers. Many people fail to vote simply because they lack a convenient or efficient way to get to their voting locations, even if they are otherwise motivated to vote. These voters need to know about ride-to-the-polls opportunities offered by the campaign. Also, there may be circumstances at the polling place itself that make it difficult for elderly or disabled voters to participate, even if they are able to reach the venue. The campaign must be aware of such barriers and be prepared to help physically challenged voters overcome them when they arrive to vote.

Social barriers often appear as legal barriers. Individuals, campaigns, and political parties often discourage voters from participating by suggesting that the act of voting is illegal unless very strict conditions are met. Voters who fear that they may run afoul of the law in the act of legally voting may be effectively disenfranchised unless they are properly informed beforehand. This is one of the GOTV processes that needs to begin well in advance of Election Day, using as many sources as possible to disseminate voting information. Topics should include:

- Know your rights
- Documents needed
- Help is available

While various community organizations may undertake voter-education programs to increase participation generally, it is imperative for individual campaigns to make certain their supporters understand clearly what their rights and obligations are in terms of voting. By targeting messages about this to new and infrequent voters who support the campaign, the impact of intimidation can be minimized. This requires that the campaign begin communicating well before Election Day about voters' rights, the registration and identification documents that voters will need to present, and the availability of help at the polling place if their right to vote is challenged.

This is another area in which a campaign's more active supporters can have a significant impact by communicating with other supporters in their social networks who are relatively new to voting and who might need information or assistance. By merely providing these activists with contact information on other nearby supporters, a campaign may increase its vote yield.

Getting the GOTV Message Out

Here's a list of the many ways that GOTV messages can be delivered; the efficacy of each one depends on the nature of the audience. If the intent of the campaign is to enhance total turnout in a precinct, for example, all methods apply, but some are more efficient than others. If, in contrast, the campaign wishes to selectively turn out voters without inadvertently causing the opposition to take notice, more targeted communications are required.

Direct mail. Targetable to the individual household level and therefore an important ingredient in selective-turnout GOTV efforts, direct mail is usually too expensive for broad, total turnout efforts. In the latter case, using door-to-door workers to distribute the same in-depth information as handouts or door hangers is a good substitute. When e-mail addresses are available for GOTV targets, they should be used as supplements or substitutes for direct mail, although it is arguable that hard-copy messages are more effective as a result of their more enduring presence.

Door-to-door. This kind of face-to-face communication between voters and campaigners is the single most effective way of increasing turnout. However, turnout is increased regardless of the candidate preference of the voter and the campaigner, so GOTV communication of this kind should be limited to known or highly likely supporters.

Phone communication. Live calls from campaign volunteers or paid operators have the advantage of being able to answer voters' questions, so this approach is highly recommended in the mix of GOTV communication with new and infrequent voters.

Automated calls are an excellent way of targeting to the household level, conveying basic voting information and persuasive arguments about why to vote. If delivered by the candidate or by individuals who have high affinity with the targeted voters, these messages can be more effective. Automated calls may also permit voters to press buttons on their telephones' keypads to request contact from the campaign (for example, about transportation or more information).

Media messaging. The ever-increasing segmentation of radio and television markets may yield effective (if not cost-efficient) methods for delivering narrow-cast GOTV communications, especially if high-affinity ethnicity is a factor in an electoral contest. Although radio is still a broadcast medium, the cable industry's ability in some markets to target to nine-digit zip code levels may make cable TV (and perhaps cable radio, in the future) a viable medium for geographically concentrated GOTV messages.

Peer networks. A campaign well-stocked with avid and energetic supporters should undertake programs that will use these activists as conduits for GOTV communication with other supporters, especially those voters likely to have special needs for information and transportation. As other forms of voter communication become more expensive and less effective, peer communication rises even higher in the array of GOTV tools.

This chapter is an ambitious exploration of GOTV strategies and tactics, but it does not pretend to exhaust the subject. At best, it should provide the reader with some concepts that will lead to more in-depth thinking about the challenges of getting advocates to vote in large numbers.

17

Independent Content

PAUL HARANG

Barack Obama's words, spoken and sung simultaneously by a variety of celebrities, soar over a simple acoustic guitar arrangement. Will.i.am, recording artist and member of The Black Eyed Peas, created the video "Yes We Can" without the support, direction, or approval of the Obama campaign. Soon after the video was published to the web, millions of people viewed it from their home computers. Not long thereafter, Obama adopted it and began using it at his rallies, sometimes in his stead. During the 2008 presidential election, thousands of these kinds of videos were uploaded to YouTube, spread through social networking websites such as Facebook and MySpace, and e-mailed through networks of co-workers, families, and friends. This powerful new generator of content became both an asset and a liability for national campaigns.

Independent content is nothing new in political campaigns. Groups unaffiliated with candidates have produced newspaper, radio, and television ads and mass mailers for years. The 2004 election saw the rise of groups known as "527s," which are unaffiliated with the campaigns and therefore free from Federal Election Commission (FEC) regulations. They broadcast their messages with traditionally financed TV spots, mailers, books, and user-distributed Internet videos.

527s

527s generally attempt to influence elections through media campaigns. The name comes from a section of the United States Tax Code, 26 U.S.C. § 527. This law was an attempt to remove the use of "soft money," or money not subject to federal limits, from political campaigns. 527s are inhibited from directly supporting or opposing specific candidates. However, they often use issue positions to make clear which candidate they favor. A distinct advantage that 527s have over other political organizations is that they can raise money by accepting contributions over $5,000.

The Bipartisan Campaign Reform Act of 2002, better known as the McCain-Feingold Act, played a role in the rise of 527s. The act amended the Federal Election Campaign Act of 1971 by further limiting soft-money contributions to federal and local political campaigns. This left 527s as the only outlet for soft-money contributions. At the time, Senate Minority Leader Mitch McConnell predicted that the act would "not take the money out of politics. It takes the parties out of politics."

Citizens United v. Federal Election Commission

On January 21, 2010, the United States Supreme Court held that the First Amendment does not limit the corporate funding of political broadcasts in candidate elections. The issue came before the Supreme Court because of a dispute over a highly political film produced by nonprofit group, Citizens United. *Hillary: The Movie* criticized Hillary Clinton's 2008 campaign for president. The feature-length film essentially functioned as a campaign commercial, and the group produced and released it without disclosing who funded it. The court held that the First Amendment allows corporations to fund independent campaign expenditures without disclosing their donors.

Heralded by many as a victory for free speech, some Democrats, most notably President Obama, publicly stated their disappointment in the ruling. Shortly after the ruling, President Obama called it "a major victory for big oil, Wall Street banks, health insurance companies, and other powerful interests that marshal their power every day in Washington to drown out the voices of everyday Americans." He said the ruling gave "a green light to a new stampede of special interest money in our politics."

Reforming campaign finance law to require these independent groups to disclose their donors became a new element of the president's legislative agenda. However, after months of debate, the DISCLOSE Act, which would have codified this requirement, failed in the Senate by one vote in September 2010, less than two months before the 2010 midterm elections.

2004

During the 2004 campaign, independent groups produced and broadcast videos in support of both presidential candidates. The most famous example was Swift Boat Veterans for Truth, a group of Vietnam War veterans who served on a U.S. Navy Fast Patrol Craft. The group attacked the military service of John Kerry, who served as a swift-boat captain for four months during the Vietnam War. The group successfully tarnished the military career of man who was awarded three Purple Hearts, one Silver Star, and one Bronze Star in the line of duty. While Kerry and his supports belatedly disputed the truth of the ads' accusations, pundits, journalists, and media scholars generally agree that the attacks had a significant negative impact on Kerry's campaign. This group's effort was so effective that any harshly negative political campaigning by an independent group has become known as "swiftboating."

An example from the left is the liberal activist group MoveOn.org, which used its 527 status in 2004 to raise money and run ads critical of George W. Bush. In 2006, the FEC fined Swift Boat Veterans for Truth and MoveOn.org for violating campaign-finance law during the 2004 election. The commission ruled that the groups crossed into the territory of political committees by explicitly attempting to influence the outcome of the election. The ruling stripped both organizations of 527 status and therefore made their donations subject to FEC regulation.

2008

During the 2008 presidential election, supporters of the presidential candidates posted to the web thousands of videos supporting and attacking candidates or causes.

On March 5, 2007, a video appeared on YouTube entitled, "Vote Different." It spoofed Apple's Orwellian 1984 Super Bowl ad that introduced the Macintosh computer. As mindless drones watch Hillary Clinton's presidential campaign announcement in a theater, a young woman, on the run from armed guards, hurls a sledgehammer into the screen. The screen explodes and fades into text, which reads, "On January 14th, the Democratic primary will begin. And you'll see why 2008 won't be like '1984.'" The video ends with the web address for Barack Obama's website. In just over two weeks, 2.3 million users viewed the ad, and television news shows ran it as well.

The video was the creation of Philip de Vellis, an employee for Democratic media firm Blue State Digital. In a blog entry on the Huffington Post two weeks after he uploaded the video, de Vellis admitted authorship and claimed that he created the video "because I wanted to express my feelings about the Democratic primary, and because I wanted to show that an individual citizen can affect the process." He then announced his resignation from Blue State Digital in order to protect the firm from charges of conflict of interest.

This video marks the first time in modern political history that a single, unfunded individual produced content with his own equipment that became central to a national presidential race. As de Vellis put it, "The game has changed."

Many independent YouTube videos followed Vote Different, earned scores of views, and captured the attention of traditional news media. The "I Got a Crush . . . on Obama" ad, produced by a small group of independent filmmakers on a shoestring budget, featured beauty pageant contestant Amber Lee Ettinger singing about her love for the presidential candidate and his qualifications for the presidency. The video became a hit, earning millions of views and even more news media attention than the Vote Different ad. The timing, the humorously catchy song, and the risqué nature of the clip made this a particularly successful viral video, turning Ettinger, popularly known as the "Obama Girl," from an unknown model into a national celebrity.

Obama recognized the impact that small groups of citizens were having on the campaign, calling the Obama Girl video "just one more example of the fertile imagination of the internet. More stuff like this will be popping up all the time." He also voiced some frustration in losing complete top-down control of campaign content, remarking that the video upset his daughters.

On Election Day 2008, some local newspapers in the southern U.S. were delivered in a plastic covering sponsored by the National Rifle Association. The covering listed candidates that the NRA supported for each election. This was a legitimate and eye-catching advertising practice that put the NRA's ticket in the hands of anyone from those communities who read the daily newspaper.

EMILY's List (Early Money Is Like Yeast), a political action committee focused on raising money to help elect pro-choice Democratic women to the House and Senate, has been called the largest PAC in the country. In 2006, this organization's support helped reelect every female Democrat in Congress and also elect ten new ones. EMILY's List supported Hillary Clinton during the campaign for the Democratic presidential nomination and endorsed Barack Obama after Clinton dropped out of the race.

2010

As a result of the *Citizens United* decision, the 2010 mid-term elections featured a record amount of independent expenditures. According to the nonpartisan Campaign Finance Institute, nonparty spending more than doubled from 2008, totaling $280 million. Independent groups outspent the Democratic and Republican parties by 20 percent.

Republicans picked up more than sixty congressional seats and took hold of the House of Representatives. They also gained six seats in the Senate, cutting the Democrats' majority to 53-47. While independent expenditures favored Republican candidates, the dramatic increase in nonparty spending did not necessarily dictate the results of the elections. In the nine most competitive races won by Republicans, nonparty spending favored the Republican candidate more than two to one. However, in the thirty-five races won by Democrats, nonparty spending favored the Republican candidates nearly four to one.

Independent Content Related to Policy, Not Elections

On September 10, 2007, the *New York Times* published a full-page ad entitled, "General Petraeus or General Betray Us? Cooking the Books for the Bush White House." Paid for by the liberal advocacy group MoveOn.org, the ad coincided with a report to Congress by David Petraeus, general of the multinational force in Iraq.

In the ad, the group claimed that Petraeus exaggerated progress made in the Iraq war between the report and the February 2007 surge of 30,000 additional troops to combat zones. It stated that the way the Pentagon collected violence and casualty data failed to account for things such as car bombings and certain types of executions.

Journalists and politicians voiced disapproval of the ad, and on September 20, Congress passed an amendment to the National Defense Authorization Act for the Fiscal Year 2008 condemning "personal attacks on the honor and integrity of General Petraeus and all members of the United States Armed Forces." The amendment passed 72 to 25.

In an example of how policy-focused independent content can impact campaigns, no candidate for the Democratic presidential nomination voted for the amendment. They were criticized by Republicans and conservative

Democrats on the Senate floor and in the press. Candidates for the Republican nomination criticized the ad and used it to highlight the views of Democratic candidates. The Rudy Giuliani campaign bought its own full-page ad in the *New York Times* and used it to counter the assertions made by MoveOn.

A Rasmussen poll conducted days after the ad found that 58 percent of Americans disapproved of the ad, compared to 23 percent who approved of it. However, the day the Senate passed the measure criticizing MoveOn.org, the organization raised over $500,000. According to *The Economist*, MoveOn raised $1.6 million in a four-day period after the advertisement. MoveOn's provocative ad effectively distracted the legislative process, created a fundraising boom for the organization, and became the central focus of the campaign for president.

Direct-Mail and Referendums

Direct-mail has been a marketing and political campaign tool since the U.S. Postal Service developed the zip code system in the 1960s. Independent groups use political mailers as a relatively inexpensive and effective way to target voters. Direct-mail by independent groups is especially effective in referendum campaigns. Referendums offer a great opportunity for independent organizations like 527s because they do not have to operate around an official campaign and can therefore exert more control over their message. In 2008, the organization ProtectMarriage.com orchestrated a direct-mail effort to convince California voters to vote "Yes" on an amendment to the California state constitution that would officially ban gay marriage. The mailers used quotes from then-Democratic presidential candidate Barack Obama and vice presidential candidate Joe Biden that illustrated their support for defining marriage as between one man and one woman, even though both Obama and Biden had stated on previous occasions that they did not support the amendment. The organization, which sponsored the petition to put the amendment on the ballot, also mailed out lists of businesses that opposed the proposition and urged a boycott.

The money spent by the opposing sides totaled over $83 million, making it the second-most expensive campaign in 2008, behind only the race for president. Donors contributed money from all 50 states and over 20 countries. For political consulting firms, the liberal campaign-finance law concerning independent groups involved in referendum campaigns provide an important source of income.

What to Do about Independent Content?

Joe Trippi, campaign manager for Howard Dean in 2004 and John Edwards in 2008, characterized the easiest way of responding to negative third-party content as "flooding the zone." Citing the outcry after Hillary Clinton claimed her airplane was forced to take evasive action because of sniper fire when landing in Bosnia in 1996, Trippi noted that the story was untrue, or at the very least exaggerated, and that user-generated YouTube videos pointing this out sprang up immediately. In response, the Clinton campaign cleverly produced its own videos with the keywords "Hillary, Bosnia, sniper fire" and uploaded them to YouTube. When users subsequently searched for videos criticizing Clinton's embellishments, they were exposed to videos providing the Clinton campaign's explanation for their candidate's controversial statement.

While the changing dynamic of third-party content can present dangers for a national campaign, it can also provide advantages. As noted earlier, the Will.i.am video, "Yes We Can," with its high production value, star-studded cast, and adoption of official campaign rhetoric, provided the Obama campaign with a popular ad that stayed on message. The campaign adopted it and used it to highlight its theme of a grassroots-oriented, new style of politics. As this video proved, the perspective provided by political outsiders can do much to refresh the strategy of a campaign, putting it more in touch with the current values and trends of the greater society.

In a media environment driven by rapidly advancing technology that focuses increasingly on user interactivity, political campaigns can no longer rely on the traditional top-down configuration of dictating campaign content and the structure of campaign participation to passive citizens. An active citizenry now has a bigger stake in the national conversation about American politics. Campaigns that understand this and try to bring this voice into their everyday considerations will be more successful than old-school campaigns that try to control every aspect of, and every outlet for, their message. The successful campaign will be the one that accepts and incorporates input on policy and strategy from this democratic force that has a louder voice every election cycle.

SUGGESTED READINGS

Clayworth, Jason. "Obama Responds to 'Crush.'" *Des Moines Register,* June 19, 2007.

de Vellis, Phil (a.k.a ParkRidge 47), "I Made the 'Vote Different' Ad." *Huffington Post,* March 21, 2007. Online at: huffingtonpost.com.

McConnell, Mitch. "Bipartisan Campaign Reform Act of 2001." *Congressional Record* 147:3 (March 19, 2001): S3860.

18

Public Journalism

DAVID D. KURPIUS

In the summer 2009, the health-care debate topped the news almost daily as Congress and President Barack Obama worked toward a solution. Town-hall meetings across the country offered citizens the opportunity to talk about the issues and engage their congressional representatives. Instead, however, the headlines were about uncivil behavior by citizens who were more interested in shouting and disrupting these meetings than working toward solutions and consensus. Everyone loses in this situation. Media covered the raucous events as sensational disruptions and some politicians decided not to even schedule a meeting, likely fearing a similar spectacle.

Rewind to the mid-1990s and look at a vastly different model of engagement. We The People, Wisconsin, a collaborative effort of local media in Madison, Wisconsin, held an issue convention on health care. People from across the state came to the new Monona Terrace Community and Convention Center overlooking Lake Mendota to learn about the issues from experts in the various areas. The local media participating in this public-journalism effort watched and listened as citizens, politicians, and issue experts discussed various aspects of health-care issues.

This effort obviously did not solve the health-care problem, but it did provide a good model for effectively trying to address pressing civic issues, and it stands in stark contrast to the meetings in 2009. The difference is that the media were providing opportunities for the discussion to go well, which helped them fulfill their role of attracting and informing viewers, readers, listeners, and the larger public. Politicians were not giving stump speeches or canned sound bites for the evening news. Instead, they were part of the conversation, which helped fulfill their role of informing and attracting voters and representing citizens in solving public problems. The people participating in the convention were there because they cared about civil discourse and solving problems, and the media covered it extensively across media platforms.

This type of event and coverage is at the heart of public journalism. One of the best and longest-running public-journalism efforts is the Madison collaborative. The Madison partnership includes the *Wisconsin State Journal,* the locally top-rated WISC-TV (CBS), WHA-TV (PBS), and WHA-FM (NPR) stations, and Wood Communications, a public-relations group that promoted the effort and helped manage citizen involvement. The partnership has ongoing financial support. In its nearly 20 years of existence, We The People, Wisconsin, has held town-hall meetings and issue conventions, formed legislative panels, and set up citizen mock courts to conduct issue "trials." It focuses on educating citizen participants on the issues before setting those citizens up for the discussion and deliberation. It also presents mobilizing information to encourage participation and engagement from an even larger cross-section of the population. We The People, Wisconsin, focuses on city issues and statewide elections. It even partners with other media across the state and is not afraid to take its show on the road to garner more diverse perspectives. The key to its success is an evolving format that keeps the program fresh and interesting, actively involves people who are often missing from civic discussions, and puts the content in the medium that will best convey the information. This keeps internal competition down and avoids perceptions of gotcha journalism.

Now that you have an idea about how this works, let's back up and define it. Public journalism (or civic journalism) started almost two decades ago with a focus on reengaging citizens and hence democratic life through newspapers and television coverage. The goal was to change coverage to involve more people in communities in civic discourse and to improve the public dialogue on issues facing the community. Political races were an early focus.

Initially, there were pockets of innovation and experimentation around the country, from Seattle, Washington, to Wichita, Kansas, to Madison, Wisconsin, to Charlotte, North Carolina. Foundations supported many of these media projects. Early adopters were part of the Knight Foundation effort called the Project on Public Life and the Press. The Pew Charitable Trusts followed with the establishment of the Pew Center for Civic Journalism. These efforts fit well with the public-media model in the United States, and subsequently the U.S. Corporation for Public Broadcasting (CPB) and PBS helped fund various projects, such as Best Practices 2000 (BP2K). Best Practices was an offshoot of public journalism that funded partnerships between public and commercial stations focused on improving political coverage.

Foundation funding was crucial to the development of these experiments. While these foundations did not provide a large amount of money, it was enough to encourage media participation. The grants from the Pew Center for Civic Journalism were about $20,000, each going to media organizations that might have multimillion-dollar news budgets.

Why We Need Public Journalism

Simply put, public journalism changed coverage patterns to include greater diversity of sources, communities, and ideas. Stories developed as journalists explored communities and issues in-depth. If you start to build a story at the level of citizens, in their communities, you end up with a different perspective and angle as compared to traditional top-down reporting.

Initial public-journalism efforts focused on projects, such as election campaigns, community-issue ballots, and community problems. Techniques included town-hall meetings, comparative coverage, and increasing the community voices in coverage. Media adopted the town-hall format early on, as it was an easy way to engage citizens in discussion and to have venues for print and broadcast coverage. Often these events were televised live. Campaigns and citizens alike quickly grasped the format. Campaigns worked to stack the audience in their favor, while some citizens came to love the attention enough that they became regulars at the town-hall meetings. To mitigate the effects of either of these efforts, media partners in many communities began randomly selecting the audience from mail-in or e-mailed forms. This ensured strong participation while limiting any entities' ability to meddle with the composition of the audience.

Another key change was toward user-friendly coverage. One 2000 study found that civic-journalism newspapers tended to use more graphics than other media when presenting issues and solutions to citizens. A common thread in civic coverage was comparative reporting. Journalists would look to other communities with similar issues to see how potential solutions might work locally and where these other solutions fell short. The comparisons were often portrayed in graphic form to make it easier for readers to digest the information and begin working toward their own viewpoints and eventually solutions. At times, citizens were invited to comment or even cast non-binding votes through a media organization as a way to gauge citizen perspectives and support for particular issues or solutions.

A core tenet of public journalism is a bottom-up approach to coverage. This usually begins with "listening tours" in diverse communities. Today, it is increasingly difficult for reporters to find time to go into less-covered communities simply to gauge the pulse of citizens and to gain perspective. In the past, when journalists changed their routines to include these efforts, their reporting tended to have more non-elite citizens as sources. This form of sourcing is more structured and purposeful than the person-on-the-street interviews commonly presented in newspapers and on television news, which ask very specific and focused questions. In contrast, civic journalists ask more open-ended questions, allowing citizens to pick their way through an issue and control the path of explanation. This leads to different information that maintains the citizen's voice and viewpoint. For example, there is a big difference in the type of response an average citizen will give to two questions on health care. If the reporter asks, "Where do you stand on President Obama's health-care plan?" the individual may tense up, worry about knowing the plan well enough, and give a short response. However, if the reporter asks, "Tell me how you think about paying for your own health care," the person is more likely to open up and the conversation can move toward the person's position on the broader issue of health care. This type of questioning begins by trying to discover where citizens are in their thinking, and not with the ultimate question the reporter seeks to answer. Citizens, unlike politicians and government elites, need time to work up to a full-fledged opinion on an issue. Asking follow-up questions eventually gets to this point, but it follows the citizen's path rather than the journalist's and the answers are likely to be much different. This approach provides a deeper, more contextual understanding of the person's viewpoint. This type of coverage not only captures more "real-people" responses, but also—if the reporter thinks carefully about where she has not gone in the community to listen—it provides more varied responses from a greater diversity of people. Factors to consider are race, socioeconomic levels, education, history, and geography.

Television public journalism did change reporting patterns. More people who were not affiliated with government or big business (non-elites) were used in public-journalism stories compared to non-civic coverage. The racial and gender diversity of sources also improved in public-journalism stories. On both television and in newspapers, public journalism increased the amount of coverage of campaigns. As part of these efforts, media organizations devoted additional airtime and space to coverage of politics. In addition, media organizations practicing public journalism tended to give more prominence to the coverage as well.

Public journalism engages citizens in the democratic process, empowering them to present ideas and give feedback, and it charges journalists with making the conversation go well. That means reporting from the perspective of citizens instead of the powerful, providing deep coverage and comparisons that illuminate problems and potential solutions, and constantly reinventing coverage to help people engage and see the value of good, reliable, meaningful information.

Ways to Engage

A key component for public journalism is engaging citizens. There is not simply one way to do it. As mentioned earlier, town-hall meetings have been popular. Some communities use a "Front Porch Forum" as a way to engage people. Still others gather at community-issue conventions or pizza parties to share ideas and address pressing problems. Not everyone can or is willing to attend a community event. For these people, media organizations provide phone banks and e-mail addresses as contacts, where citizens can both get information and express their viewpoints. Surveys explore the broad boundaries of issues and focus groups tunnel deeper into the same issues to provide context and broader understanding. The point is that there are multiple and varied ways to engage people, with the focus on attracting the greatest possible breadth of community perspectives. Much can be learned by campaigns from these efforts, as more and more election work in campaigns focuses on organizing and mobilizing supporters on the ground.

How Public Officials Can Use Public Journalism

Politicians were initially reluctant to participate in this new type of media coverage. In a business focused on controlling images, statements, and presentations of the candidate, it seemed that too much was left to chance. Going into an open forum without a sense of who exactly would be asking questions, or even what topics might come up, can be daunting. However, the structure of these events makes it difficult for candidates to say no. This is particularly true given that the media partners usually make it clear to candidates that the audience will be told which candidates were invited and did not attend. In the early days, a few candidates avoided these events. However, it quickly became clear that nonparticipation was not well received by potential voters.

In the town-hall meetings or similar events, it is difficult for candidates to duck questions. When a citizen asks a direct question, she expects a direct answer. Sometimes candidates will talk their way around an issue, and citizens are not always comfortable with asking a follow-up question. In these cases, journalists often step in to ask the citizen if he thinks the candidate answered his question. If not, the candidate is given another opportunity to respond.

There is no doubt that these free-flowing citizen-candidate events are challenging for the campaigns. Often, the mission seems to be to get the candidate off-message and relaxed enough to have a real conversation. However, with the cameras rolling and the reporters taking copious notes, that is difficult to do. It also does not necessarily serve the campaign simply to stay on message when citizens are asking questions that demand more complex, contextual answers.

There is a positive side to public journalism events for candidates and government officials. In the age of short, often disconnected sound bites, these venues provide an opportunity for candidates to elaborate on the complexities of an issue or to explain how they developed their positions. When the town halls focus on community issues rather than campaigns, the opportunity to listen to citizen input and hear potential solutions is invaluable. In many ways, public journalism–focused media do a much better job of both fostering citizen participation and sharing the conversation with those who are interested but cannot attend the event than their non-civic counterparts.

In the best scenarios, civic journalists conduct comparative coverage. This coverage looks outside of the area or region for other places facing similar issues. The goal is to not reinvent the wheel, but to look at the successes and failure of other communities, weigh the trade-offs, and work toward a well-reasoned solution. Comparative reporting brings new information into the dialogue and helps people reconsider their own positions, as well as consider other alternatives. Daniel Yankelovich calls this the "working-through process."

There Is a Future

National news networks have adapted civic elements to their coverage, including citizen panels and feedback loops both on the Internet and via phone banks to solicit citizen comments and reactions. ABC's *Nightline* has conducted several town-hall meetings on issues. There also are more partnerships on political coverage. This is one of the big lessons from public journalism that the economic downturn of 2009–2010 has helped push forward. Media partnerships work, and they are a good way to explore better multimedia political coverage in the future.

Campaign Meets Public Journalism: Advice for Candidates

The first reaction of many campaigns to public journalism, particularly town hall meetings, is that they are not going into an unstructured arena. That approach can easily backfire, however, making it appear that the campaign and candidate are refusing to respond to potential voters. The better advice for candidates or campaign strategists is to study previous public journalism efforts. Then, get prepared. Have a strategy and anticipate questions. The appearance that you are dodging a question will likely work against you. You want to be seen answering questions directly, though you will likely have the opportunity to put the answer in context. It is less likely that you will be tied to short sound bites in a public journalism event, but that is not a reason to go overboard. Be as clear and concise as possible.

It is also important to be at ease in the town-hall setting. Research the area and the types of citizen who are likely to attend the meeting. Think about the types of questions they might ask, and formulate your probable responses. If possible, engage citizens before the meeting begins. Get comfortable and help them see you as a well-intentioned, good person.

The campaign will also want to get its supporters in the meeting. This is not easy, as many media partnerships now select citizens randomly from requests for admission. You also don't want to go overboard, as that will make it look like you stacked the deck.

When answering questions, be conversational. Ask the citizen to clarify his or her question if needed, and listen well. Look for opportunities for casual engagement. In this forum, citizens get to judge your body language and personal reactions.

Finally, know the media participants, their key employees, and the structure of their political coverage. This will tell you a lot about how the forum will run and how problems will be handled during a live event. See this as a great opportunity to earn good media coverage. Don't forget to monitor the citizen feedback online and in coverage after the event to assess your performance.

Good public journalism events are the antithesis of the screaming episodes seen in some of the 2009 congressional town-hall meetings. Such antagonism simply goes against the core purpose of helping the civic conversation at the heart of democratic life go well.

SUGGESTED READINGS

Coleman, Renita, and Ben Wasike. "Visual Elements in Public Journalism Newspapers in an Election: A Content Analysis of the Photographs and Graphics in Campaign 2000." *Journal of Communication* 54, no. 3 (Sept. 2004): 456–73.

Kurpius, David D. "Sources and Civic Journalism: Changing Patterns of Reporting?" *Journalism & Mass Communication Quarterly* 79, no. 4 (Winter 2002): 853–66.

Yankelovich, Daniel. *Coming to Public Judgment: Making Democracy Work in a Complex World.* 1st ed. The Frank W. Abrams Lectures. Syracuse, N.Y.: Syracuse University Press, 1991.

19

Online Political Advertising

MONICA ANCU

Political advertising is undoubtedly the main communication tool between candidates and voters during political campaigns. Dwight Eisenhower pioneered the use of television advertising in his 1952 campaign for the U.S. presidency on the advice of his campaign strategist, Rosser Reeves, who noticed that ads are "brief, to the point, and difficult to avoid" compared to other forms of political communication, such as speeches or campaign literature.

From 1952 to 2000, candidates disseminated political ads through print, radio, and television. In 2004, the Internet became a significant distribution channel for ads, creating both challenges and opportunities for political communicators. First, the Internet required the invention of new advertising formats to take advantage of the multimedia and interactive potential of the medium. Online advertising now means far more than the simple conversion of television spots to digital. Producers now must completely reinvent the formerly static broadcast and print-media formats and adapt it to this revolutionary new medium. Second, the low to nonexistent cost of online advertising opened the political arena to voices and publics that previously could not afford advertising, given the exorbitant rates charged by the mainstream media. Small-budget political groups, political bloggers, and even individual citizens have evolved into political advertisers, sometimes attracting numbers of viewers that rival those who see the official campaign ads on television. Third, Internet advertising allows candidates unprecedented, unmediated access to supporters and very strict control over the timing and context of ads. In addition, hyperlinks, communication tools, donation and volunteering forms, and other interactive features—easily incorporated into online ads—have changed the role of political advertising. On television, advertising is simply a way to disseminate information. On the Internet, political messages have become a powerful grassroots mobilization tool.

Perhaps the low cost of online advertising is its most attractive feature for political campaigns. In the 2004 election, the two presidential candidates and all congressional and local candidates combined paid $29 million for online communication. In comparison, those same candidates spent about $600 million on TV commercials. In the 2006 congressional election and the 2008 presidential election, a mere 1 percent of all ad spending went online. To date, Barack Obama is the candidate who has spent the most money on online advertising. By November 2008, his online ad bill was $16 million, with $7.5 million (or about 45 percent) of that total allocated to Google pay-per-click searches, another $1.5 million to Yahoo, and the rest used for banner ads on websites and in video games. By contrast, Senator John McCain's campaign devoted only about $4 million to web ads.

Online Ad Formats

Candidates can choose from several forms of online advertising to promote themselves. *E-mail advertising.* E-mail advertising is the electronic version of direct mail and covers all messages transmitted to the audience with the intention of nurturing sender-receiver (or, in this case, candidate-voter) relationships. E-mail advertising is the favored method of online promotion by most political campaigns, primarily due to its reduced cost and the low technical complexity of creating messages. On average, political campaigns allocate about 80 percent of their online ad spending to e-mail advertising.

E-mail has the enormous benefit of giving advertisers complete control over the message: who receives it, and when. The chief rule is that the advertiser needs receivers' permission before sending messages. Once a candidate overcomes this obstacle and persuades voters to share their e-mail addresses, campaign e-mail is extremely successful in reaching its target audience. In political campaigns, e-mail advertising is an efficient way for candidates directly and personally to reach supporters and like-minded individuals. Research on political e-mail shows that this form of promotion is most frequently used to inform supporters about campaign events, to solicit supporter involvement through donations and volunteering, and to direct readers to the candidate's website, where voters are exposed to additional campaign communication. Asking receivers to forward a message to family and friends is also one of the most common features of political e-mails. Overall, e-mail advertising is predominantly positive in tone, focused on candidate promotion rather than opponent attack. The 2008 Obama campaign set the example for how e-mail advertising can be used to its full potential by developing an unprecedented list of 13 million e-mail addresses.

Search-engine advertising, also called search-engine marketing (SEM). An advertiser buys keywords ranging from single words to full phrases. When Internet users type those keywords into a search engine, the search engine returns a list of free results, together with the advertiser's paid ads, which are displayed at the top or on the side of the page and usually marked with the words "sponsored links." The search engine charges the advertiser only if the user clicks on the advertised links. Regardless of user clicks, search-engine advertising is highly efficient and should be overlooked by no political candidate, given that it reaches all Internet users (supporters, undecided voters, and supporters of the opponent alike) who actively search for information about a particular candidate or issue. Millions of searches occur every minute in the United States, mostly through Google, Yahoo!, and Microsoft search engines. These search engines act as both gatekeepers and disseminators of information, determining which websites Internet users visit. Research shows that a majority of Internet users will not go beyond the first page of search results; in fact, they will not go farther than 10 results from the top. Search-engine ads therefore offer candidates a chance to display their message on the first page—where it counts—and to reach an already highly interested audience.

Once again, Barack Obama was the first candidate to demonstrate the potential of pay-per-click (PPC) engine searches. His campaign spent about half of his entire online-ad budget on Google AdWords, which is the major PPC system in the U.S., followed by Overture, Yahoo! Search Marketing, and Microsoft adCenter. Hillary Clinton and Bill Richardson were the only other Democratic candidates in the 2008 primaries to use PPC engine searches. On the Republican side, 5 out of 8 primary candidates invested in PPC, with Rudy Giuliani and John McCain running most of this type of advertising. The Obama campaign understood that PPC searches are particularly effective in directing users to candidate-endorsed websites and in driving traffic to campaign websites. Because most Internet users tend to click only the first hyperlinks on the search page, and because sponsored links are always listed as at the very top of the results list, these subtle advertisements increase the chance that people will navigate to candidate-endorsed pages rather than to pages with possible hostile content. Therefore, this technique can prove extremely valuable for counteracting attacks and for reputation management. For example, Google users who typed the word "Obama" into that search engine in September 2008 were exposed to a message saying, "Join Team Obama. Obama for America." That message linked to Obama's official campaign website and minimized the risk of users going to web pages attacking Obama. Similarly, searches for John McCain's name resulted in a sponsored result saying, "John McCain 2008. Get Involved and Support Senator John McCain," and also linked to McCain's official website.

In addition to using name-based keywords, political candidates can buy issue-centered keywords, such as "national security," "unemployment," "health care," and so on. A combination of candidate names, including common misspellings, and policy-issue keywords are often very effective in ensuring that Internet users looking for information on those issues are pointed to candidate-sponsored web pages. To illustrate, a candidate named Joe Smith who wants to direct voters to his views on Medicare reform would create an ad that links to a targeted website, such as JoeSmith.com/Medicare. This technique can also be used to attack an opponent by linking the opponent's name to harmful pages. However, a content analysis of political PPC searches during the 2008 primaries revealed that negative messages were almost nonexistent at the time and that most ads were positive in tone.

Website advertising. Buying space on third-party websites to display content in the form of video or banner ads qualifies as website advertising. As of April 2006, this form of online advertising is regulated by the Federal Election Commission (FEC) through FEC 11 CFR, Parts 100, 110, and 114. The FEC rule declares that "Internet communications placed on another person's website for a fee are General Public Political Advertising." As a result, online website ads must include a disclaimer and be paid with money adhering to federal campaign contribution and spending limits.

Online political video ads gained mainstream attention in 2002, when the Democratic National Convention's website posted a spot about Social Security. In the spot, President George W. Bush appeared to be pushing an elderly lady down some stairs, which were actually a graph of the stock market. The clip was shown on nightly newscasts, and the resulting traffic to DNC's website caused its server to crash. In 2003, MoveOn.org launched a political advertising contest challenging voters to create a 30-second TV ad that "tells the truth about George Bush." About 1,500 entries were received, 150 of them were posted on a website called *Bush in 30 seconds,* and the winning ad ran on television. These two events marked the beginning of political video advertising on the Internet. In 2004, Bush and John Kerry were the first major candidates to make use of online video advertising by digitizing their TV commercials for web distribution and also by producing original web-only clips.

Campaigns use online video ads in several ways. For instance, campaigns embed video clips in e-mail messages to guarantee that supporters view the ads. As a candidate in the 2004 primaries, Howard Dean used online ads as a fundraising tool. He produced online ads and then asked supporters to donate the money required to buy air time to broadcast the clip. Web ads can also gain a viral character as people e-mail these messages to their pre-existing social network of friends and colleagues, helping to spread the message across the Internet. Individuals who otherwise may not have been interested in a particular commercial are drawn to it by the tacit endorsement of a friend or family member, as well as by the promise of entertainment, since many of these clips are humorous. Undecided voters, late deciders, and voters with low-information-seeking habits in particular are more susceptible to interpersonal communication and political advertising than other categories of voters.

Video-game advertising. In October 2008, Barack Obama became the first political candidate to advertise in a video game. His campaign used Microsoft's Xbox360 network to reach video-game players in battleground states. According to market research data, about 72 percent of the U.S. population played video games in 2007, with Microsoft Xbox subscribers accounting for about 20 percent of that market. The ads were displayed on virtual billboards inside car racing and sports games such as Burnout Paradise, Madden 09, the popular Guitar Hero, and other games produced by Electronic Arts. Although common among commercial advertisers, video-game ads had never been tested in a political environment prior to 2008.

Independent-Source and Citizen-Produced Online Ads

Inexpensive and unsophisticated video editing technology and the almost-universal penetration of the Internet into American households gave private citizens the means to create and distribute their own political advertising. In 2004, citizen-sponsored messages were seen by millions of voters; some had more traffic than the candidates' websites. The most notable example is the animated clip *This Land,* produced by two brothers known to the Internet community as JibJab. The clip showed Bush and Kerry dancing and singing together while exchanging musical epithets such as "sissie," "liberal wiener," and "right-wing nut job." In spite of this highly unusual political rhetoric, the media's attention and the web traffic to the page hosting the animation was overwhelming. Web metrics data from Nielsen/NetRatings indicate that about 50 million people saw the clip during the general-election period.

After JibJab's success, many political activists have used online advertising to make their voices heard. The multitude of controversial events in recent years—such as the war in Iraq or the possible privatization of the Social Security system—gave many people the motivation to speak up. Since 2004, an unprecedented number of PACs, 527 organizations, issue groups, and civic advocates have cluttered the political arena. These groups have small media budgets that prohibit television advertising and therefore push them toward web advertising. Despite small budgets, political analysts credit some of these third-party groups, such as Swift Boat Veterans for Truth and Progress for America Voter Fund, with influencing election outcomes mainly due to their web advertising. Swift Boat Veterans produced some of the most controversial television and online advertising of the 2004 campaign, a series of television ads (carried widely on the Internet) attacking Kerry's patriotism and war record. The Progress for America Voter Fund created the most advertised political spot on television in 2004, called *Ashley's Story*, a video clip originally posted on the group's website as a fundraising tool.

Research into third-party and citizen-produced ads in 2004 and 2008 revealed that these messages are overwhelmingly negative in tone, often involve attacks on candidates' character, and include unethical computerized alterations of candidate visuals and sound bites. Such findings raise concern about the ads' credibility and effects on voters, given that these clips attract a significant number of viewers.

Summary

With the Internet rivaling television for the amount of time people spend using media, advertising online has become an essential part of the political communication mix. Unlike television, online political advertising comprises a multitude of formats, from the traditional 30-second video clip to longer video streaming, banner ads, search-engine ads, dynamic ads embedded within other forms of online content, and several other formats.

When used efficiently, online advertising can be as powerful and effective as televised advertising. Online ads reach people on websites where they are likely to research an issue or candidate before voting. Imagine an ad for a candidate placed on a news website. Interested voters will read the news about the campaign and also see the candidate's ad. The ad has information on the candidate, links to the candidate's website, possibly links to fundraising, and supporter mobilization tools. Additionally, online ads can be customized and targeted to the audience to a degree that television ads cannot. When people go online, advertisers know their geographic location (based on their computer's IP address), their interests (based on the sites they visit and the keywords they use for engine searches), and their demographics (through registration and subscription accounts). Such information can be used by political candidates to specifically tailor their message and make sure the right message reaches the right audience. In short, online advertising in all its formats must be part of every smart political campaign.

SUGGESTED READINGS

Cornfield, Michael, and Kate Kaye. "Online Political Advertising." In Costas Panagopoulos, ed., *Politicking Online: The Transformation of Election Campaign Communications.* New Brunswick, N.J.: Rutgers University Press, 2009, 163–78.

Mosher, Mark. "Mixing New and Old Media: The Integrated Campaign to Save San
Francisco General." *Politics* (formerly *Campaigns & Elections*) (June 2009): 34–38.

Schroeder, Chris. "Online Ads." *Politics* (formerly *Campaigns & Elections*) (Feb. 2004): 38–39.

20

Evaluating Campaign Websites

MICHAEL XENOS

Presidential campaigns have featured cutting-edge and highly visible websites since the 1990s. Further down the ballot, there has been more variation, but it is likely that we have reached a saturation point in this area of campaigning. For a variety of reasons, we may never see a world in which every candidate for every office creates a campaign website. Some lack enough resources even for a basic site, while others, such as some extremely safe incumbents, may simply not need one. Nevertheless, it is now fair to say that all serious campaigns must have a web presence of some kind.

Any attempt to evaluate campaign websites must begin by recognizing that precisely because they are so common, the website is seldom a make-or-break element of the typical campaign. Although the history of Internet campaigning surely contains many war stories of candidates who claim that they simply could not have won without their campaign website, and one can often find commentators willing to say that a particular candidate's web strategy definitely won them the race, those searching for correlations between campaign-site features and electoral success are often frustrated. It is easy to pick out differences between any given pair of websites (in overall look or perceived sophistication, for example). But it is often very difficult to identify major differences in the kinds of information or basic functionality provided by most campaign websites. As a wealth of research on campaigns and elections makes clear, it is largely factors completely unrelated to the online campaign that make any given race a slam-dunk for the favored candidate, a contest so close that in the end anything could be cited as the deciding factor, or something in between.

Despite this caveat, however, there are general principles that can be used to assess practices of web campaigning. They range from the basic features required for a site to appear "normal" as compared to most others in the genre, to more advanced guidelines for effectively integrating the newest bells and whistles available. Given that new media are constantly changing, although they are developed through specific examples, the latter principles are intended to be generally applicable, even as feature-sets and technology continue to evolve.

Covering the Basics: Must-Have features

As mentioned at the outset, there are a number of basic features that are commonly found on the vast majority (at least three-quarters) of state- or district-level campaign websites. These "must-have" features include the following:

- Candidate biography
- Issue position statements
- Contact information
- Photos of the candidate and his/her supporters
- Donation and volunteering links

These features form the bedrock of most useful information for supporters and potential supporters alike, and they are at the heart of how the Internet has dramatically increased the ability of the average voter to learn about and get involved with campaigns. As noted, this list is probably best understood as fluid and it will likely change or grow in the future, but the general principle is that campaign sites—like all website genres—tend to homogenize around a current set of practically defining features. Because these features are so common, users come to expect them in some form on all candidate websites. Unlike television or radio advertisements, websites require users to navigate toward them in the first place, and the very nature of web surfing puts the user in more control of what they see. Thus the first principle is to provide the basic staples users expect, so that they do not become dissatisfied and navigate elsewhere.

To be sure, there are better and worse ways of implementing each item on the list. For example, biographies are generally more engaging when written in a personable, first-person style. Similarly, captions are an often-overlooked tool for making photos more effective at drawing a site visitor into the world of the campaign. But it is unlikely that minor differences in font or design will alter the functionality of these features, which serve to make basic information about the candidate accessible on-demand to anyone with an interest in the campaign.

Beyond the Basics: What You See Is What You (Should) Get

Familiar to amateur web developers everywhere as a term describing software that enables one to create websites with little or no technical programming expertise, the principle of "what you see is what you get" (or WYSIWIG) can also be used to distinguish better from worse uses of web technology in political campaigns. What is more, this principle is not feature-specific; rather, it can apply to virtually any tool that might be incorporated into a web campaign, including tools that have yet to be even invented.

As noted earlier, the menu of widely available web features is always expanding, and in their own time, candidates have largely kept pace with broader trends in online tools. For example, as weblogs (or blogs) have grown in prominence and popularity, more and more candidates have opted to create campaign blogs. Similarly, following the popularization of social networking websites such as Friendster, MySpace, and Facebook, a growing number of candidates have been featuring links to profiles within these networks as part of their online campaigns. Furthermore, just as web users have come to expect certain things from campaign websites, they also have tangible expectations for other widely recognizable web genres, such as blogs or social-networking profiles. At some level, one might expect candidates naturally to conform to these expectations in an effort to engage such users. In many cases, however, the adoption of these features in online campaigning has proceeded in ways that render the campaign versions of these popular web practices virtually unrecognizable to people accustomed to their day-to-day use, outside of the world of politics.

Example: Blogs

Like most web forms, blogs have taken on a set of essential characteristics.that are easily recognizable to those who frequent such sites. In the technical sense, most definitions of "blog" include reference to a web page comprised of periodic "posts," which are dated and published in reverse-chronological order. Such posts can serve as diary entries or—more often in the political blogosphere— as instances of commentary on current events. One of the key words here is "periodic." As anyone who regularly reads at least one blog knows, there is little point in returning unless it has been updated since one's last visit. There are certainly other signature characteristics of blogs, but providing information or commentary and doing so on a regular basis are surely near the top of the list.

For their part, candidates often create web pages that might be labeled as "blogs" and that bear the visual markings of the blog genre, but do not necessarily adhere very closely to dominant blog conventions. This is less often the case with presidential campaigns, but it is often seen in U.S. House and Senate or gubernatorial races. Perhaps the most common deviation is infrequent updates. Just as in an earlier era many candidates produced campaign websites that were relatively static, one-shot brochures, candidates in recent campaign cycles have often created a blog and seeded it with an initial entry or two, only to leave it inactive for long periods. The difference, however, is that even the most casual observer can easily identify the age of the last blog update, since it is typically clearly marked. Another example is blogs that serve merely as a collection of press-releases, calendar events, or photos, rather than the regularly updated stream of more informal commentary and information that those who read blogs produced by others have come to expect.

The point here is not that campaigns are foolish in their use of blogs. In fact, campaigns have very good reasons to be cautious about highly interactive web tools that allow site visitors to actually co-produce the site's content by leaving comments or creating posts of their own. Given the importance of message discipline in campaigning, candidates are rightly reluctant to relinquish broadcast-like control over blog content through an open comment feature, and many users likely understand this necessity. However, it is possible to split the difference. Exceptional campaign websites represent clever negotiations and compromises between the competing demands of campaign strategy and the open-ended nature of interactive web communication. For example, a number of sites allow comments, but only from users who have registered with the site as supporters or even volunteers. This enables the campaign to retain some control over content, but most importantly avoids leaving the impression of a bait-and-switch, which can unnecessarily turn off some visitors.

Example: Social Networking

Social-networking profiles have, to date, been subjected to relatively less-careful research about generic tendencies or defining elements. However, as tools that offer any user an extremely straightforward mechanism for producing a personalized web presence, social-networking sites carry their own set of basic instructions. Standardized forms present users with spaces for sharing innocuous information with friends, such as favorite books, music, television shows, movies, quotations, and other details about one's life and personal interests.

We can look to the 2008 crop of presidential candidates for exemplary cases. Democratic candidates Barack Obama and Hillary Clinton, for example, produced Facebook profiles that showed an earnest adoption of local norms within that area of the Internet. Through these pages one could learn that Obama watches ESPN's *SportsCenter* and is also a fan of *The Godfather,* or that Clinton enjoys crossword puzzles and has special attachments to movies such as *Casablanca* and *The Wizard of Oz.* Though John McCain did not feature as much personal information as the others, his Facebook profile included a comment wall and other common ways of interacting with other users of the site.

Further down the ballots, however, many congressional and gubernatorial candidates simply use the Facebook page as a new receptacle for familiar campaign website content. Like a campaign blog that is merely a distribution center for press releases, these profiles likely deviate substantially from the expectations of such sites held by their regular users. Moreover, in the 2008 cycle, many candidates featured a now-familiar array of icons for the most popular social-networking websites—Facebook, MySpace, or Flickr—somewhere on their homepages. Yet, in a substantial proportion of cases, many of the icons were virtual dead ends, taking site visitors either nowhere or to the homepages of sites on which the candidate had no profile or presence.

Regardless of the particular feature involved, the principle of "what you see is what you get" points to key relationships between web campaigns and different kinds of Internet users browsing for candidate information online. For those with relatively low rates of using the Internet for political information, departures from standard formats in the use of many web technologies may not pose much of a problem. However, it is possible that many candidates may miss important opportunities with potential voters for whom the Internet is more frequently and actively woven into their daily lives. Content is always the most important part of any website; but the sense in which form and function constitute distinct yet indirect languages of their own is also a unique part of online communication.

* * *

After numerous cycles in which Internet campaigning has been said to have come into its own, it is fair to say that campaign websites have become a permanent and regular fixture of modern campaigning. While the "state of the art" in candidate sites will likely continue to be a moving target, declining costs and increasing availability of web development technology are also working to flatten out many differences between the most and least technologically advanced sites. Going forward, the process of evaluating political campaign websites will likely be driven as much by how candidates deploy various technical features as it is by whether they have a site at all or what particular features are included on that site. Through variations in these execution strategies, candidate sites hold the potential to forge distinctly different patterns of interaction and engagement with site visitors.

SUGGESTED READINGS

The eVoter Institute, evoterinstitute.com, provides research reports on the use of the web in campaigns.

The Pew Internet and American Life Project, pewinternet.org, provides reports on many aspects of Internet use, including politics.

Foot, K., Schneider, S. *Web Campaigning.* Boston: MIT Press, 2006.

Gulati, G. J., and C. B. Williams. "Closing the Gap, Raising the Bar—Candidate Web Site Communication in the 2006 Campaigns for Congress." *Social Science Computer Review* (Winter 2007): 443–65.

Xenos, M. A., and K. Foot. "Not Your Father's Internet: The Generation Gap in Online Politics." In L. Bennett, ed., *Civic Life Online: Learning How Digital Media Can Engage Youth.* Boston: MIT Press, 2007. 51–70.

21

Online Social Networks and Political Campaigns

MONICA ANCU

"Today's audience isn't listening at all—it's participating," writes William Gibson, the science-fiction writer who coined the term "cyberspace." Nowhere on the Internet is this observation more accurate than on social-networking websites, where the dividing line between message senders and receivers has been blurred into a collective, free-for-all, continuous, and instant dialogue. Also labeled as social media or Web 2.0, social-networking websites were created shortly after the 2004 U.S. general election, pioneered during the 2006 congressional midterms, and became the backbone of online political campaigning in the 2008 presidential race. The most popular such sites include Facebook and MySpace, Twitter (a cell phone–driven website), YouTube (the leading video-sharing website in the world), LinkedIn (a professional social network), Flickr (a photo-sharing website), and FriendFeed (also a content-sharing network). Facebook, Twitter, and YouTube are in the top 10 most visited websites on the Internet, attracting an average of 10 percent of all Internet users worldwide on any given day.

Online social networks are websites composed of personal, self-presentation pages of their members. Visitors usually fill out a standard template-based public profile composed of self-descriptive content, such as interests, hobbies, likes and dislikes, photos and multimedia materials, links to websites of interest to them, their favorite music, movies, TV shows, books, and so on. Users also create a list of other users with whom they share a personal, professional, or other type of connection. The social connections to other users in the network constitute the core of online social networks. User interaction—establishing and maintaining social relationships with other individuals—is the single most attractive feature of social networks.

Short History

Among the most popular social-networking websites, both in the U.S. and worldwide, are MySpace and Facebook. MySpace launched in 2003 under the slogan "A place for friends"; by 2006, it had registered about 106 million unique members, claiming the number-one spot among social-networking websites. Facebook launched in 2004 as an exclusive network for college students and attracted only about 7 percent of all social-networking users in the U.S. until September 2006, when it opened its membership to everyone with an e-mail address. Soon after, Facebook's user base boomed to an audience of 124 million unique visitors per month as of May 2008. Given that the record voter turnout in a U.S. presidential election is about 127 million voters, the individual audience of each website is both impressive and significant. According to audience demographics studies from February 2010, about 73 percent of teens, 72 percent of young adults, and about 41 percent of people over the age of 40 use these social-networking websites. Overall, 47 percent of all U.S. Internet users over the age of 18 have established a social-networking profile.

Candidates in the 2006 U.S. congressional election pioneered the use of Facebook and MySpace for political campaigning. During the election, Facebook took the initiative to create profiles for all Senate, House, and gubernatorial candidates and invited the candidates to personalize and manage these profiles. Supporters could also register with candidates and become "friends." About one-third of Senate candidates and one-tenth of House candidates took advantage of the Facebook invitation and joined, attracting visits from about 1 million users during the election period. Facebook estimated that 1.5 million users connected to either a candidate or a political group during this first attempt at political campaigning through online social media. During the same election, congressional candidates also joined MySpace but in smaller numbers. Only one-fifth of Senate candidates and a mere 3 percent of all House candidates used this social website to reach supporters. On the whole, it was mostly the Democrats, the Senate candidates, the challengers, the better-financed, and candidates in very competitive races who pioneered political campaigning through social media. In this regard, the adoption of social media mirrors the adoption of every new technology for political campaigning. Candidates with more money can afford better and larger staffs, and this surplus of resources makes them more likely to experiment with new technologies. In contrast, minor-party candidates and those financially challenged were less likely to be early adopters of new technology.

By the time of the 2008 primaries, all political candidates had adopted social websites into their campaign communication mix, with Barack Obama setting the example for the efficient exploitation of these new types of sites. At the same time, the taste for online social networks as political tools had grown significantly among U.S. voters. Visits to MySpace and Facebook for the purpose of gathering political information and getting involved with political campaigns ranked in the top three most popular online activities during the 2008 presidential campaign, together with watching political videos and making online donations.

The Obama Story

Social-networking websites were to Barack Obama what television was to John F. Kennedy. Kennedy's 1960 victory over Richard Nixon is credited, in part, to the introduction of television as the main medium for campaign communication. Similarly, Barack Obama's 2008 presidential victory is attributed to his innovative use of social websites for information dissemination, supporter mobilization, and fundraising. Using all of the top social websites at once, Obama directly engaged millions of supporters in ways unequalled by any other candidate. By Election Day 2008, Obama had about 2.5 million supporters on Facebook, about 850,000 friends on MySpace, approximately 115,000 followers on Twitter and 34,000 on FriendFeed, close to 117,000 YouTube subscribers, and 50,000 Flickr friends. On all these websites, Obama outnumbered his rival John McCain by at least 300 times in terms of supporter connections and amount of available content.

How were online social networks beneficial to Obama and to political campaigns in general? Current research has identified some notable ways, listed below.

Direct communication between candidates and voters at very low cost. Among all online forms of communication—websites, blogs, podcasts, and the like—social sites stand out for their exceptional communication potential. A variety of easy-to-use communication tools—such as direct messages, public comments, instant messaging, and e-mail—are available for free to all users. One research participant confessed to streaming a live speech of his political candidate from his home computer while simultaneously asking questions via the candidate's Facebook page and participating in real-time polls.

Social websites can serve several communication purposes. First, they can at least complement, if not replace, expensive communication tools such as voter lists, phone banks, direct mail, or print and television advertising. Candidates with lower budgets for communication can now easily reach constituents through social-media websites, which are not only free to use but also allow distribution of any type of message form (text, graphics, audio and video, and even streaming, which allows for competition with live television coverage).

Second, social websites help candidates bypass the filter of the traditional press and disseminate messages that mainstream media would either edit or overlook, such as fundraising requests or live audio or video streaming from campaign events. Equally, social media can be used to disseminate or complement mainstream media content. For instance, during the 2008 presidential primaries, candidate and former Democratic senator John Edwards announced his presidential candidacy in New Orleans in front of mainstream television cameras, while his advisers posted a YouTube video outlining his campaign. Similarly, Democratic candidate Hillary Clinton held three online chats with supporters following the announcement of her presidential bid.

Third, social websites can reach supporters promptly in situations when reaction time is critical, such as responding to an attack. To respond to anonymous accusations regarding his stand on abortion and gay rights, 2008 Republican primary candidate Mitt Romney produced and distributed a rebuttal video through A-list conservative blogs within 8 hours of the original attack. Reputation management through social media was pioneered during the 2003 presidential primaries by candidate Howard Dean and his campaign manager, Joe Trippi. Dean and Trippi were among the first political communicators to realize the power of social media to counteract attacks or disperse rumors by targeting thousands of individuals with specific, accurate, and controlled campaign messages.

Fourth, communication through social websites is a two-way dialogue that allows for the collection of feedback from the audience. Fostering bidirectional talk and online interactivity between a campaign and its supporters is one of the guaranteed ways to attract goodwill. Young voters and those with college educations especially favor the use of online communication tools by candidates and have declared themselves more likely to support candidates who employ these technologies.

Politicians must realize that social-networking websites move communication toward an era of electronic media immersion, in which consumption of political news and political engagement start to overlap. A perfect example of how the audience engages with the message is President Obama's video message to the citizens of Iran, recorded in March 2009. The video clip, distributed through the White House's official YouTube channel, was downloaded by users in both Iran and the United States, edited, remixed with comments and additional clips, and redistributed, also through YouTube. Research on political campaigns shows that voters who engage in political activities are more likely to vote than passive ones. Political candidates who allow audience participation through social networks could therefore increase supporter turnout on Election Day.

Both in 2006 and 2008, candidates used MySpace and Facebook profiles mainly for self-promotion and positive rhetoric rather than for attacking opponents. Well-known candidates focused their messages on discussing policy issues, while less-established candidates centered their profiles around character presentations, with the obvious intention of making themselves known to voters. However, very little content on a social-networking profile comes from the owner of the profile. Most content is created by visitors to that page, which means that online social websites force campaigns into the delicate situation of sharing control over the message with supporters. Even though most political candidates screen the user-generated content posted on their social-networking pages, users of those pages are still greatly empowered in their communication abilities. Instead of the candidate communicating messages to voters, now the voters directly address not only the candidate but also, at the same time, other supporters of that candidate.

Voter mobilization and engagement. Voters report increased political engagement and campaign interest after being connected to a candidate through social media, due to the appearance of so-called "parasocial" feelings toward the candidate. The online interaction with candidates gives voters the feeling of a personal bond and friendship with the candidate, making them more likely to actively donate, volunteer, or vote for that candidate. About 42 percent of MySpace and Facebook users in 2008 claimed that social websites made them feel more connected to candidates, compared to 23 percent of non-users. Because social-networking websites create a sense of connection and engagement, they may be just the right tool to reach a disengaged (or even apathetic) electorate, such as the young voters who form the main public on social sites.

Candidates who want to reach the younger demographics as well as to induce group organization and engagement must integrate social-media communication into their campaign mix. Online social networks not only connect candidates to voters, but they also allow supporters to interconnect and self-organize. Visitors to MySpace candidate profiles during the 2008 primaries declared that the main attraction of the website was the opportunity to meet other supporters of their candidate. The need to socialize with like-minded peers was the number one motivator to access a candidate's MySpace profile, followed by the need to find information about the candidate and the need to find entertainment. Supporters also reported taking advantage of the interactive communication features of social websites to promote their candidate to other voters, including voters who were not subscribers to MySpace or Facebook, or subscribers who were not officially registered with the candidate. Such promotional activities on behalf of a candidate peaked during the 2008 primaries, when several candidates were fighting for their party nomination.

Reaching the opinion leaders. Adult users of social media over age 18 tend to be more educated, more engaged in social life, more active in their community, and skillful, early adopters of technology. They are well-connected, maintain profiles on multiple social networks, and use social media to keep in touch with old friends, make new friends, and make plans for offline activities. Regular social-media users connect to their networks multiple times a day, both consuming and producing content. These engaged citizens constitute most of the audience of online social networks, and they are desirable targets for campaign communicators. In addition, social websites have been embraced by numerous political pundits, activists, and political junkies, people who are leaders in their own offline communities and have huge numbers of followers and friends on social networks. These are influential opinion leaders who, many times, will relay a candidate's message to the less active members in their group.

Conclusion

Not everyone is enthusiastic about the value of social networks to political campaigns. A study from Temple University found that while popularity on blogs is correlated to high ranking in opinion polls, popularity on social media outlets such as MySpace or YouTube is not related to a candidate's chances of victory. For instance, Republican presidential candidate Ron Paul had the biggest number of mentions on both YouTube and MySpace during the 2008 primaries, yet he lost the nomination to Senator John McCain. The connection between Facebook and MySpace and a candidate's share of votes is also unclear so far. While several studies show that exposure to a candidate's MySpace or Facebook profile can improve candidate ratings, evidence that social networks increase the number of people who vote for a certain candidate is scant. In addition, the same attributes that make social media a powerful campaign tool, if used correctly, can also bring doom to a candidate's campaign. During the 2006 mid-term elections, the Republican senator from Virginia, George Allen, lost his seat after a recording captured him labeling a minority citizen a "macaca." The video spread virally on YouTube. Candidates and their consultants must be aware of both the challenges and the opportunities of this interactive, rapidly evolving medium.

Despite this criticism, consultants and pundits tend to agree that online social networks are a game-changer in political campaigning. On the electorate side, these websites engage voters, allowing them to establish direct connections with the candidate and like-minded supporters. On the candidate side, social networks offer cheap and efficient tools to disseminate information, to engage voters, and to mobilize supporters into grassroots campaigning. However, social websites are still in the emerging phase with plenty of room for innovation and creativity in campaign communication. Undoubtedly, future campaigns will find new uses for these channels, possibly with more focus on video-sharing and distribution following the transition from analog to digital television in 2009 and the wide adoption of broadband Internet. We also expect to see an increase in mobile social networks such as Twitter, made possible by the popularity of multimedia-enabled smartphones.

SUGGESTED READINGS

Gibson, William. "God's Little Toys. Confessions of a Cut and Paste Artist." *Wired*, July 13, 2005. Online at: wired.com/wired/archive/13.07/gibson.html?tw=wn_tophead_7.

Harfoush, Rahaf. *Yes We Did: An Inside Look at How Social Media Built the Obama Brand*. Berkeley: New Riders Press, 2009.

Trippi, Joe. *The Revolution Will Not Be Televised: Democracy, the Internet, and the Overthrow of Everything*. New York: William Morrow, 2004.

Constituencies

22

Older Voters

ROBERT H. BINSTOCK

During election campaigns, especially presidential elections, political consultants and journalists focus on older persons as an important voter demographic. During the 2008 election campaign, for instance, the prominent political consultant Mark Penn wrote, "America as a nation has never been older and the power of the senior vote has never been greater." And a perennial journalistic cliché is, "Seniors are a key battleground in this election."

This chapter addresses many topics regarding older voters in the context of national campaigns and elections. First, it discusses two possible explanations for the considerable attention that older people receive from political consultants and journalists—their comparative level of participation in elections, and the presumption that they are a government-benefits-program constituency. Second, it describes campaign strategies used for targeting senior voters. Next, it documents the fact that older persons do not vote as a cohesive bloc, and addresses the widely held notion that it is politically fatal for elected officials to cut (or attempt to cut) benefits in governmental old-age programs. The chapter then explains why older people do not vote as a bloc and why, nonetheless, the myth persists that they do. Finally, it suggests lessons from the behavior of older voters in the 2008 presidential election that should be of use to political consultants and campaigners on an ongoing basis.

Level of Electoral Participations

Why has the notion that older voters are an especially important electoral constituency developed among politicos and journalists? One reason is that older persons have a high voting participation rate and therefore seem to pres-

Figure 1
Voting Turnout, by Age Groups,
in U.S. Presidential Elections, 1972–2004

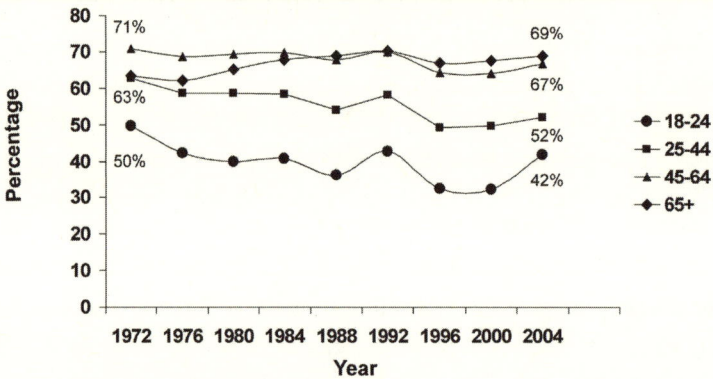

Source: National exit polls (1972-2004)

ent a rich resource of votes to be mined. The 1972 election is an appropriate baseline frame of reference for comparing the turnout of age groups because that was the first national election following the 26th Amendment to the U.S. Constitution, which established the right to vote for 18-year-olds in all of the states. As shown in Figure 1, since the 1972 presidential election, people aged 65 and older have generally been increasing their turnout rate while the rates for all other age groups have become lower than they were in the early 1970s. Moreover, since 1992, older voters have participated at a higher rate than the other age groups although participation by voters aged 45–65 has been nearly as high during that period.

But the fact that older voters participate in elections at a higher rate than younger voters does not, by itself, account for the attention they receive. As Figure 2 indicates, older people are far from the largest age group in the electorate. In the 2008 presidential election, for example, Americans aged 45–64 cast 38 percent of the vote, and those aged 25–44 accounted for 36 percent, compared with only 16 percent by persons aged 65 and older. However, the percentage of older voters will grow substantially in the decades ahead. According to U.S. Census Bureau projections for 2030, when all baby boomers will have reached the ranks of old age, persons aged 65 and older will be slightly more than 23 percent of the voting-age population.

Figure 2
Percent of Total Vote Cast by Age Groups
in U.S. Presidential Elections, 1972–2008

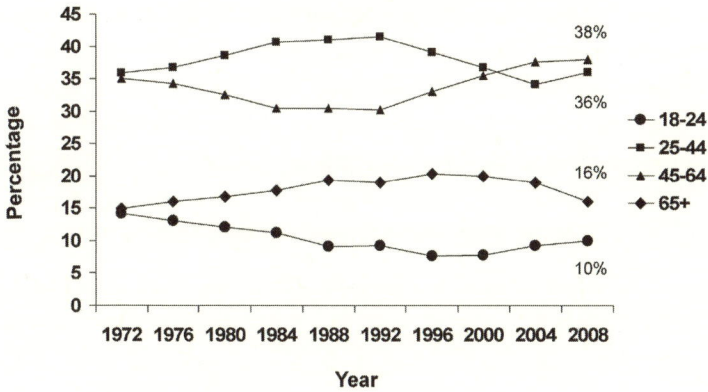

Source: National exit polls (1972-2008)

A "Benefit-Programs" Constituency

Another factor that makes it easy to understand why older voters get so much attention from campaign consultants and strategists is that they are a readily identifiable benefits-program constituency that has been created by the very existence of Social Security, Medicare, and other old-age polices. Seniors are therefore a tempting electoral target—the "senior vote"—because in theory they may be swayed by campaign efforts focused on old-age-benefits issues. Because issues regarding major old-age benefit programs are most prominent in presidential elections, this chapter will focus on those elections rather than on state and local elections.

Presidential candidates have frequently addressed "senior issues" on the campaign trail, usually to portray themselves as champions for old-age benefit programs and to make sure that their opponents do not best them in this strategy. Senior issues were not especially prominent, however, in the 2008 campaign. To the extent they were mentioned by John McCain and Barack Obama, they were overshadowed by issues concerning the economy and the wars in Iraq and Afghanistan. But in the 1996 campaign, both Senator Robert Dole and President Bill Clinton claimed that they had "saved Medicare" during the previous 12 months (even though the former had led the Senate's enactment of a bill to cut the program's benefits, and the latter had vetoed the bill). In the 2000 presidential campaign, both candidates—Vice President Albert Gore and Texas governor George W. Bush—promised to secure insurance coverage for prescription drugs within the Medicare program. And in 2004, although President Bush promoted his proposal for partially privatizing Social Security, he took pains to assure current seniors (and also "near-seniors") that they would be protected from benefit reductions. Not surprisingly, his opponent, Senator John Kerry, implied in campaign speeches that Bush's proposal would lead to large benefit cuts for these same groups.

Overall Strategies for Targeting Senior Voters

Since John F. Kennedy's campaign for president in 1960, senior-citizen committees, "senior desks," and other types of special structures targeting older voters have been established within election campaigns. Their aims are to register older voters, maintain and enhance the allegiance of older voters through the substance of issue appeals, and then ensure that seniors turn out to vote. To do this, senior campaigns promulgate issues intended to appeal to older persons through methods commonly used to target other voting constituencies—robocalls, e-mail blasts, direct mail, and television and radio ads; letters to the editor (vetted by higher echelons in the campaign); and appearances by the candidate or surrogates before targeted audiences. In the 2008 election, for instance, surrogates included members of Congress, state and local office holders, academics, and celebrities.

Such common efforts to reach out to particular groups of voters have some dimensions that are special in the case of seniors. One such dimension is that events featuring candidates and surrogates can be held in a great many venues where retired older voters can be easily targeted and—unlike voters who are still in the labor force—are available as audiences on weekdays. These venues include senior centers, congregate meal sites, retirement communities, public-housing projects for the elderly, assisted-living facilities, nursing homes, AARP conferences, and the like. One of the reasons that members of Congress readily favor federal support for senior centers and congregate meal programs is that these provide pre-assembled, targeted audiences when candidates are running for reelection.

In contrast, the present cohorts of senior voters are more difficult to reach through the use of relatively new social media. For example, according to Flickr (a photo-sharing web site), only 10 percent of persons who use

Twitter are aged 60 and older. However, as more and more baby boomers join the ranks of older voters, they should be easier to reach through social media than are today's elders. In 2009, 36 percent of Twitter users were in the 51–60-year-old category, and 47 percent were aged 41–50. Similarly, according to the market research firm NPD Group, 61 percent of baby-boomer Internet users in 2008 visited sites that offered streaming or downloadable video, and 41 percent had visited social networks such as Linked-In, Facebook, and MySpace. On average, boomers visited such sites 8 times a month.

Another dimension of strategies to target older voters is that some swing states with large numbers of electoral votes also have a higher proportion of older persons than the national average. Consequently, campaign efforts in those states to capture the votes of seniors are potentially more rewarding than elsewhere. For instance, Florida had 27 electoral votes in 2008, and 25 percent of its voting-age population was aged 65 and older; Pennsylvania had 21 electoral votes, and 23 percent of its voting-age population was in this age range. In contrast, although 22 percent of West Virginia's voting-age population was age 65 and over, that state had only 5 electoral votes.

Still another special dimension of planning strategies to target senior voters is the importance of distinguishing among the varied constituencies within the older population that have distinct concerns and political leanings. Even within the broader Hispanic community, for instance, it is important to distinguish among Chicanos, Cubanos, and Puerto Ricans—as well as other native and foreign-born Latinos. For instance, poor and wealthy older Americans have substantially different stakes in issues concerning Social Security. Social Security benefits account for 83 percent of income for older persons in the lowest income quintile, while they are only 18 percent of income for those in the highest quintile. Similarly, in planning campaigns aimed at seniors in specific geographical locales, it is important to pay attention to the differing long-term political attachments of the elders residing there. Older persons who have migrated to the east coast of Florida to retire, for example, have preponderantly come from the Northeastern states and have Democratic leanings. Retiree migrants on the west coast of the state are more likely to have come from other, more Republican-leaning parts of the country.

Seniors Don't Vote Cohesively

What impact do these senior strategies have on older voters? Because election returns are not reported by age or any other demographic characteristic, the best available sources of information on age and voting decisions are nation-wide election-day exit polls conducted for the media. Over many years these polls have tracked votes by age groups, consistently using age 60 and older to define the oldest group (although off and on they have used age 65 as well). Although age 65 and over is commonly used to categorize "seniors," age 60 is a cutoff point that is highly relevant to old-age benefit policies. Persons aged 60 and over are eligible for social and legal services, transportation, and meal programs provided through the Older Americans Act. They are old enough to anticipate the health-insurance benefits of Medicare when they turn 65. And they are also on the cusp of eligibility to choose early retirement benefits under Social Security at the age of 62. (The early retirement option is elected by about two-thirds of those who receive retirement benefits from the program.) Despite campaign strategies that specifically woo seniors, exit polls reveal that targeting older persons does not seem to have had much impact on their electoral choices. Over many decades, this constituency has split its votes among candidates in much the same pattern as the electorate as a whole and members of other age groups. As sociologist Debra Street has concluded, "There is no credible evidence that age-based voting blocs are a feature of national election landscapes." Figure 3 shows that from 1980 through 2004, the percentage of votes for the Republican candidate from persons aged 60 and over was often about the same as and never more than 3 percentage points different from the percentage cast by the electorate as a whole. (Possible reasons for the broader spread in the Obama-McCain election of 2008 are discussed below.)

When the votes of various age groups are compared (see Figure 4), the percentages cast for Republicans have often been virtually identical for the 30–44, 45–59, and 60 and older age groups, and it never exceeded a difference of 3 percentage points during the 1980–2004 period. Only the 18–29-year-old voters have deviated substantially from the others. To the extent that attachments to political parties exist among voters in this youthful age range, those allegiances are relatively new and have not been reinforced over a long period of time. One consequence of this fact is that members of the youngest group of voters are far more inclined to vote for independent candidates than are their elders. In the 1980 election, the 18–29 age group cast 11 percent of their votes for Independent candidate John Anderson, and in 1992 and 1996 they gave Independent candidate Ross Perot 22 and 10 percent of their votes, respectively. The overall insignificance of differences in age-group vote distributions can be appreciated by comparing them with the distributions of other demo-

Figure 3
Percent of All Voters and Voters Aged 60+
Voting for Republican U.S. Presidential Candidates, 1972–2008

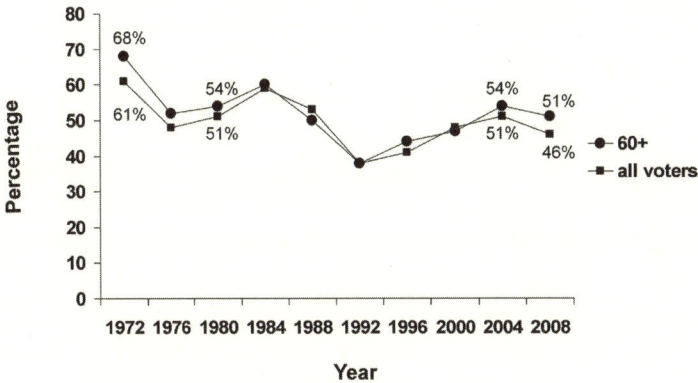

Source: National exit polls (1972-2008)

graphic groupings. Over the same seven elections (1980–2004), for example, men consistently cast a higher proportion of their votes for Republicans than did women, with the difference ranging from 7 to 10 percentage points (except in 1992, when a great many white men deserted the Republican Party to vote for Perot). This gender gap has held true, as well, among older men and women. A far more dramatic gap has persisted between African Americans and whites. Throughout the same period, African Americans of all ages were a very cohesive voting bloc. They never cast more than 12 percent of their votes for the Republican candidates, while the white percentage for Republicans ranged from 64 to 40 percent (the latter figure in 1992, when, as noted above, usually Republican white men gave considerable support to Perot).

The "Third-Rail" Myth

In spite of the overwhelming evidence to the contrary, the notion lives on that there is a distinctive senior vote that responds to pocketbook issues involving old-age benefit programs. For instance, print and television media repeatedly assert that politicians who try to take benefits away from older voters will face dire consequences when they run for reelection. Perhaps the most familiar of these journalistic warnings is that Social Security is the "third rail" of Ameri-

Figure 4
Percent Voting for Republican U.S. Presidential
Candidates, by Age Groups, 1972–2008

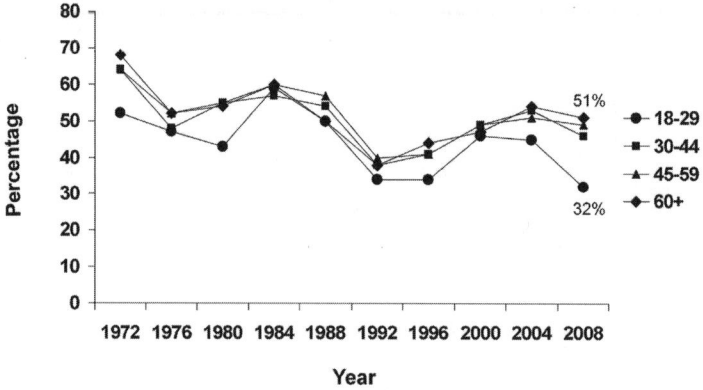

Source: National exit polls (1972-2008)

can politics because politicians who "touch it" will be "dead" politically. Yet a dramatic test case in the 1980s belied this cliché.

During his first term, President Ronald Reagan signed legislation that eliminated a year's cost-of-living increase in Social Security benefits. In addition, he proposed a general cut in Social Security benefits (an idea that was rejected by the Senate). When he ran for reelection in 1984, Democrats were confident they could gain votes from older persons because they had strong grounds for portraying Reagan as an enemy of Social Security and the elderly. But just the opposite happened. People aged 60 and older voted for Reagan *more heavily* in 1984 than they had in 1980, increasing their percentage for him from 54 percent to 60 percent. In doing so, they were right in line with the electorate as a whole, which gave Reagan 59 percent of the vote. So, even though Reagan "touched" Social Security, he was far from "dead" politically with older Americans! In fact, there is no evidence that self-interested older voters have wreaked revenge on any other American politician in recent history. Moreover, a great deal of evidence indicates that the situation has been similar in European nations, where many pension reforms have been undertaken.

Why Isn't There a Senior Vote?

There are many reasons why the senior-vote model is wrong in assuming that older persons vote on the basis of self-interest, especially with regard to benefits made available by old-age programs. One reason is that candidates are on the ballot, but issues affecting Social Security, Medicare, and other national old-age policies are not. Candidates are, first of all, individuals who may elicit feelings of trust or distrust and respect or disdain. Voters respond to a variety of individual traits—candidates' personalities, appearances, backgrounds, and performances to date.

In addition, candidates usually identify themselves with a broad range of issue positions. Old-age policies are only one possible set of issues in any election. Also in the mix are issues related to the economy, national defense, foreign policy, homeland security, taxes, civil liberties, abortion, the environment and natural resources, energy, immigration, education, scientific research, public health and health care, agriculture, welfare, and myriad others. Older persons, like younger and middle-age persons, may respond to any one or more of these types of issues.

Candidates also, of course, have political party affiliations. Older persons who identify with parties have strong partisan attachments because they have been reinforced over a long period of time. So the candidates' parties may be a more important consideration for an older voter than positions on old-age policies or other sets of specific issues.

Most important, a central assumption of the senior-issues vote model— that political attitudes and behavior of older people are predominantly shaped by common self-interests that derive from the attribute of old age—breaks down for a variety of reasons. There is no sound reason to expect that a birth cohort—diverse in economic and social status, labor force participation, gender, race, ethnicity, religion, education, health status, family status, residential locale, and every other characteristic in American society—would suddenly become homogenized in self-interests and political behavior when it reaches the old-age category. Old age is only one of many personal characteristics of aged people, and only one with which they may identify themselves. Moreover, as suggested earlier, self-interests among the elderly in relation to old-age policy issues—as well as the intensity of those interests—may vary substantially.

Why Does the Voting Bloc Myth Persist?

Despite these facts, the image of older persons as bloc voters swayed by "senior issues" persists because it serves certain purposes. First, it is marketed by the leaders of old-age-based interest groups, such as the 40 million–member AARP. Although these organizations have shown little capacity to swing voters, they have a strong incentive to inflate the voting power of the constituency for which they purport to speak. Alternatively, the image of the senior vote is used as a "straw man" by some interests who would like to see greater resources allocated to their causes and therefore find it useful to depict a collective selfishness of older voters as a root of many societal problems, such as inadequate support for children's programs. This image is also purveyed by journalists as a tabloid symbol that helps them reduce the intricate complexities of politics down to something easy to write about.

Most important, as political scientists Steven Peterson and Albert Somit have observed, politicians share the widespread perception that there is "a huge, monolithic, senior citizen army of voters." This perception is reinforced by the fact that there are a great many older citizens who are generally quite active in making their views known to members of Congress, especially when proposals arise for cutting back on Social Security, Medicare, or other old-age benefits. Hence, politicians are wary of, and eager to capitalize on, a perceived potential cohesiveness of older voters. They strive to position themselves in a fashion that they think will appeal to the self-interests of older voters, and they usually take care that their opponents do not gain an advantage in this arena. So even though older persons do not vote as a bloc, they do have an impact in shaping election campaign strategies and often lead incumbents to be concerned about how their actions in the governing process can be portrayed to the elderly in subsequent campaigns for office. For example, in the years before the annual cost-of-living adjustments in Social Security benefits were established in the mid-1970s, members of Congress customarily voted increases in benefits just prior to their biennial efforts to be reelected.

Lessons from the 2008 Election

As noted earlier, issues designed to appeal to the self-interest of older voters were not prominent in the 2008 campaign. Nonetheless, older voters displayed distinctive behavior in this election. Obama won the national popular vote by a margin of 53 percent to 46 percent. Yet seniors were the only age group to vote for McCain. Persons aged 60 and older favored McCain by 51 percent to 47 percent, and persons aged 65 and older preferred McCain by 53 percent to Obama's 47 percent. What drew a majority of older voters to McCain in an election that Obama won by 7 percent of the popular vote (which included a minority of seniors)? Some of the answers to this question suggest that the features particular to a given election may sometimes be as important, or more important, than old-age issues when developing strategies for courting the votes of seniors.

Old-Age Affinity

There is some evidence that voters in the then-72-year-old McCain's particular age group positively identified with his age. When the exit poll asked voters whether the ages of the candidates were factors in deciding their votes, an overwhelming majority (83 percent) responded that age was of little importance or no importance, and the percentage of seniors who chose these responses was among the very highest. But when the pollers asked about judgment and experience, characteristics often popularly associated with older ages, the results were quite different. Forty-seven percent of respondents aged 65–74 said that "only McCain" had "the right judgment to make a good president" (as compared with 37 percent who chose "only Obama"). Moreover, this age group's choice of "only McCain" was 13 percentage points higher than that response from those aged 75 and older, and 10 points higher than that response from those in the 60–64 year-old age range. Similarly, 49 percent of voters in the 65–74 age range said that "only McCain" had "the experience to serve effectively as president" (compared to 27 percent for Obama). This "only McCain" response received 7 points less from 60–64-year-olds, and 4 points less from voters aged 75 and older.

Race

Another feature particular to the 2008 election, of course, was the candidacy of an African American. Older voters, like all voters, stated overwhelmingly that race "was not a factor at all" in their choice between candidates. In fact, the percent of seniors who chose this response was even higher than the 82 percent aggregate response for all age groups. Yet white older voters joined the other members of their race aged 30 and older in voting strongly for McCain. The tallies were 58 percent among persons aged 65 and older, 56 percent in the 45–64 year-old age group, and 57 percent among those aged 30–44. (Only 44 percent of whites 18–29 voted for McCain.)

The Importance of Paying Attention to Birth Cohorts

Still another reason for McCain's strong showing among seniors was that a particular birth cohort within the 2008 older population has a relatively strong preference for Republican presidential candidates. Beginning in their early teens, this cohort was socialized to politics during the eight years of Dwight Eisenhower's presidency. Eisenhower was the first Republican president in 20 years, following the five consecutive terms served by Democrats Franklin Roosevelt and Harry Truman. The comparatively strong affinity for Republican candidates for president within this Eisenhower cohort of older voters was displayed in both the 2004 and 2008 elections.

In the 2004 election, both candidates were white, and there was no significant difference between their ages. Table 1 indicates that the age 60–64 group of voters was exceptionally strong in favor of George Bush in his contest with John Kerry, giving 57 percent of its vote to the Republican president. In comparison, only 52 percent of the group aged 65 and older voted for Bush, and only 51 percent of those aged 45–59 favored him. Four years later, most

TABLE 1.

Nationwide Percentage of Votes for U.S. President, 2004, by Selected Age Groups

Age Group	Bush	Kerry
All ages	51	48
65+	52	47
60–64	57	42
45–59	51	48
30–34	53	46
18–29	45	54

Source: Edison/Mitofsky Exit Poll (2004)

TABLE 2.

Nationwide Percentage of Votes for U.S.
President, 2008, by Selected Age Groups

Age Groups	McCain	Obama
all ages	46	53
75+	51	46
65–74	54	45
60–64	48	50
45–59	49	49
30–39	46	52
18–29	32	66

Source: Edison/Mitofsky Exit Poll (2008)

of this Eisenhower cohort had become members of the age 65–74 category. Table 2 shows that in the 2008 election this particular age category was the strongest for McCain, giving him 54 percent of their votes. The impact of this particular cohort can be appreciated by noting that the age group immediately older and the age group immediately younger provided noticeably less support for the Republican. Among voters aged 75 and older, only 51 percent were for McCain, and voters aged 60–64 voted in favor of Obama, not McCain.

There is a lesson in this for political consultants who are focused on older voters. The mix of birth cohorts that constitute the older population changes over time, and their political propensities through various stages of the life course can be taken into account in planning campaign strategies. In 2008, for instance, registration and turnout efforts targeted particularly to persons aged in their late 60s (in key swing states) might have been especially helpful for Republicans.

Just which party might benefit from such a strategy in the future will depend upon the changing mix of birth cohorts that join the ranks of older voters. Over the next two decades, 76 million baby boomers born over a 19-year span—from 1946 through 1964—will be entering the old-age category. Although pundits have commonly written about boomers as if they are a homogeneous group, politically they are heterogeneous. In the 2008 election, for instance, they gave both Obama and McCain 49 percent of their votes.

Moreover, the ages at which "early boomer" cohorts and "late boomer" cohorts formed their partisan political attachments have been during different historical periods, so there are likely to be different political birth cohorts among elderly boomers in terms of their partisan predispositions. Political consultants will be well advised to pay attention to the specifics of these differences when formulating campaign strategies targeted at seniors in forthcoming elections.

SUGGESTED READINGS

Binstock, Robert H. "The Boomers in Politics: Impact and Consequences." In Robert B. Hudson, ed., *Boomer Bust: Economic and Political Dynamics of the Graying Society.* Vol. 1: *Perspectives on the Boomers.* Westport, Conn.: Praeger, 2009. 135–52.

Binstock, Robert H. "Older Voters and the 2008 Election." *The Gerontologist* (in press). 382–84.

Campbell, Andrea Louise. *How Policies Make Citizens: Senior Political Activism and the American Welfare State.* Princeton, N.J.: Princeton University Press, 1993.

Campbell, Andrea Louise, and Robert H. Binstock. "Aging and Politics in the United States." In R. H. Binstock and L. K. George, eds., *Handbook of Aging and the Social Sciences,* 7th ed., 265–79. San Diego: Academic Press, 2011.

Goerres, Achim. *The Political Participation of Older People in Europe: The Greying of Democracies.* New York: Palgrave Macmillan, 2009.

Macmanus, Susan A. *Young v. Old: Generational Combat in the 21st Century.* Boulder, Col.: Westview Press, 1996.

Schulz, James H., and Robert H. Binstock. *Aging Nation: The Economics and Politics of Growing Old in America.* Baltimore: Johns Hopkins University Press, 2008.

23

The Religious Conservative Voter

LISA K. LUNDY

Religious conservatives, as described by Charles H. Cunningham in the first edition of this guide, are "people of faith who have a personal relationship with God and who turn to him to help make decisions in their daily lives." While religious conservatives vary from Orthodox Jews to Roman Catholics, the largest and most visible group in recent American politics has been evangelical Christians. Politically, evangelical Christians tend to be socially and fiscally conservative. As such, most have affiliated themselves with the Republican Party in recent years. It is increasingly difficult, however, to characterize evangelical Christians as a cohesive group.

Based on a 2008 study from the Pew Forum on Religious and Public Life, 26.3 percent of adults in the United States belong to evangelical Protestant churches. These are primarily Baptist, nondenominational, and Pentecostal churches, but also include Lutheran, Presbyterian, Methodist, and other churches with an evangelical tradition. These voters are concentrated most heavily in the Southeast region of the U.S., with the heaviest concentrations in Oklahoma, Arkansas, and Tennessee.

While evangelical voters have often been characterized as a homogenous group, they are increasingly diverse and reluctant to be identified as part of the "religious right" or the Moral Majority. While these terms grew out of conservative movements, some evangelical leaders want to avoid association with what have become pejorative terms. Some of this discussion is led by influential evangelical leaders who defy traditional labels. For example, Rick Warren of Saddleback Church in Lake Forest, California, would likely oppose categorization as part of the religious right, but he often supports politically conservative policies and is often attacked by the secular left for being too conservative. Yet he has also been criticized by conservatives for reaching out to liberals. When Warren delivered the invocation at President Obama's inauguration ceremony in January 2009, he was attacked by some conservatives for aligning himself with Obama. Interestingly, liberals also attacked Obama for aligning himself with Warren.

Evangelical Christians are ethnically diverse. While many evangelical Protestant congregations are primarily white, African Americans and Latinos are generally more religious than the U.S. population as a whole. According to the Pew Research Center's Forum on Religion & Public Life, 79 percent of African Americans say religion is very important in their lives, compared with 56 percent of all U.S. adults. It is important for political candidates aspiring to communicate to evangelical Christians to understand the diversity of their audience.

Evangelical Christians, while typically assumed to affiliate overwhelmingly with the Republican Party, are diverse in their political ideology. A 2008 Faith in Public Life poll taken just after the 2008 Democratic primary uncovered several interesting findings about evangelical voters. One in three evangelicals voted in the Democratic primary. This indicates that Democratic candidates may be overlooking hundreds of thousands of voters in some states if they are not communicating with evangelical voters. This poll also found that the majority of evangelical voters, regardless of party, sought an agenda that went beyond abortion and same-sex marriage to issues such as ending poverty, protecting the environment, and fighting HIV/AIDS.

Issues that Motivate Religious Conservatives

The issue of defining marriage has taken center stage in recent elections for religious conservatives. This issue is an example of the role that age plays in determining how evangelicals view politics and political issues. A Religion & Ethics NewsWeekly/United Nations Foundation survey conducted in September 2008 found that while only 9 percent of white evangelicals aged 30 and over agreed that "same-sex couples should have the same legal rights to marry," 26 percent of white evangelicals aged 18–29 agreed with the same statement. An additional 32 percent of this group said that same-sex couples should be offered the same protections and benefits of marriage. Candidates can relate to evangelical audiences by communicating the value they place on families. While this may include addressing the institution of marriage, it may also extend to tax provisions for married couples, the minimum wage, health insurance, and education.

The prohibition of abortion continues to be a key issue for religious conservatives. While younger evangelical voters appeared less conservative than their elders on several issues in the 2008 election, a Religion & Ethics NewsWeekly/United Nations Foundation survey found almost no difference on the issue of abortion. Thirty-six percent of evangelical voters surveyed by the Pew Forum on Religious and Public Life said that abortion should be illegal in most cases, with an additional 25 percent asserting that abortion should be illegal in all cases. President Barack Obama has chosen to communicate with voters on this issue by discussing policies to reduce the number of abortions. He has identified this as a common desire of people who disagree on the issue of abortion. In a 2009 commencement speech at Notre Dame University, Obama addressed Americans on both sides of this issue: "So let's work together to reduce the number of women seeking abortions by reducing unintended pregnancies, and making adoption more available, and providing care and support for women who do carry their child to term." This is a good model for candidates who oppose prohibiting abortion.

In recent years, some evangelical leaders have attempted to bring a broader spectrum of issues to the forefront of the evangelical agenda. For example, Jonathan Merritt has worked in recent years to increase concern about environmental issues among evangelicals. Merritt's father, James, is a former president of the Southern Baptist Convention, and Jonathan Merritt launched the Southern Baptist Environment and Climate Initiative. Of his efforts, Merritt remarked to the *New York Times* in 2008, "I learned that God reveals himself through Scripture and in general through his creation, and when we destroy God's creation, it's similar to ripping pages from the Bible." Candidates can speak to this issue by communicating an appreciation for natural resources and a commitment to protecting them. This is also an area where candidates can relate to voters on a more personal level. Discussing one's love for the outdoors and particular outdoor activities can help candidates seem more relatable to voters. This can, in turn, lead into a discussion of protecting natural resources.

Evangelical leaders are also speaking out on the issue of poverty in America and abroad. Rick Warren's website emphasizes mobilizing the church across the world to help with issues such as poverty and HIV/AIDS. Bill Hybels, founder of the Willow Creek Association of more than 12,000 churches, emphasized a broad range of issues for the church in a 2007 article in the *New York Times,* remarking, "If there is racial injustice in your community, you have to speak to that. If there is educational injustice, you have to do something there. If the poor are being neglected by the government or being oppressed in some way, then you have to stand up for the poor." Many political candidates participate in initiatives to help the poor, both in the U.S. and internationally. Many evangelical voters are interested in hearing about these efforts and, in particular, about faith-based initiatives to help the poor.

Communicating with Religious Conservatives
Mass Media

Evangelical media is media produced and/or consumed by evangelicals. According to the Barna Group, a media research organization, the audience for evangelical media tends to include more females than males. Also, African Americans use evangelical media more than any other ethnicity. Users of evangelical media tend to have lower incomes and tend to be more politically conservative. Protestants use more evangelical media than Catholics, and southerners use more evangelical media than residents from other areas of the U.S. Several media have great potential for reaching religious conservatives.

Radio

According to Murray State University journalsim professor Bob Lochte, Christian radio in North America, in terms of the number of stations, has doubled in size in the last twenty years. Christian radio typically follows one of two formats: contemporary Christian music (CCM) or preaching/teaching programs. CCM is the seventh most programmed radio format in the U.S., with almost 700 full-time stations. Almost 90 percent of the audiences for the preaching/teaching programs are 35 years old or older, and nearly 60 percent are 50 years old or older. Key players in Christian radio are the Moody Bible Network, Salem Communications, and K-Love. Operating out of Chicago, the Moody Bible Network began broadcast service in 1925 with a weekly program on WGES in Chicago. By 2007, Moody owned 31 stations in 14 states, with several hundred affiliates, translators, and satellite transmitters. Most of the $13 billion in the network's annual operating costs are underwritten by the Moody Bible Institute.

Based in Camarillo, California, Salem Communications owns Salem Radio Networks, which syndicates talk, news, and music programming to approximately 2,000 affiliates. The company owns and operates approximately 100 radio stations, including stations in 23 of the top 25 markets. According to its resource guide, "Salem Communications is America's leading broadcaster specializing in themes related to family, faith, news, and culture." Syndicated talk radio hosts include Bill Bennett, Mike Gallagher, Albert Mohler, Cal Thomas, and Richard Land. The Salem Radio Network News (SRN News) provides radio news to over 2,000 affiliates, with a presence in every major market and all 50 states. Salem Web Network publishes a number of websites with over 100 million page views per month and over 2 million e-mail subscribers.

With studios in Santa Rosa, California, transmitting via satellite, K-Love operates 230 stations and translators serving all 50 states, as well as an online stream at klove.com. K-Love is a ministry of the Educational Media Foundation (EMF) and is listener-supported. Christian radio also has a strong presence on satellite radio. Sirius offers several channels for Christian music as well as FamilyNet Radio, which is described as "faith-based, family-friendly, programming from the official broadcast voice of the Southern Baptist Convention." James Dobson hosts daily broadcasts of his *Focus on the Family* program on Sirius and XM, as well as radio stations across the U.S. Many ministers of large evangelical churches are also communicating directly to interested listeners via podcasts.

Television

In 2005, the Barna Group found that 45 percent of all adults had watched some Christian programming on television during the past month. Trinity Broadcasting Network (TBN) is the self-proclaimed largest religious network, providing 24 hours of commercial-free programming for a variety of Christian denominations. TBN has over 77 million cable/satellite subscribers, and it offers a variety of programs. Church services are among the highest-rated programs on Christian television. TBN also offers programming for children and teenagers, as well as a 24-hour multi-denominational Spanish-language faith channel. While much of TBN's programming is commercial free, political candidates may seek the endorsement of individuals like Pat Robertson of the *The 700 Club*. One example of this is from the 2008 presidential campaign of Rudy Giuliani. Not only did Robertson endorse Giuliani, but he also shared his endorsement in speaking to the National Press Club and explained why Giuliani was his candidate of choice despite their differences on abortion and gay rights. Seen in 97 percent of U.S. television markets, *The 700 Club* reaches an average daily audience of 1 million viewers. Candidates should also look for TBN-sponsored programs that may overlap with their own initiatives. For example, TBN partnered with Corrections Corporation of America (CCA) in

2008 to provide rehabilitative programming to inmates. Candidates may be able to partner with TBN in such initiatives.

Magazines

There are hundreds of print-based periodicals targeted at religious conservatives. The Evangelical Press Association (EPA) and the Associated Church Press (ACP) produce over 400 periodicals with a combined circulation of more than 25 million. Some evangelical publications are direct-mail pieces for members or supporters of organizations. For example, *Decision* is published by the Billy Graham Evangelistic Association and mailed to 800,000 supporters. World Vision publishes a quarterly magazine for its 500,000 supporters. About half of all Christian magazines are published by mission agencies, parachurch groups, or Christian schools. Other publications are subscription-based and are supported by advertisers.

Christianity Today is a monthly magazine representative of American evangelicalism. It was founded in 1956 by Billy Graham as a way to bring the evangelical Christian community together. Its circulation is 140,000, and its readership is estimated at 294,000. Additionally, its website (all print articles appear online) attracts 11.8 million visitors monthly, 2.3 million of whom are unique visitors. *Christianity Today* (christianitytoday.com) characterizes its readers as influential evangelicals. According to its website, most subscribers attend churches with a weekly average attendance of 841, and more than half of its subscribers serve as a pastor, deacon, elder, teacher, committee leader, business administrator, or hold another leadership position within their church. The majority of subscribers are married and male (62 percent), and their median age is 55.1 years.

Today's Christian Woman is a monthly magazine geared toward Christian women; it has a circulation of 210,000 and a readership of 420,000. The median reader age is 45.9 years with a household income of about $74,072. Its subscribers are avid readers; most read for about 10.6 hours per week. They tend to be socially active and community-minded women—70 percent are involved in community and civic groups, 21 percent hold leadership roles, 41 percent sign petitions, and 17 percent will call government officials if they feel strongly about issues. Ninety-two percent of readers are faithful church attendees.

For reaching a younger audience, communicators can turn to RELEVANT magazine. RELEVANT includes a monthly print magazine with a circulation of

75,000 and a total readership of 225,000, an online magazine, a weekly podcast, and e-mail newsletters. On average, RELEVANT readers spend at least two hours reading the magazine. According to FOXNews, RELEVANT is "the premiere media outlet covering faith, pop culture and life in your 20s." The median age for readers is 28; readers are 61 percent male.

Baptist Press is a daily (Monday through Friday) international news wire service. With a central bureau in Nashville, Tennessee, *Baptist Press* has five partnering bureaus in Richmond, Atlanta, Nashville, Washington, D.C., and London. It circulates to Baptist newspapers in 40 states, with a combined circulation of 1.16 million, and is the largest religious news service in the United States. *Baptist Press* also operates a website with updated news and provides news feeds for other websites (bpnews.net).

The Internet and Social Media

Religious conservatives are just as active in online media as other groups, and in some cases are more so. In fact, about two-thirds of all Americans with Internet access have used the Internet for spiritual or religious purposes. Google lists over 17 million pages using the word "evangelical." According to a May 2008 study done by the Barna Group (barna.org), Christians used social media in nearly the same proportions as non-Christians surveyed. Bryan Auday and Sybil Coleman found in 2009 that nearly 50 percent of evangelical college students surveyed reported spending between 1 and 7 hours a day using Facebook, in addition to other forms of social media. Evangelicals are also heavy users of podcasts. In the study, 38 percent of evangelicals had listened to a sermon or church teaching via podcast, compared with 17 percent of other adults surveyed. One out of every 4 adults surveyed said they had downloaded a church podcast in the previous week.

The key for political candidates in reaching evangelicals via online and social media is a willingness to engage in a dialogue. During Barack Obama's candidacy in 2008, he did not hesitate to target evangelical voters, despite his Democratic affiliation. He spoke openly with *Christianity Today* about his faith and participated in Rick Warren's Saddleback Civil Forum on the Presidency, responding to questions about a range of issues.

Candidates who connect with supporters on Facebook have the opportunity to quickly expand their social network through the existing networks of their supporters. As of January 2011, Republican Governor Bobby Jindal of Louisiana had over 68,000 supporters on Facebook, using the platform to provide updates on his initiatives, give links to speeches, and maintain relationships with his supporters.

Candidates may consider posting messages relevant to evangelical audiences on tangle.com, formerly known as GodTube, a site similar to YouTube for evangelical audiences. Tangle.com has more than 2.5 million monthly unique visitors and more than 8 million monthly video streams, with an average session time of 13 minutes. Tangle.com also offers advertising opportunities. Politicians can use Twitter to connect with and understand evangelical audiences. Candidates running for state or local office can follow ministers of large evangelical congregations. This is a good way to see what issues are important to congregants and to begin building a network of contacts in this arena.

Grassroots Communication

Some candidates have effectively reached out to evangelical audiences by going straight to the source: churches and church services. Most recently, candidates like Sarah Palin and Louisiana's Bobby Jindal have generated support for their candidacies and policies by speaking at evangelical churches, often about their own conversion experience. One note of caution for candidates: it is important to be respectful of the separation of church and state when pursuing any religious voters. Candidates, particularly those already in office, should avoid using taxpayer funds to fund travel to speak in churches. Jindal, for example, came under a great deal of fire (even from some religious leaders) for using state money to travel to churches throughout Louisiana. Candidates should also be aware that, according to a 2008 Pew Research Center survey, 50 percent of conservatives express the view that churches should stay out of politics. This is up from 30 percent just four years ago.

If, as Fordham University political scientist Monika McDermott suggests, evangelical voters use religion as a shortcut in developing presuppositions about candidates, it follows that candidates who self-identify as people of faith would do well to share that fact with evangelical voters. Regardless of party affiliation, candidates can speak to voters about their faith, but authenticity is important. In a 2007 *Time* article, Hillary Clinton remarked, "Maybe we're getting back to where people can be who they are. If faith is an element of who you legitimately, authentically are, great. But don't make it up, don't use it, don't beat people over the head with it." In reaching out to evangelical voters, candidates should emphasize points of agreement rather than focusing on points of division. Discussing the 2008 presidential campaign, CNN's Roland Martin said, "If the Democratic Party is serious about fostering a relationship with the faith community, they are going to have to come to grips with the fact that there are Democrats of faith who are pro-life and against gay marriage, but who are in agreement on other social issues such as the response to the rapid rise of HIV/AIDS and eradicating poverty." This may help mitigate the threat Notre Dame political scientist David Campbell discusses, that evangelicals feel they are surrounded by a society that does not respect their beliefs.

Candidates can also use direct mail to reach key groups with targeted messages. Because voters receive so much mail at election time, direct-mail pieces are most effective when they grab the reader's attention and/or resonate with voter values. One political candidate who successfully used direct mail in a recent election took advantage of consumer data to identify swing voters who might be interested in his candidacy. According to a 2006 *Business Week* article, Democrat Tim Kaine of Virginia used consumer data in his 2005 gubernatorial campaign to reach out to voters. Kaine, a former missionary, targeted voters with a message emphasizing values, education, and transportation. He was successful in earning the votes of a traditionally Republican voting bloc.

Candidates seeking to reach evangelical audiences may find it helpful to enlist a consultant such as Burns Strider, who worked with Hillary Clinton, or Shaun Casey, who advised Barack Obama, in the 2008 presidential campaign.

In April 2009, *Newsweek* editor Jon Meacham penned a cover story entitled "The End of Christian America." Meacham pointed to research showing a decline in the number of Americans who claim no religious affiliation as evidence that America is becoming an increasingly secular nation. According to the American Religious Identification Survey, the number of Americans who self-identify as Christians has fallen since 1990 from 86 to 76 percent. If this is case, there may be a stronger pull for evangelicals to look to faith-based media for information, encouragement, and escape from mainstream media sources. If political communicators wish to reach evangelicals, it will be important for them to identify and understand the sources that evangelical voters are using.

24

Young Voters

KATHERINE KNOBLOCH

For decades, scholars and politicos have argued over the efficacy of reaching out to young voters. While campaigns have attempted to lure young people to the polls with gimmicky slogans and flashy media operations, some analysts have written off young Americans as a lost cause, citing decades of low turnout rates. Tactics such as the "Vote or Die" campaign spearheaded by celebrities and promoted by the MTV organization for the 2004 presidential election have lacked on-the-ground substance, appearing to have been rather ineffective at increasing turnout. Similarly, some Internet-based offensives—such as Howard Dean's presidential primary campaign in 2004—have unraveled without the supervision of a tightly run campaign organization.

Even when campaigns do manage to engage young voters, the resulting support can be detrimental if not properly directed. Although the Dean campaign managed to gain a strong youth following based on its ability to tap into the Internet's grassroots organizing potential, the campaign failed to use that support strategically. When masses of college students swarmed into Iowa in the weeks preceding that state's caucus, many potential voters were turned off by their in-your-face-tactics and huge orange hats.

The Obama campaign learned from Dean's mistakes and coupled web-based networks with localized and directed organizational development. In the 2008 election, this translated into utilizing already established online social networks, such as Facebook, Twitter, and YouTube, to connect with young people and to build an on-the-ground support system of dispersed campaign volunteers, who were trained and loosely managed by the central Obama organization.

While the 2008 presidential election and the campaign of Barack Obama certainly seem to suggest the benefits of engaging citizens between the ages of 18 and 29, doubts still linger about the efficiency of expending resources on a youth population largely considered apathetic to politics. The central problem remains: campaigns must figure out how effectively to engage youth in ways that will lead to turnout at the polls and increased participation in the political process.

Below, a brief summary of the history and characteristics of the youth vote is presented, followed by a number of suggestions for how and when to reach out to young people with the goal of increasing their turnout at the polls and their participation in the larger political process. As will be evident, today's version of youth participation differs from earlier versions, oscillating between virtual and local networks, which in turn coordinate their efforts to maximize the skills of each individual volunteer. Though increasing the youth vote does appear to require the utilization of resources outside of the normal channels used to mobilize older generations, the benefits can be significant, both in immediate electoral victories and long-term political stability.

The Rise of the Youth Vote

The granting of the vote to 18-year-olds serves as a good starting point for a discussion of young voters. Beginning with World War II, politicians and young people began arguing that those old enough to serve in the military were old enough to vote. Leading the crusade, West Virginia congressman Jennings Randolph (D) became an ardent supporter of lowering the voting age from 21 to 18, and in 1942 he introduced in the U.S. House of Representatives an amendment to lower the voting age nationwide. The fight was not easily won, however. Randolph would reintroduce the legislation 10 more times before the amendment would succeed. It was not until the Vietnam War that his proposal received widespread popular and political support. A generation already affected by an unpopular draft began to protest the discrepancies between national policies that made 18 an age old enough to fight and die for one's country but not old enough to take part in the electoral process. In 1971, after years of struggle, the 26th Amendment lowered the voting age from 21 to 18.

The first presidential election after the passage of the amendment saw significant youth turnout, as newly enfranchised young people mobilized in response to the draft and the Vietnam War. That initial spurt, however, dissipated

Figure 1
Turnout among 18–24 Year Olds, 1972–2008

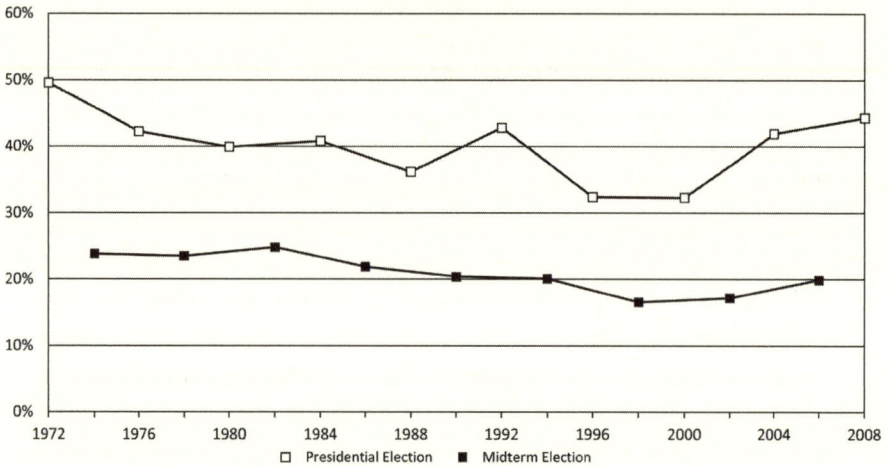

as youth voting rates gradually declined in subsequent decades, particularly in local elections, which generally see much lower levels of youth turnout. Although the 1992 election saw a temporary surge in young voters in the race between Bill Clinton and George Bush, it was short-lived. The 1996 election saw a continued decline; voting rates for 18- to 29-year-olds dropped to 37 percent.

While this period marked a low point for youth turnout, the number of young voters has increased dramatically since then. According to the Center for Information and Research on Civic Learning and Engagement (CIRCLE), using estimates from the U.S. Census Current Population Survey, voting rates began rising gradually with the 2000 presidential election, which saw a youth voting rate of 40 percent. The rise continued in the 2004 election, as youth voting rates increased to 49 percent. This increase was particularly significant for 18- to 24-year-olds, who typically vote at lower levels. In the 2004 election, their vote increased by 10 percentage points over 2004, reaching 42 percent. In 2008, turnout for 18- to 29-year-olds reached a 52 percent turnout rate, the highest since the 1972 election, which was the first election after 18-year-olds won the right to vote. A resurgence in youth interest in local politics may be emerging as well. For the decisive midterm congressional elections of 2006, young voters turned out in higher numbers than in the 1998 and 2002 elections, helping give Democrats control of Congress and influencing many state and local races.

Characteristics of the Youth Vote

During the 2008 presidential election, 44 million young people were eligible to vote, representing over one-fifth of the total population of eligible voters. According to CIRCLE, using statistics from the National Election Pool Exit Poll, this generation appears to differ significantly from older generations. Young people are generally better-educated than their elder counterparts, with about one-fifth of this voting bloc currently enrolled in college, but they are less likely to be married or to have served in the military. Although men represent a larger share of those eligible to vote, women are slightly more likely to vote. In addition, this segment represents the most diverse generation of citizens, including larger numbers of racial, ethnic, and sexual minorities than older generations. Campaigns would be wise to recognize the diversity of this population, as well as the potential benefits that reaching out to the youth vote can have in building long-term relationships with a broader spectrum of citizens.

This lesson about diversity applies to partisan and ideological divides as well. The majority of today's youth—like the majority of older generations—identify as independents, leaving room for candidates and campaigns of all ideologies to make headway with this segment. Current trends, however, point toward a liberal bent. According to 2008 studies conducted by the Pew Research Center, young people who identify as Democrats or lean toward the Democratic Party outnumber those who identify as or lean toward Republicans by 23 percentage points. Still, even though recent elections appear to signify an overwhelmingly liberal youth vote, young people have not always been so closely affiliated with liberal policies. Effective candidates from any party could potentially use the youth vote to their advantage.

Perhaps most significantly, many of today's young people grew up immersed in new communication technologies. According to a 2009 study by the Pew Research Center, 93 percent of young adults aged 18 to 29 are online, and nearly three-quarters of young people online use social-networking sites. The integration of telephone and online technologies is equally important, allowing young people to be constantly connected to their expanding social networks. Candidates and campaigns hoping to reach young people must find ways to utilize these already established communication networks and to integrate them into their everyday campaign practices.

How to Reach Young Voters

Recent increases in youth turnout appear to be tied to massive get-out-the-vote efforts, coupled with campaign strategies that employ web-based networks to organize on-the-ground supporters. Successful utilization of these strategies may even be credited for Barack Obama's electoral victory. According to exit polls, Obama won 66 percent of voters between the ages of 18 and 30. Among older voters, the race was much tighter, with McCain winning 54 percent of the voter ages 64–75 to Obama's 45 percent. The key to this outreach is effective communication. Campaigns need to build organizational and inter-personal structures that actively engage youth, recognize the different ways in which young people are utilizing mediums of communication, and speak specifically to young people about issues that are of concern to them.

The Internet and Social Networking

The most significant medium for reaching the youngest generation is the In-ternet. Campaigns that are serious about increasing youth turnout must invest in a significant Internet presence that can translate into localized organization and turnout. According to a 2008 study conducted by the Pew Research Cen-ter, young people increasingly go to the Internet for new information, with the web serving as their top source for daytime news. Without some type of net visibility, candidates risk never reaching these young citizens.

Campaigns must take advantage of the multiple outlets through which young people find information on the web. Straightforward information is needed, but candidates must also recognize the ways that young people use communication technologies to interact. Young people expect web features that allow them to upload their own content and provide avenues for two-way communication. Chris Hughes, a cofounder of Facebook, led the Obama team's efforts at online outreach and took advantage of his knowledge of social networking: Obama's campaign Facebook page registered over 2 mil-lion supporters. The centerpiece of the online outreach was the website My.BarackObama.com, where supporters could find information, create their own content (including fundraising pages), and connect with other supporters across the country. Campaigns should construct profiles on social-networking sites, such as MySpace and Facebook, that post information about the candidate or issue as well as provide avenues for two-way communication between the campaign and its followers. These sites, along with blogs and micro-blogs such as Twitter, can serve as places for the direct dissemination of campaign information, urging supporters to contact officials or show up at a rally, or reminding them of registration deadlines. MTV's ongoing Rock the Vote campaign, designed to mobilize young people to register and turn out at elections, similarly takes advantage of trends toward user-generated content, providing a voter registration tool that individuals or groups can upload to their websites or social-networking profiles. Those who download the tool then serve as an arm of the organization, registering new voters through their already established social networks.

Streaming video is also key to connecting with young people. Sites such as YouTube, along with candidates' social-networking profiles and campaign webpages, can be used to post videos in which candidates or campaign officials speak directly to their supporters. During the 2008 presidential primary campaign, Hillary Clinton solicited questions from her young supporters through her website and then answered selected questions in videos posted on YouTube. Obama used similar tactics and has continued the tradition in his presidency, posting weekly video addresses that allow him to speak directly to the public without the interruption or interpretation of the news media.

These new mediums provide the opportunity for young people actively to organize, allowing them to communicate with candidates and each other. It is this virtual interaction that is essential to engaging young people and building networks—networks that can carry over well after the campaign has ended. More than five months after the election, Obama's Facebook supporters had swelled to more than 6 million, and the site still serves as a place both to disseminate information and to organize and mobilize supporters.

E-mails and Texting

In addition, many members of this generation do not have land-lines and are heavily reliant on cell phones and e-mail for communication. Because this contact information is not publicly available, young people must provide their contact information directly. Campaigns must continuously construct lists of phone numbers and e-mail addresses in order to try to reach as many young people as possible. Again, the 2008 Obama campaign serves as a good example. During the campaign, the Obama team compiled contact information while registering voters and at campaign rallies, and it continually added to these contact lists as the campaign progressed. Before picking Joe Biden as his running mate, Obama asked his supporters to send a text message to the campaign, with the promise of alerting them of his choice via text before breaking the news through traditional media outlets. In doing so, Obama energized supporters and captured their phone numbers for future use.

Throughout the campaign, text messages served to connect Obama directly with his young supporters. Texts were used to mobilize volunteers and remind supporters of important upcoming events, but they served another critical purpose as well. Texts, and similar tools of social networking, allowed Obama to send messages directly to his supporters without the interference of the news media. The ability to communicate in this fashion created a bond between Obama and his supporters, who were able to feel they had a personal connection to the candidate.

The emphasis here is that candidates and campaigns must be vigilant in their attempts to reach young people through new technologies. During the 2008 presidential election, the Obama campaign recognized the ways in which youth were communicating and acted to capitalize on that knowledge, utilizing text messaging, e-mails, and social networking in their campaign efforts and even placing ads in online video games. Candidates and campaigns must keep up with current technology and media trends and communicate with young people through the avenues that they are already using.

On-the-Ground Organization

Getting young people actively involved in the campaign process is crucial to voter turnout. Young people are not only a resource on Election Day; they also can be a resource throughout the campaign. The youngest generation often has time and motivation that politicians can tap into, aiding both the young people, who can use these opportunities to build their resumes and create professional networks, and campaigns, which can harness and direct these resources to their benefit. Involving youth in campaigns provides opportunities for young supporters to connect and build ties with one another that strengthen a network of young activists who are committed to serving the campaign and who can serve as ambassadors to members of the youth community.

Social networking, both online and interpersonal, is essential to recruiting a volunteer base and to the volunteers' ability to aid the campaign. As campaigns establish online networks, they must continually work to transform web-based support into local participation. Having already established connections with young people through online social networking, campaigns can use these connections to call for volunteers and keep supporters informed of the opportunities for participation in their areas.

Young volunteers can be utilized through call centers and canvassing, and they appear to be particularly useful at registration efforts. They can also represent campaigns at events, such as concerts and sporting matches, providing opportunities for candidates to reach large numbers of young people who otherwise may never have contact with a campaign representative.

In addition to building a cadre of young volunteers within their own campaigns, candidates should establish connections with youth organizations, such as student-based party organizations and the League of Young Voters, which already have a mobilized membership base of potential supporters and volunteers. The important point is actively to involve young volunteers in ways that encourage them to become an integral part of the campaign process—that is, allowing them to represent the campaign to other members of their community.

Finally, part of an on-the-ground organization includes creating a presence within youth culture. Campaigns should draw on youth culture to bring young people into their campaigns and get young people excited about political involvement. The Rock the Vote campaign illustrates the ways in which drawing on youth culture can energize young voters about the political process. Founded in 1990, the campaign integrates music, fashion, and popular youth culture with politics, drawing on celebrity endorsements, clothing sales, promotional concerts, and MTV specials to encourage youth turnout and embed political participation in popular culture. Coupled with online and on-the ground mobilization and outreach efforts, such as the voter registration tool discussed above, Rock the Vote's integration of politics and youth culture allows young people to incorporate politics into their personal and social lives.

Mobilization

Personal contact is an essential tool of youth outreach, and face-to-face forms of voter contact are the most effective means of increasing turnout. According to research compiled by Young Voter Strategies, a research organization funded by Pew and based at George Washington University, door-to-door canvassing and lengthy phone conversations are the most efficient ways of boosting youth turnout rates, while impersonal methods—such as automated telephone calls and direct mail—appear to be largely ineffective and have dismally low cost-efficiency rates. While robocalls and direct mail may seem enticing based on low costs, their impersonal nature allows young people to ignore their message more easily. The interpersonal avenues work because they provide opportunities for young people to connect with others like themselves, allowing them to identify with the campaign and understand it in terms that are familiar to them. And although these more personalized strategies may seem to require more resources, canvassing costs can be reduced by visiting places where young people are already concentrated, such as youth apartment communities and college neighborhoods. By targeting these areas, campaigns can reach more young people with less effort.

Similarly, phone campaigns can rely on young volunteers, who use personal time and their own phones to conduct conversations with potential supporters. In 2008, the Obama campaign implemented this strategy, using its website to allow volunteers to download a list of names, phone numbers, and addresses of potential voters. Callers used targeted scripts that allowed the campaign to maintain control over the message. Through this method, the campaign employed a network of dispersed, self-directed volunteers who could offer traditionally costly interpersonal contact for free. As this example suggests, building a strong core of young volunteers is both vital to achieving the personal contact necessary to reach the youth vote and cost-efficient for the campaign.

Youth Issues

Central to all of this outreach must be a message that relates to young people. Young people will not be excited about a campaign that does not speak to issues that are important to them. Candidates and campaigns must recognize issues that are pertinent to younger generations and create messages that are easily understandable and relate to these voters' real lives. A 2008 poll conducted by MTV and CBS News indicated that young people generally tended to be concerned about the same issues as older generations, with the economy and the war in Iraq listed as the primary concerns for young people. Still, young people have a unique perspective on these issues. In the same poll, young people indicated that the biggest problem facing the nation for the next 20 years will be the economy, an issue that profoundly affects young people entering the workforce.

Aside from the economy, issues such as college loans, job opportunities, same-sex marriage, immigration, foreign policy, health care, Social Security, energy policy, and global warming are all relevant to young people and affect them differently than older generations. The youngest voters tends to be called into combat at a disproportionately higher level than older generations; thus, issues of foreign and military policy can be deeply personal, particularly for young members of the military community. In addition, global warming and energy policy may not seem like immediate threats to an older generation, but younger generations looking toward the future see global warming as an even larger threat than the war in Iraq and list it as the second-largest threat facing the nation in the future.

While this list is by no means exhaustive, all of these issues affect young people's lives currently or are a cause of concern for their future. Campaigns should take the extra step in their platforms by emphasizing how issues will affect younger generations. Campaigns must also create policy stances that connect with youth, structuring them in such a way that tells younger Americans why these issues are significant to their generation.

Key Points of Contact

Each of these avenues for youth engagement is important, and all of them require a prolonged effort on the part of campaigns. Still, there are several key moments crucial to increasing youth turnout: voter registration, absentee voting, and Election Day. In each case, young voters need to be aware of deadlines and procedures for properly ensuring that their vote counts. For many young people, voting is new, and therefore young citizens may have not formed voting habits. They may be unfamiliar with both how and when to vote. Campaigns must constantly strive to ease this process by instructing young voters on the steps necessary to successful voting.

Registration

Facing the challenges of increased mobility and low levels of information, people between the ages of 18 and 29 are less likely to be registered to vote than those 30 and older. Many young people are not registered, and most must do so well in advance of Election Day, when they may not be acutely aware of the election. Because missed deadlines are among the primary reasons that young citizens fail to register, campaigns must make every effort to inform young people about these deadlines. In addition, many young people are mobile and may be registered in a district other than the one in which they currently reside.

Through media campaigns and interpersonal contact, campaigns should invest resources to register new voters and increase awareness of registration procedures. Campaigns should utilize mail-in, online, text-based, and in-person registration to increase youth participation. Text-based and online efforts appear to be particularly effective at registering young voters. By March 2008, Rock the Vote had registered over 500,000 18- to 29-year-olds through its online registration tool, and the number has likely increased significantly since then. By offering online and text-based registration options, campaigns and candidates can ease the registration process by positioning it in a communication structure already familiar to young people.

Absentee and Early Voting

Absentee or early voting is also essential to increasing turnout. Because so many youth are highly mobile, significant numbers of young people vote absentee—as many as 14 percent, according to a 2008 estimate from CIRCLE. Campaigns must ensure that they know the circumstances that permit them to vote absentee. Young people must know how to vote absentee, and they should be informed about important deadlines and procedures relating to absentee or early voting. In addition to providing young citizens with information about eligibility requirements, campaigns should ensure that these voters understand how and when to request absentee ballots. In the end, efforts aimed at registering young people at their current residences may eliminate the need for aggressive absentee-voting campaigns.

Election Day

Finally, campaigns must continually work to ensure that young people turn up at the polls on Election Day. Campaigns should invest resources in familiarizing young people with local voting procedures, voting locations, and ballot design. If young people are not aware of how or where to vote, they may simply opt out. According to a 2006 report by Young Voter Strategies, by building young people's confidence in and familiarity with the voting process, candidates can achieve significant increases in youth turnout. For example, campaigns could have a countdown to Election Day posted on their webpages and online profiles, and they could remind their supporters via text message and e-mail that the day is approaching. In addition, text messages, e-mails, and personal contact from field teams on Election Day can instruct registered voters about their polling locations and hours, reminding young people to vote and providing them with the informational resources to do so.

The key to all of these efforts is continual, active involvement. Young people should be involved in all stages of the campaign process, and campaigns must reach out to young voters through media currently utilized by the youth. While engaging young people may require additional resources and a committed, continual effort to adapt outreach efforts to their habits, the long-term benefits can be significant. Voters' preferences when casting a ballot for the first time appear to affect their vote choices later in life. While the youth of the New Deal supported Democrats fairly consistently, those who were young during the Reagan administration appear to generally favor Republicans. By engaging young voters, candidates and campaigns can create loyalty that exceeds individual elections and provides dividends in future years.

SUGGESTED RESOURCES

CIRCLE: The Center for Information and Research and Civic Learning and Engagement. Online at: civicyouth.org.

The League of Young Voters. Online at: theleague.com.

New Voter Project. Online at: newvoters.org.

SUGGESTED READINGS

Green, Donald, and Alan Gerber. *Get Out the Vote: How To Increase Voter Turnout.* Washington, D.C.: Brookings Institution, 2004.

Greenberg, Eric H., and Karl Weber. *Generation We: How Millennial Youth Are Taking Over America and Changing Our World Forever.* Emeryville, Calif.: Pachatusan, 2008.

Winograd, Morley, and Michael D. Hais. *Millennial Makeover: MySpace, YouTube, and the Future of American Politics.* New Brunswick, N.J.: Rutgers University Press, 2008.

25

The Latino (Hispanic) Voter

MELISSA MICHELSON

Latinos account for more than half (50.5 percent) of the population growth in the United States since 2000, a figure driven more by natural increase (births minus deaths) than by immigration. The community is clustered in the Southwest and Northeast, plus Florida, but considerable percentage increases are to be found throughout the country and particularly in the South, making Latino voters relevant to almost any modern political campaign. The most recent U.S. Census estimates find that Latinos comprise about 15.5 percent of the population, making them the largest minority group in the nation. Over the next four decades, the size of the Latino population is expected to triple, accounting for most of the nation's population growth and growing in proportion to almost a third (29 percent) of the U.S. population by 2050.

Latinos are concentrated in metropolitan areas, although the Latino Diaspora includes all 50 states. By far the largest population center is California, particularly Los Angeles County, and half of the nation's Latinos live in California or Texas. Major concentrations also are found in Florida, Illinois, and New York. Considerable Latino communities in all areas of the country, with consequences for political campaigns and agendas, marks a dramatic change from just a few decades ago, when Latinos were by and large concentrated in just a few geographic areas.

Latinos are less likely to vote than Anglos (non-Latino whites) and African Americans, but their strategic position in traditional battleground states and their reputation as swing voters have earned them the "sleeping giant" nickname and increased attention from candidates and the major political parties. Nationwide, less than a third of Latinos vote in presidential elections, while less than one-fourth participate in congressional elections. Latinos lag in their rates of participation at every level of the process: the voting rate based on the voting-age population, the voting rate based on the voting-age citizen population, and the voting rate based only on registered voters. Some, but not all, of this discrepancy in participation can be attributed to low rates of citizenship among Latinos, as well as the relatively low socioeconomic status (SES) and high rate of noncitizenship (about 40 percent) of the Latino population. Another strong explanatory factor is the relative youth of the Latino population. Compared to Anglos and African Americans, Latinos are much more likely to be first-generation immigrants, which further reduces their tendency to be citizens, to be proficient in English, and to vote.

Despite all of these qualifications and limitations on their potential political power, Latinos are an increasingly popular target of political mobilization efforts and campaigns by political candidates. In 2004, the two major political parties spent a combined $8.7 million on Latino-voter outreach; in 2008, the Obama campaign alone committed $20 million. This increasing attention is due to the increasing size of the Latino population, making them a larger "prize" to be won, and also to their deserved reputation as swing voters, willing to cross partisan lines to support individuals with whom they share issue positions and ideologies. While Latinos tend to be concentrated in states that are considered safely Democratic (California, New York, Illinois) or Republican (Texas), they are also a significant proportion of a crucial swing state (Florida) and other battlegrounds (Colorado, New Mexico, Nevada). Thus, despite their propensity to abstain from the political process, scholars and pundits for years have noted the potential power of the Latino sleeping giant to influence election outcomes. In fact, dramatic increases in Latino turnout in 2008 combined with bloc voting for Barack Obama gave the Democratic candidate the margin of victory in several key states, including Florida, where increases in turnout by Puerto Ricans overwhelmed Cuban American support for Republican John McCain.

In 2003, Latinos surpassed African Americans as the largest minority group in the United States. While African Americans are largely loyal to the Democratic Party and are concentrated in non-battleground states, Latinos by comparison have been historically more likely to consider Republican candidates and are located more strategically in the context of presidential campaigns. Thus candidates for elected office are more likely to spend resources courting Latino voters—and increasingly so as the Hispanic population continues to grow.

Latino Subgroups

The pan-ethnic label "Latino" includes a variety of national-origin groups with very different political histories and proclivities. The largest Latino group in the United States by far is the Mexican-descent population (64 percent), but Mexicans have lived in the Southwest since before the Mexican-American War (1846–1848), making this community a mix of both new immigrants and fifth- and sixth-generation Americans whose ancestors lived in areas once ruled by Mexico but ceded to the United States after the war. Puerto Ricans make up the second-largest subgroup (9 percent). The island of Puerto Rico was taken by the United States in the Spanish-American War (1898) and later given special status as a commonwealth rather than being granted either statehood or independence. In 1917, Puerto Ricans in the mainland United States were granted citizenship. Thus, while members of other Latino national-origin groups must negotiate the citizenship process in order to have voting rights in the United States, Puerto Ricans are automatically granted such rights upon migration to the United States from the island.

For decades, the third largest Latino national-origin group in the United States has been Cuban Americans, with political muscle beyond their numbers (3.4 percent) due to their high levels of political participation and their strategic location—about two-thirds of all Cuban Americans live in Florida. Cubans are distinctive not only for their partisanship—they lean heavily towards the Republican Party, unlike most other Latinos—but for their wet-foot/dry-foot policy, which means that immigrants from Cuba who are intercepted at sea (wet foot) are returned to Cuba, while those who make it to the shores of the United States (dry foot) are allowed to stay as political refugees. The complexity of this process and the importance placed upon it by the Cuban American community were laid bare to the general public with the scandal surrounding the return of Elián González to Cuba in 2000. The boy was picked up at sea but local Cuban American officials refused to return him to the island, and his forced repatriation by the Clinton administration is cited by some observers as contributing to the Democrats' loss of Florida that November.

Other Latino national-origin groups, however, are gaining on Cubans. Dominicans were estimated to comprise 2.8 percent of the Latino population in the United States in 2006, and they are projected to surpass Cubans in terms of overall population size as early as 2010. Cuban American political power is also decreasing due to the increasing diversity of the Florida Latino population overall, including increasing numbers of Democratic-leaning Puerto Ricans. Younger generations of Cuban Americans also seem less loyal to the Republican Party than their older co-ethnics, although the community overall still leans heavily to the GOP.

Partisan Inclinations

Latinos tend to affiliate with the Democratic Party, with the notable exception of Cuban-descent Latinos, who generally prefer the Republican Party. This pattern of partisan affiliations is generally attributed to the perception among Latinos that the Democratic Party and its policies are more favorably inclined towards minorities in general and Latinos and immigrants in particular, and to the Republican Party's traditional hard-line stance on communism, which is more salient to Cubans than to other Latinos. About two-thirds of Mexicans, Puerto Ricans, and Central Americans identify as or lean toward the Democratic Party, while more than two-thirds of Cubans identify as or lean toward the Republican Party. This pattern was first noted by the 1989–1990 Latino National Political Survey, and it persists generally unchanged two decades later. Latino partisanship is more explicitly political than that of Anglos, who tend to be socialized into their political affiliations. Latinos with more education are more likely to be Republicans than Democrats, while Latinos with liberal opinions on abortion, affirmative action, school vouchers, and government-funded health insurance are more likely to be Democrats. Those with more positive economic perceptions are more likely to be Democrats, but income does not affect partisanship. Latino partisanship, compared to Anglo partisanship, is more likely to be influenced by short-term factors such as economic and issue preferences.

Some have argued that Latino social conservatism (for example, commonly held positions on abortion and homosexuality) and socioeconomic mobility will move them toward the Republican Party; but research indicates that this is unlikely. While newly arrived Latino immigrants may not learn partisanship through intergenerational transmission as do Anglos, they learn the preferred partisanship of their national-origin group over time. Newly arrived immigrants tend to not associate with either major political party, but exposure to the American political system over time socializes Latino immigrants into the dominant political affiliation of their peers. Subsequent generations of Latinos become more likely to be Democrats and strong partisans, due to the Democratic Party's image of being more supportive of policies favoring minorities. Partisanship also increases with education, citizenship, and abandonment of plans to return to the country of origin.

Still, pooled biennial National Election Studies reveal that there has been a marked shift toward the Republican Party in recent decades. From 1978 to 2002, Republican identification increased from 15 percent to almost 38 percent, while Democratic identification declined from 68 percent to 53 percent. Latinos who are evangelical or mainline Protestants, in particular, are more likely to identify as Republicans than their Catholic counterparts, and they are also more likely to vote. In 1976, 82 percent of Latinos voted Democratic (Jimmy Carter) and 18 percent voted Republican (Gerald Ford), while in 2000, 62 percent voted Democratic (Al Gore) and 35 percent voted Republican (George W. Bush). While some exit polls conducted during the 2004 election put Latino support for Bush at 44 percent, this figure has been discredited by subsequent research. More likely it was closer to 39 percent, which is still an increase from Bush's share of the Latino vote in 2000. Does this mean that Latinos are shifting to the Republican Party? Reagan received 37 percent of the Latino vote in 1984, but four years later, George H. W. Bush received only 32 percent of the Latino vote, and in 1996 Bob Dole received a mere 21 percent of the Latino vote. Further skepticism is warranted by the 31 percent of the Latino vote received by John McCain in 2008. Even in Florida, which is dominated by GOP-leaning Cuban American voters, the Republican nominee garnered just 43 percent of Latino votes. In sum, while Latinos' reputation as swing voters is warranted to some degree, there is a clear tendency for large majorities of Latino voters to support the Democratic Party.

For most Latinos, as with most non-Latinos, partisanship is a clear and strong predictor of vote choice. However, Latino voters will cross party lines to support a co-ethnic or to support a candidate with whom they share issue positions, particularly in a nonpartisan setting. Ethnicity plays a key role in vote choice, but it does so indirectly through partisanship, ethnic-related issue positions, and candidate evaluations. In some circumstances—for example, to support their preferred political party—Latino voters will choose the non-Latino candidate over the co-ethnic candidate. Other factors, such as issue positions and symbolic cues, also play a role. Low-education Latinos are more likely than high-education Latinos to use non-policy cues when evaluating a candidate—for example, if the candidate speaks Spanish or uses Spanish-language advertisements, if the candidate promises to appoint Latino officials or campaigns in Latino neighborhoods, or if the candidate is Latino and not Anglo. However, high-education Latinos are more likely to use policy and ideology cues. Overall, however, Latino issue concerns are not significantly different than those of non-Latinos. Latinos in the United States are concerned about the war in Iraq, the economy, education, jobs, and so on. While they are more attuned to issues concerning immigrants and immigration, as illustrated by their participation in the March 2006 marches on immigration reform, their vote choices and partisan inclinations are more heavily influenced by mainstream issues. The exception to this rule, however, is in political contexts of anti-Latino or anti-immigrant sentiment, such as that of the early 1990s in California and at the national level in 1996. In these situations, Latinos are more likely to be concerned with immigration policy and thus to be attentive to candidate and party positions on immigration-related issues when making their vote choice decisions.

The fact that Latinos prefer to support co-ethnics rather than non-Latinos does not also mean that Latinos are unwilling to vote for individuals from other groups. During the 2008 presidential campaign, much was made of the alleged difficulty Obama would face winning Latino votes (despite evidence from his Illinois campaigns that he was actually quite good at winning over Latino voters). Polling in late 2007 found that Hillary Clinton was the preferred candidate of 59 percent of Democratic Latinos, while Obama was preferred by only 15 percent. A year later, however, the willingness of Latinos to support a black candidate was made very clear—67 percent of Latinos voted for Obama and only 31 percent for John McCain. Other elections have also seen strong support for black candidates by Latino voters, including mayors Harold Washington (Chicago), David Dinkins (New York), Wellington Webb (Denver), and Ron Kirk (Dallas), and members of the U.S. House of Representatives Charles Rangel (D-NY) and Maxine Waters (D-CA).

There is also some, albeit limited, evidence that using Latino surrogates can influence Latino vote choice, particularly in favor of Republican candidates. One study has shown that outreach by Latino canvassers on behalf of non-Latino Republican candidates can increase Latino votes for the Republican Party. Evidence from the 2008 presidential primary season suggests that Latino surrogates were able to increase support for Barack Obama. Increased use of Spanish-language television and radio in recent years has increased speculation about the impact of Latino-oriented media (LOM) on Latino voters, but existing research is mostly speculative. Television-based outreach is particularly important when targeting Latino voters, as this is more likely to be their source of political news than is the case for non-Latinos. Contrary to popular belief, however, most Latinos get their political news from English-language stations rather than Spanish-language stations, and it is unclear to what degree exposure to English-language advertisements influences Latino political behavior. Research on media effects finds that Spanish-language advertisements by candidates affect Latino turnout, and Spanish-language radio clearly contributed to the participation by thousands of immigrants in the spring 2006 immigrant-rights marches. And yet we still know very little about how the use of LOM affects Latino vote choice.

Both political parties now campaign aggressively for Latino votes, but whether this targeted outreach influences vote choice remains an open question. Massive sums spent on Spanish-language television and radio spots are potentially important in terms of Latino turnout and vote choice, but existing research remains speculative. However, Latino voters contacted by Latino Republicans are more likely to support Republican candidates, and Latino voters contacted by Latino Democrats are more likely to support Democratic candidates, while parallel effects are not found for Latino voters contacted by non-Latino partisans. This suggests that endorsements by Latinos for Latino candidates made through the mass media (for example, via television advertisements or direct mail) should also impact Latino vote choice.

The effectiveness of different types of surrogates also remains an open question. Research on the use of heuristics by low-information and high-information Latino voters suggests that low-information Latinos can be swayed by celebrity endorsements, while high-information Latino voters are more open to endorsements by trusted Latino politicians, mirroring the influence of endorsements found in studies of the general public. Certainly the May 2008 endorsement of Obama by Bill Richardson, a longtime Clinton affiliate, swayed many Latino voters. Endorsements by Latino entertainers such as Jessica Alba and George Lopez, in contrast, were likely more limited in their impact. And while McCain was endorsed by at least one Latino celebrity, Daddy Yankee, there is no evidence that this swayed any Latino voters to cross party lines.

Turnout and Targeting

Recent years have seen a surge of interest in the power of mobilization efforts to increase Latino political participation. As with non-Latinos, direct efforts such as live phone banks or door-to-door canvassing have been found particularly effective at encouraging turnout, even among low-propensity Latinos in low-income neighborhoods and for low-salience elections. Blandishments to vote by co-ethnics seem to be more compelling than those made by non-Latinos. Latinos are also more likely to vote if there is a viable Latino candidate on the ballot or if they are represented by Latino elected officials, and also if issues or events in the political environment are salient to Latino voters, such as the anti-immigrant Proposition 187 on California's November 1994 ballot or local battles over English-only policies.

Mobilization efforts by political parties and candidates have also increased significantly in recent years. While the explosion of the Internet and micro-targeted cable television channels makes it increasingly difficult to reach non-Latino voters, the heavy use of Spanish-language television and radio stations by Latinos in the United States, combined with the relatively low number of such media outlets, makes targeting Latino voters easier. In addition, advertising rates for top-rated Spanish-language outlets such as Univision tend to be lower than that of the major English-language stations.

Conclusion

As Latino political participation and clout continue to increase, observers are learning more about how Latinos think and act in the political arena. Historically, most Latinos have preferred the Democratic Party, with the notable exception of Cuban loyalty to the GOP. Despite little to no knowledge of United States partisan politics on their arrival, Latino immigrants quickly learn the "preferred" partisanship of their national-origin group, and there is little evidence that Republicans are making inroads into the non-Cuban Latino population. Latino participation lags behind that of other groups, with the notable exception of attendance at local meetings, but their participation is steadily increasing in both electoral and non-electoral settings. In 2008, Latinos constituted 9 percent of the electorate, with significant gains in the battleground states of New Mexico, Florida, and Nevada. When targeted by mail, telephone, or door-to-door campaigns, Latino turnout increases significantly. Latino voters are particularly more likely to be receptive to appeals to participate when those appeals are made by co-ethnics and by co-partisans. Latino participation is also influenced by political context, including anti-Latino legislation, Latino representatives, and the presence of viable Latino candidates. Other research indicates that Latinos are willing to cross party and ethnic lines for a candidate they support, either for partisan, ethnic, or other reasons, such as ideology and issue positions. When deciding how to vote, low-education/low-information Latino voters are more likely to use non-policy cues (such as speaking Spanish), while high-education/high-information Latino voters are more likely to consider ideology and issue positions.

SUGGESTED READINGS

Abrajano, Marisa A. "Who Evaluates a Presidential Candidate by Using Non-Policy Campaign Messages?" *Political Research Quarterly* 58, no. 1 (March 2005): 55–67.

Alvarez, R. Michael, and Lisa García Bedolla. "The Foundations of Latino Voter Partisanship: Evidence from the 2000 Election." *Journal of Politics* 65, no. 1 (Feb. 2003): 31–49.

Barreto, Matt. "¡Sí Se Puede! Latino Candidates and the Mobilization of Latino Voters." *American Political Science Review* 101, no. 3 (Aug. 2007): 425–41.

de la Garza, Rodolfo O., Lewis DeSipio, F. Chris Garcia, John Garcia, and Angelo Falcón. *Latino Voices: Mexican, Puerto Rican, and Cuban Perspectives on American Politics.* Boulder, Col.: Westview Press, 1992.

Hajnal, Zoltan, and Taeku Lee. "Out of Line: Immigration and Party Identification among Asian Americans and Latinos." In Taeku Lee, Kathrick Ramakrishnan, and Ricardo Ramírez, eds., *Transforming Politics, Transforming America: The Political and Civic Incorporation of Immigrants in the United States.* Charlottesville, Va.: University of Virginia Press, 2005. 129–150.

Michelson, Melissa R. "Meeting the Challenge of Latino Voter Mobilization." *Annals of Political and Social Science* 601 (Sept. 2005): 85–101.

Nicholson, Stephen P., Adrian Pantoja, and Gary M. Segura. "Explaining the Latino Vote: Issue Voting among Latinos in the 2000 Presidential Election." *Political Research Quarterly* 59, no. 2 (June 2006): 259–71.

Wong, Janelle S. "The Effects of Age and Political Exposure on the Development of Party Identification among Asian American and Latino Immigrants in the United States." *Political Behavior* (Dec. 2000). Vol. 22, No. 4, pp. 341–371.

26

Race and Southern Politics

WAYNE PARENT

While the interplay between race and southern politics remains thick and complicated, three simplifying themes have emerged by the end of the first decade of the twenty-first century. First, white racial resentment remains relevant, even as its influence is waning. Second, black mobilization is a significant, powerful, but as of yet only intermittent force. Third, non-native southerners and younger voters are shifting the political racial landscape in ways that have very obvious impacts for the future.

White Racial Resentment

The relevant headlines in the immediate aftermath of the 2008 elections focused on the dramatic result of an African American presidential candidate winning North Carolina, Virginia, and Florida. However, the media analysis a few days later began to focus on another trend. Barack Obama had fared dramatically worse in some other southern states. The places where Obama's appeal was weaker than Democratic presidential candidate John Kerry's had been four years earlier were concentrated in the white, mostly rural South. Most analysts pointed to white racial resentment or prejudice as the reason. Since most of these areas have a history of this racial dynamic in politics, it is an understandable conclusion.

White resentment is tough to measure. Today candidates don't air blatantly racist ads and, as a rule, people don't tell surveys that they vote a certain way because they are racists. However, blatant racism has not always been so taboo in politics. In the fairly recent past and in some states more than others, political successes were often the result of campaigns where there was no attempt to even thinly camouflage anti–African American prejudices and policies.

Three such elections stand out. During the middle of the twentieth century, race politics held center stage both nationally and in the South. The first of these national elections was in 1948, when Strom Thurmond ran on a states'-rights platform against passing any form of civil or voting rights legislation. In 1964, after three elections in which the major contenders had muddled, nondistinct stands on civil rights, Republican Barry Goldwater (who, for reasons that may have had little to do with racial prejudice, nonetheless did not support civil rights or voting rights legislation) ran against Democrat Lyndon Johnson, who ran an explicitly pro–civil rights platform. Finally, right after the passage of that landmark race legislation, George Wallace ran in 1968 as an independent with an explicitly racial message. These three elections provide a good guide to the strength of the roots that underlie the message of racial resentment.

Only a handful of states in the nation supported any of these three candidates. None of the three had any chance in the election, and all lost in landslides. However, Alabama, Mississippi, and Louisiana supported all three. Georgia and South Carolina supported two of the three, and Arkansas supported George Wallace. Except for Goldwater's win in his home state of Arizona in 1964, these six states are the only states in the Union that voted for presidential candidates that clearly opposed voting rights and civil rights for African Americans at a time when the issue was at the forefront of the American political agenda. It is also these states that have among the highest proportion of African American voters. Race politics boiled in the mid-twentieth century, and it appears that racially motivated resentment politics continues to be a significant part of the political dynamic today.

Today, older white voters, who presumably voted in elections or were attuned to the political dynamics of the 1960s, would logically be those likely to vote against the first African American presidential candidate. Exit polls provide some striking evidence in the 2008 election. According to statewide CNN exit polls of the presidential race between Democrat Barack Obama and Republican John McCain, the percentage of white voters for Obama was lowest in Alabama (10 percent), second-lowest in Mississippi (11 percent), and third-lowest in Louisiana (14 percent). Georgia was a distant fourth, at 23 percent. The national average was 43 percent. In Alabama and Mississippi, 98 percent of African Americans voted for Obama; in Louisiana, it was 94 percent. The most cautious interpretation of this data would simply highlight the racial polarization of voters. However, the histories of these states suggest that more is at play. While the degree of black mobilization and support for Obama was fairly uniform across the country, the extent of white opposition was clearly not as uniform. And the causes for that overwhelming white opposition may be seen as a logical continuity of decades of white racial voting patterns.

The three states—Alabama, Mississippi, and Louisiana—where fewer than one in seven white voters voted for Barack Obama are also the only three states that fifty years earlier voted for Strom Thurmond, Barry Goldwater, and George Wallace. These numbers alone make the point well: southern white resentment remains a significant force in southern politics.

Black Mobilization

A second trend in race politics in the American South is the increasing, but sporadic, significance of black mobilization. This writer's interest in black mobilization in the South led to his first major research project, an analysis of voter registration in New Orleans after the election in 1981 of Ernest "Dutch" Morial, the city's first black mayor, when it was a black minority city. The conclusion at that time was that political efficacy in the black community leads to higher participation. It remains relevant today. When black voter constraints are removed, black registration and participation rise significantly when African American politicians have a chance at winning. After Morial's election, voter registration skyrocketed in the black community. The real possibility that an African American would be elected president of the United States in 2008 had the same effect on black registration and turnout—black mobilization.

Since concrete statistics on black turnout remain unavailable at the time of this writing, less exact measures of the phenomenon will be used. Evidence of increased black mobilization in the South for the presidential election is ample and widespread. The first indication of the significance of turnout in the black community came during the Democratic primaries in the South, when then-Senator Barack Obama was in a tight contest with then-Senator Hillary Clinton.

Several party primaries that were pivotal to Obama's win were in the South. They were a result of high turnout and almost uniform support in the black community. Obama's initial win in the Iowa caucuses on January 3 was followed by a stunning setback to Clinton in New Hampshire on January 8.

The next significant primary was South Carolina, where African American mobilization was crucial to Obama's 55 percent resounding victory over his main two opponents, Senators Clinton and John Edwards from neighboring North Carolina. Black support for Obama, well above 70 percent in most estimates, was the crucial factor and brought Obama's campaign back into the forefront. The same pattern continued after the February 5 Super Tuesday, where both Obama and Clinton were perceived to have roughly equal momentum. The critical post–Super Tuesday run of wins by Obama was highlighted by resounding wins in several southern states and was clearly due to overwhelming black support, as blacks make up an overwhelming proportion of Democratic voters in the South. Obama won Louisiana on February 9, then Virginia on February 12, and finally, on May 6, 56 percent of the vote in the North Carolina primary.

African American Democratic candidates before Obama, most notably Jesse Jackson in 1984, had won Democratic presidential primaries in the South in the same way, with overwhelming black support among Democrats. This was a fact noted by President Bill Clinton, who was roundly criticized for airing it during the heat of the nomination campaign. The difference in this election cycle was that while black mobilization and support in the South helped Jackson become a major figure in the party and provided him with the credentials necessary to play a key, visible role at the national convention, Obama's support in the South was coupled with support outside the region. Therefore, the same phenomenon had a much larger effect. Indeed, it was one of the crucial components of his nomination victory strategy. Never before had black support in a Democratic primary had the effect of helping a black candidate to become the party standard-bearer. Merle and Earl Black in their classic book *Politics and Society in the South* spoke convincingly of the "limited effect of a franchised minority." This conclusion about the impact of black voting rights on election results seemed like one that would hold for at least a century after the landmark enfranchising 1965 legislation. After the 2008 Democratic presidential primaries, the conventional wisdom was that while black voters in the South might well be a crucial part of a winning coalition for a white candidate, these voters would not be a crucial part of a winning coalition for black candidates—and thus, they had limited leverage. The 2008 Democratic presidential primaries busted that limitation at the highest level of politics, and did so much sooner than almost anyone would have predicted.

While Obama won only three of the eleven states that were part of the Old

Confederacy in his decisive national win, two of those three victories dramatically illustrate how solid, mobilized black support can be decisive. The wins in Virginia and North Carolina, and to a lesser extent the win in Florida, were wins where an almost uniform enthusiastic black support was crucial. Again, exit polls provide conspicuous evidence. In North Carolina, Obama carried 95 percent of the black vote and only 35 percent of the white vote. He carried 92 percent of the black vote in Virginia, while carrying only 39 percent of the white vote. In Florida, he carried 96 percent of the black vote and 42 percent of the white vote, a proportion almost the same as the national average. North Carolina and Virginia illustrate the significance of black mobilization in more traditional southern states where white support for the Democratic candidate was very low.

Accounts of black mobilization were accentuated by the record-busting number of African Americans who voted early in states in the South, both those won and lost by Obama. Georgia, North Carolina, Virginia, Louisiana, and Florida all reported remarkable early turnout numbers among African American voters.

While the significance of black support as a part of winning coalitions, almost exclusively for Democratic candidates, has been widely accepted and understood, the countervailing notion—that this support had limitations—has been equally well accepted and understood. In the South, black support can cause a reactive and overpowering white counter-support. Most often that counterbalancing support occurs when the black-favored candidate is an African American. Examples of this conventional wisdom have been described several times and in several places, reinforcing Merle and Earl Black's thoughtful and convincing 1987 conclusion that while widespread African American enfranchisement provided a powerful voice for a repressed group of citizens, the political leverage was limited. Over thirty years later, in the 2008 presidential election, those limitations weakened considerably.

Changing South

The first two racial dynamics in the South discussed—white racial resentment and black political mobilization—have existed since the civil rights movement. The third is new and, while it may not immediately revolutionize southern race relations, it is slowly but definitely having a profound impact upon them. White, younger southerners and non-southerners don't show the same political racial attitudes and behavior as their older and more native counterparts. This, in turn, may affect black attitudes and behavior as well.

At first glance, in the three most racially polarized states in the South in 2008—Alabama, Mississippi, and Louisiana—the exit polls indicates that the age factor is too large to be believable. And in some ways it is. In Alabama, fully 50 percent of 18- to 29- year-olds voted for Obama; in Mississippi, 56 percent did so; and in Louisiana, 48 percent. After further analysis, it becomes clear that African Americans are a younger part of the electorate. This is a significant point in and of itself. It does not, however, necessarily point to a dramatic change within the races.

Further analysis illustrates the extent to which younger white voters are different from older white voters and younger black voters are different from older black voters in these southern states. First, as is probably expected, black voters did not vary in any meaningful way by age. There are some noticeable differences among white voters, however, in the three Deep South states with the most strident racial histories. In Louisiana, 14 percent of all white voters voted for Obama, and a modestly higher number of 17 percent of 18- to 29-year-old white voters were Obama supporters. In Alabama, 10 percent of all white voters and 13 percent of young people voted for him. In Mississippi, the difference was most dramatic. Only 11 percent of all white Mississippians supported Obama, but fully 19 percent of younger voters, over 70 percent more, were Obama voters.

In North Carolina and Virginia, the age factor is much more pronounced. In North Carolina, Obama won 74 percent of 18- to 29-year-olds and didn't even reach a majority in any other age group. In Virginia, the story was somewhat similar. Obama won 60 percent of the youngest age group and squeaked a 51 percent majority from those aged 30–64, losing only the age group over sixty-five.

The age-group difference among only white voters in North Carolina is remarkable. Overall, just 35 percent of white voters in North Carolina voted for Obama. Among 18- to 29-year-old white voters, a decisive majority—fully 56 percent—supported the African American candidate. In Virginia, the dynamic is not at all as pronounced. Among white voters in that state, Obama carried only slightly more younger voters, 42 percent, than the 38 percent of white voters overall.

The different dynamics in these two states, both noteworthy wins for the Democrat in the South, suggest another trend, one in which the evidence is less precise. In both states, but in Virginia more prominently, Obama's support appears to have been disproportionately from those citizens who are new residents, likely non-southerners. Obama's relatively easy win in Virginia was grounded in two demographically identifiable parts of the state: heavily African American urban areas and the high-growth suburban counties surrounding Washington, D.C. In those counties—Loudon, Fairfax, and Prince William—the impact of non-native southerners on the political racial relations in the South is glaring. In North Carolina, the so-called "research triangle" counties surrounding Raleigh, Durham, and Chapel Hill gave Obama disproportionate white support. The same pattern can be seen in isolation in other southern states, even in the historically more polarized states, where, for example, Obama won the higher-growth, majority-white county (parish) of East Baton Rouge in Louisiana. These examples can be found scattered around places in the South, logically, where non-southerners with no ingrained history of racially polarized politics have an impact.

Finally, another ethnic dynamic is significant. Hispanics remain a small but growing proportion of the electorate in most Deep South states. In Georgia, for instance, they made up 3 percent of the presidential exit-poll proportion. In Texas and Florida, however, their numbers are much bigger: 20 percent in Texas and 14 percent in Florida. In 2008, that was a boon for the Democrats, with Obama carrying 63 percent of the vote in Texas and 57 percent in Florida.

Continuity and Change

Race politics continue to play a significant role in southern politics. White resentment and variations in black mobilization still are the hallmarks that define them. As the civil rights generation ages, however, the impact of white resentment lessens, although slowly. Black mobilization is associated with efficacy, and the election of the nation's first African American president is likely to increase political efficacy across several types of elections in the United States over time. Again, however, the trend is likely to be a slow and somewhat sporadic one.

As the citizens of the civil-rights generation grow older, and as more and more southern voters participate in elections who have no visceral connection with those highly emotional times, the impact of white resentment should certainly decrease, and evidence found in the 2008 elections indicates that such a decrease is beginning to occur. In the states of the South where the historical context of racially polarized politics is strongest—Alabama, Mississippi, and Louisiana—changes will occur more slowly.

In the areas of the South with higher population growth than those outside the South, such Virginia, North Carolina, and Florida, racially polarized politics are diminishing rapidly. The electoral victory of Barack Obama in those three states of the Old Confederacy is an eye-catching exclamation point on the story of these changes. As non-southerners and younger southerners change not only the numbers of voters who exhibit traditional southern racial attitudes, but also perhaps the entire political context, affecting even traditional southerners, politics transforms.

SUGGESTED READINGS

Bartels, Larry M. "What's the Matter with *What's the Matter with Kansas?*" *Quarterly Journal of Political Science* 1 (2006): 201–26.

Black, Earl, and Merle Black. *Politics and Society in the South.* Cambridge, Mass.: Harvard University Press, 1987.

27

Informing Insiders

CHARLIE COOK

For almost as long as there have been politics and printing presses, there have been publications that cover politics and government. Over time, a demand was created, and filled, by highly specialized publications that provided in-depth coverage of government, politics, and elections, as well as insights into the backstage intrigue for those who either needed such detail professionally or were simply fascinated by the inner workings of politics and government.

On one level are authoritative weekly magazines like the *Congressional Quarterly Weekly Report*, founded in 1945, and *National Journal*, started in 1969 by a group of former *CQ* staffers who wanted to cover the Executive Branch with the same amount of detail and authority that *CQ* afforded to Congress. Over time, the two publications have evolved to cover comprehensively both ends of Pennsylvania Avenue for their elite subscribers—primarily corporations, trade and professional associations, labor unions, think tanks, governmental agencies, and elected officials, who pay in excess of $1,000 a year for subscriptions (though academics can get reduced rates). Both publications focus primarily on policy and the process behind policy development, but both also cover politics and elections, though on a more objective basis. In addition to their flagship weekly magazines, *Congressional Quarterly* and *National Journal* also publish *CQ Today* and *CongressDailyAM*, respectively—printed daily newsletters when Congress is in session, covering developments on Capitol Hill in great detail.

Beyond the heavier-weight and more authoritative *Congressional Quarterly* and *National Journal*, there are three semi-daily newspapers that cover Capitol Hill and politics. The original Capitol Hill newspaper, *Roll Call*, was published for 31 years by Sid Yudain as more of a light-hearted, neighborhood publication that covered the people who worked on Capitol Hill. In 1986, Yudain sold *Roll Call* to Arthur Levitt, Jr., the former chairman of the American Stock Exchange, who invested heavily in the paper and turned it into a more substantive publication. Upon his nomination by President Bill Clinton to be chairman of the Securities and Exchange Commission, Levitt sold *Roll Call* to the Economist Group, publisher of *The Economist* magazine. *Roll Call's* monopoly status was challenged first in 1994, when *The Hill* newspaper began publication, and again in 2007, when *POLITICO,* a third competitor, joined the fray. Though each are slightly different in style, all three approach their coverage of Capitol Hill, the White House, and politics less somberly than *CQ* and *National Journal* and focus more on both breaking news and regular columnists. All three publications are striving to develop both their print and web products. Their print editions are aimed more at Washington insiders, particularly those older and less inclined to look to the Internet for their news, while their websites attract both younger inside-the-Beltway readers as well as those outside the Beltway. *POLITCO,* the youngest of the products, has been the most aggressive about promoting its web product, as well as seeking radio and television partnerships.

The Hotline, published by *National Journal,* is the only truly unique product. It began in 1987 as an electronic political-clipping service that compiled the most important new stories of the day. It was initially distributed by fax and eventually moved online. In its earliest days, *The Hotline* relied on stringers to fax articles to its offices; later it encouraged reporters to file copies of their articles directly to *The Hotline.*

With the proliferation of the web, young *The Hotline* staffers now arrive at work before dawn to peruse newspaper websites from all 50 states in search of the most relevant articles. They then condense them down for inclusion in *The Hotline,* which publishes just after noon Eastern Time each weekday. Over time, *The Hotline* has also included other special features, such as tracking advertising buys, documenting how much time prominent politicians spend on cable and broadcast news programs, and even providing excerpts from the monologues of late-night comedians. With a substantial subscription price of several thousand dollars per year, *The Hotline* subscribers are almost universally institutions, corporations, trade and professional associations, labor unions, government entities, news organizations, party committees, and major campaigns. The U.S. Congress also has a subscription, so all members and staff have access to the publication.

But in the days long before the Internet and *The Hotline*, before *Roll Call* became more formidable and before *The Hill* and *POLITICO* began, there was an appetite and a market for a different sort of political publication that was more insider-oriented and approached politics from the perspective of well-connected reporters and columnists, former campaign strategists, and political scientists. Some of these publications traded more on insider gossip, featuring behind-the-scenes detail and relying less on traditional on-the-record reporting. Others were more analytical, sifting through polls, election returns, and congressional floor voting patterns.

When I moved to Washington in 1972 as a freshman in college who worked part-time on Capitol Hill, veteran newspaper columnists Rowland Evans and Robert Novak had already been publishing the Washington, D.C.–based *Evans and Novak Political Report* for five years. The two, and later just Novak, would parcel out the product of their prodigious reporting between two separate syndicated newspaper columns and their newsletter, using and abusing sources that other political reporters would kill to have. It was not unusual to have senators, congressmen, Cabinet members, and their staffs leak tidbits and rumors to Evans and Novak. They would float trial balloons, settle scores, or curry favor with the extraordinarily influential journalists, who would put the more general-interest items in their newspaper columns and keep for their newsletters the morsels that only the true political aficionados would appreciate. The *Evans and Novak Political Report* published for nearly 42 years, from 1967 until January 2009, when health problems forced Novak's retirement, almost eight years after Evans's death.

Another pair of well-connected political reporters, Jack Germond and Jules Witcover, published the *Germond-Witcover Political Report* for a few years in addition to their syndicated column of almost a quarter-century. Their true passion and success, though, lay in their newspaper columns, articles, and books.

A very different newsletter with a decidedly more analytical and less insider mission began publication in 1971. After the 1969 publication of his book, *The Emerging Republican Majority*, Kevin Phillips, a campaign strategist for Nixon's 1968 campaign, began publishing *The American Political Report*, a biweekly Bethesda, Maryland–based newsletter that sifted through reams of polling data and election results and wove a cogent analysis of political trends. In addition to trend analysis, *The American Political Report* also distilled the most important political developments culled from newspapers from each of the 50 states, something that sounds mundane in this Internet era but was remarkably helpful in the days when tracking political events from coast to coast was much more difficult. Both the coverage and analysis of political developments around the country became invaluable to practitioners and observers alike, particularly since it reflected not the approach of a journalist but instead one of the most brilliant analysts of the day. Phillips published *The American Political Report* until 1998, when he retired to Connecticut to focus on writing books.

The other major insider newsletter, *The Baron Political Report,* was launched in 1976 by Alan Baron, a former Democratic strategist who had worked for, among others, Senator George McGovern. For ten years, until health problems forced his retirement, Baron analyzed polls, election results, and backroom maneuvering.

A regular reader of these three publications would have an inside track over most other folks when it came to knowing the who, what, when, where, and, most important, why of almost any political event in Washington and around the country.

With the demise of the *Evans and Novak Political Report,* the last remaining printed Washington-based political newsletter is *The Rothenberg Political Report,* which focuses on U.S. Senate, House, and gubernatorial races. First published in 1975 by conservative leader Paul Weyrich and his Free Congress Foundation as *The Political Report,* the original intent was to provide objective analyses of congressional elections for Weyrich, his foundation, and his conservative political-action committee, the Committee for the Survival of a Free Congress. Stuart Rothenberg, then a Bucknell University political scientist, was hired in 1980 as an assistant editor and was later promoted to editor. Rothenberg bought the publication in 1989, taking it independent and renaming it *The Rothenberg Political Report.* In each issue, Rothenberg and his colleague, Nathan Gonzales, spotlight three or four different races with two or three pages of narrative analysis on each contest, based on interviews with candidates, campaigns, party operatives, and local sources. They also rate races on the basis of their competitiveness.

With much the same focus as *The Rothenberg Political Report, The Cook Political Report* was a print-only publication from its 1984 inception until 2004, when it converted to online only. *The Cook Political Report* rates every congressional and gubernatorial race in the country on a scale of Solid, Likely, or Lean Democrat, Toss Up, Lean, Likely, or Solid Republican. It also provides narrative analyses of races, and it has developed the Partisan Voting Index

(PVI), a statistical measurement that indicates the presidential voting pattern of every congressional district compared to the nation as a whole.

Campaigns and party committees closely follow both publications for their ratings and analyses of congressional races, and both publications are intended to be and are widely seen as impartial and nonpartisan.

Every current and former political newsletter has had its own recipe and approach. Since 1984, *The Cook Political Report* has evolved from a one-man shop, publishing a biweekly printed newsletter, to a five-person, online publication, with weekly e-mail updates (more often during the run-up to a general election) and thousands of pages of current and archived content.

The Cook Political Report's Senate and gubernatorial editor is Jennifer Duffy, who has worked in one capacity or another for the publication since 1988, focusing primarily on Senate races for all but four of those years. David Wasserman is the House editor; he joined the newsletter in June 2007, replacing Amy Walter, who had edited the House section for nine years before leaving to become editor of *The Hotline*. Wasserman had interned for *The Cook Political Report* during the summer of 2005 while a student at the University of Virginia.

In covering these races, Duffy and Wasserman meet regularly with candidates, and they also talk with campaign staffs and consultants, party operatives from the House and Senate campaign committees and state parties, and local political reporters. In addition to those sources, they use their own knowledge of politics in states and districts, track campaign developments, and interpret both publicly available and privately shared polling data in an effort to know, to the greatest extent possible, what is going on in each contest, who is more likely to win, and why.

The candidate meetings each run about an hour and usually begin with the candidate sharing his or her biographical narrative, walking Duffy and Wasserman through his or her professional and political career. There is a brief discussion of issues before the candidates are questioned about the political dynamics in the race, the strengths and weaknesses of their own candidacies, and the strengths and weaknesses of their opponents. As a little-known state senator from Illinois who had just started his long-shot bid for the U.S. Senate, Barack Obama met with Duffy in our offices in September 2002, 26 months before he eventually won that seat and five years before he launched his presidential campaign.

Although political newsletters like *The Cook Political Report* and *The Rothenberg Political Report* still exist, the advent and popularization of various cable-news networks and the Internet have made such publications substantially less important. However, they still fill a niche for providing very detailed analyses of congressional, gubernatorial, and presidential election campaigns.

The importance and relevance of these publications over the years lies in the fact that they helped develop what became the conventional wisdom among the political elites inside the Beltway, in state capitols, and across the country. To the extent that members of Congress, governors, other elected officials and their staffs, the White House staff, journalists, lobbyists, and other insiders read the same publications and saw the same data and interpretations, these political newsletters became an important part of the political dialogue, suggesting how events and trends were perceived.

Some of the newer and increasingly important kids on the political-communication block are daily political newsletters that have been developed by the television networks. Initially for the internal use of their producers, show bookers and correspondents, they now have become important outlets of their respective political units and are avidly read by other journalists, political operatives, and elected officials. The original was "The Note," developed in 1999 by then-ABC News political director Mark Halperin and his deputy, Elizabeth Wilner, who moved to NBC News in 2003 as the network's first political director and there began publishing "First Read." CNN followed in 2006 with the Political Ticker, and *POLITICO*'s Mike Allen started "Playbook" in 2007.

These briefings are generally five to eight pages long. They include a summary of the major political news stories of the day, with web links and some interpretation by the network political staffs, who all try to be proactive by anticipating what will be happening and making news that day. Presidential campaign and national party committee staffers often lobby these political units hard, since the content is followed so closely by other journalists and often drives the direction and interpretation of events of the day.

C-SPAN and, more recently, CNN, Fox, MSNBC, radio talk shows, the network political newsletters, and the broader Internet have dramatically changed the flow and nature of political conventional wisdom, making it far more small 'd' democratic. The information and knowledge gap between true political insiders and participants on the one side and political junkies on the other has narrowed significantly, though a distinction should be made between those shedding light, information and understanding, and those generating heat and controversy or fanning partisan and ideological flames.

More people have access to more information, insights, and varied interpretations faster than ever before, which has substantially broken down the concentric circles of information access. A television viewer, talk-show listener or reader of blogs thousands of miles from Washington, D.C., who may never have even visited the city, can now know and understand things that he or she never could have a generation ago.

Various cable news programs and guests have replaced the insider-oriented political newsletters of a generation ago, while analytical websites such as Pollster.com and Fivethirtyeight.com have taken the place of others, leaving a niche for analysis of specific congressional elections to Washington-based political newsletters such as *The Rothenberg Political Report* and *The Cook Political Report*.

But even in that narrow area, the Internet is having an impact, with websites like DailyKos.com and MyDD.com devoting substantial coverage to the Senate and House races collectively and individually. Swingstateproject.com focuses almost exclusively on individual Senate and House contests. While certainly approaching these subjects from a heavily partisan (Democratic) and ideological (liberal) point of view (and some contributors doing little more than cheerleading and talking up the prospects of one side while ignoring promising developments that favor the other party), some of the contributors have become quite sophisticated in their analyses, and even veteran analysts can pick up something of value now and again. More important, some of these websites have demonstrated the ability to raise money among activists, at least on the left, for individual congressional races. In some cases, they have channeled much-needed money into long-shot candidacies before the Democratic Party apparatus has embraced them or establishment analysts have recognized their potential.

All of three of these sites are written from the more liberal and pro-Democratic perspective, reflecting a more developed interest in and focus on specific races from the liberal side of the Internet. One view is that this reflects the fact that the left was out of power and desperately wanted to get back in, while conservatives and Republicans were in power and more lethargic about hanging onto it. Presumably, now that the left and Democrats are in and the right and Republicans are out (as of 2010), we will see a rise in the importance and sophistication of conservative political websites that focus on races as opposed to issues and broader ideological topics. There is certainly no shortage of conservative-oriented political websites, but it is clear that they focus more on issues and national political themes than on who is running in specific Senate and House races, where upsets might occur and where gains can be made.

Freed from the printing or mailing costs once associated with political newsletters, and with the price of admission to the Internet, the real growth in political information has occurred on the web, where there are now sites and blogs focusing on the politics of specific states and even some cities. Now, virtually every state has at least one—and in some cases, a dozen or more—websites devoted to covering the state capitol, statewide and state legislative contests, and behind-the-scenes maneuvering.

Some of these sites seem relatively objective; others have very clear partisan or ideological axes to grind, or are basically fronts for one political party, faction, or candidate. Some, such as PolitickerNJ.com and New Mexico Politics with Joe Monahan, have become must-reads for political players in their states, and others are more the random musings of armchair campaign managers. Today's political junkie can peruse a half dozen or so websites in less than five minutes, scanning for items of interest from a multitude of sources and accelerating the flow of information and rumors to a degree that would have been unheard of a generation ago.

The result is a political news cycle that changes from minute to minute, allowing a single event, statement, or misstep to take a state or the nation by storm and shaping the dialogue in a way that would have taken days or weeks just a few years ago. The greater anonymity afforded by the Internet has also changed the tenor of political discourse and blurred the distinction between rumors and facts.

The distinctly partisan and ideological nature of some of these political websites and the tendency of many web users, like cable news viewers and radio talk-show listeners, to read, watch, and listen to those sites, networks, and shows with which they largely agree also has the effect of intensifying viewpoints. There are fewer dissenting voices heard, which has resulted in greater ideological and partisan polarization.

Still, whether based in fact, rumor, or interpretation, elite opinion can shape public opinion, and in politics, that matters. Whether it is insider newsletters, shows, or websites, opinions are formed and politics shaped by what is said and by whom.

Contributors

Monica Ancu received her Ph.D. from the University of Florida. She conducts research on the use of online and digital communication for political campaigning. In particular, she studies online social media, campaign websites, blogs, and online political advertising.

Robert H. Binstock is Professor of Aging, Health, and Society at Case Western Reserve University. A political scientist, he has served as director of a White House Task Force on Older Americans, and has analyzed and written about the politics of aging for over four decades. The latest of his 25 books is *Aging Nation: The Economics and Politics of Growing Older in America*, coauthored with James H. Schulz.

Charlie Cook is publisher of *The Cook Political Report*, a weekly columnist for *National Journal* and CongressDailyAM, and a political analyst for NBC News.

Louis A. Day is an Alumni Professor at the Manship School of Mass Communication at Louisiana State University, Baton Rouge, where he teaches courses in media law, ethics, and philosophy. He has coauthored books on electronic media and journalism ethics (published in Spanish for use in Latin America) and is the author of one of the leading college textbooks on media ethics, *Ethics in Media Communications: Cases and Controversies*.

Thomas N. Edmonds is president of Edmonds Associates, a northern Virginia–based political consulting firm specializing in campaign media strategy for presidential, senatorial, congressional, and statewide candidates. He spent 30 years at newspapers in Detroit, Denver, and northern New Jersey before joining the trade association in 1998. He retired in 2009 and started his own consulting business, specializing in connecting newspaper media buyers and sellers with a special focus on helping newspapers capture more of the lucrative political advertising revenue and market share.

Malcolm P. Ehrhardt is president of the Ehrhardt Group in New Orleans. He has conducted focus group research in the Gulf South for political campaigns and candidates for more than 15 years. In addition, his firm conducts qualitative research for more than 20 commercial clients in industries ranging from banking and real estate to home building products. He also conducts workshops on strategic planning and crisis communications.

Bill Fletcher, Jr., is a writer, photographer, musician, and film and video director. He is CEO of Fletcher Rowley Riddle, Inc., a Nashville-based firm specializing in political and corporate communications consulting and media production. The firm has produced media for more than 500 political campaigns in 41 states. "Fletch," a graduate of East Tennessee State University, also had an extensive career as a newspaper reporter, photographer, columnist, and editor. He is also a former vice president of Cumberland University in Lebanon, Tennessee.

John Franzén has headed his own campaign media firm in Washington, D.C., for more than thirty years, serving progressive candidates and organizations nationwide. He also served for fifteen years on the board of the American Association of Political Consultants, where he launched an oral history project that records the recollections of some of the industry's pioneers. He can be reached at *www.franzenco.com.*

Ron Garay was the F. Walter Lockett, Jr., Distinguished Professor at the Manship School of Mass Communication at Louisiana State University, Baton Rouge. He received his Ph.D. in mass communication from Ohio University in 1980. He has written a variety of articles and book chapters on radio and television history and regulation and is the author of *Congressional Television: A Legislative History, Cable Television: A Reference Guide to Information, Gordon McLendon: The Maverick of Radio,* and *The Manship School: A History of Journalism Education at LSU.*

Robert K. Goidel is the director of the Manship School of Mass Communication's Research Facility, which includes the Public Policy Research Lab and the Media Effects Lab. As senior public policy fellow of the Reilly Center for Media & Public Affairs, he directs the annual Louisiana Survey and provides analysis to government, organizations, and the media. He works closely with diverse constituencies to develop survey instruments, analyze data, prepare reports, and present research findings. His received his Ph.D. in political science from the University of Kentucky and is the author of two books and numerous journal articles. He is a professor in the Manship School and the Department of Political Science at Louisiana State University, Baton Rouge.

Paul Harang earned his master's degree from the Manship School of Mass Communication at Louisiana State University, Baton Rouge. He is Deputy Director of Research for the City of New Orleans Office of Intergovernmental Relations.

Bud Jackson is the president of Jackson Group Media, LLC, a strategic communications firm located in Alexandria, Virginia. He currently serves as president of the American Association of Political Consultants Mid-Atlantic chapter, which represents political professionals in Washington, D.C., Pennsylvania, Virginia, Maryland, Delaware, New York, and New Jersey.

Lynda Lee Kaid is Professor of Telecommunication and a Research Foundation Professor at the University of Florida, where she specializes in political communication. A three-time Fulbright scholar, she has also done work on political television in several European, Asian, and Latin American countries. She is the author or editor of more than 25 books, including *The Encyclopedia of Political Communication, The Handbook of Political Communication Research, Videostyle in Presidential Campaigns*, and *Political Advertising in Western Democracies*.

John E. Kimball is the former Chief Marketing Officer at The Newspaper Association of America. He spent 30 years at newspapers in Detroit, Denver, and northern New Jersey before joining the trade association in 1998. He retired in 2009 and started his own consulting business specializing in connecting newspaper media buyers and sellers with a special focus on helping newspapers capture more of the lucrative political advertising revenue and market share.

Katherine Knobloch is a doctoral student in the Department of Communication at the University of Washington and a graduate of the Manship School of Mass Communication. She studies young people and the formation of civic identities, as well as the role of the citizen in the democratic process.

David Kurpius is an associate professor and associate dean of undergraduate studies and administration at LSU's Manship School of Mass Communication. He is the author of numerous articles and book chapters on filling the gap in media coverage of civic discourse, including the areas of civic journalism, statewide public-affairs television, and hyperlocal media.

Lisa K. Lundy is an assistant professor the Manship School of Mass Communication at Louisiana State University, Baton Rouge. Her research focuses on health, science, and agricultural communication. Her professional experience includes public relations for the University of Florida's College of Agricultural and Life Sciences and designing and writing publications for the March of Dimes. In 2006, she received the Tiger Athletic Foundation Teaching Award, which recognizes teaching excellence on campus. She currently serves as chair of the editorial board for the *Journal of Applied Communications*.

Robert Mann is a professor of mass communication at the Manship School of Mass Communication at Louisiana State University, Baton Rouge. A former newspaper journalist and press secretary to two U.S. senators and a U.S. governor, Mann is the author of six books, including political histories of the civil-rights movement, the Vietnam War, and American wartime dissent.

Melissa Michelson is an associate professor of political science at Menlo College. From 2006–2009, she was principal investigator for the evaluation of the James Irvine Foundation's California Votes Initiative, a multiyear effort to increase voting rates among infrequent voters—particularly those in low-income and ethnic communities—in California's San Joaquin Valley and targeted areas in southern California. Her two major strands of research include Latino political incorporation and field experiments in voter mobilization of ethnic and racial minorities.

Wayne Parent is the Russell B. Long Professor of Political Science at Louisiana State University, Baton Rouge. He is author of *Inside the Carnival: Unmasking Louisiana Politics*. He has served as both department chair and associate dean of the College of Arts and Sciences at LSU.

Trevor Parry-Giles is a professor in the Department of Communication at the

University of Maryland, where he is also an affiliated scholar with the Center for American Politics & Citizenship and the Center for Political Communication & Civic Leadership. He is the author or coauthor of *Constructing Clinton: Hyperreality and Presidential Image-Making in Postmodern Politics, The Prime-Time Presidency:* The West Wing *and U.S. Nationalism,* and *The Character of Justice: Rhetoric, Law, and Politics in the Supreme Court Confirmation Process.* Parry-Giles also has worked as a political writer for presidential, congressional, statewide, and initiative candidates and campaigns.

David D. Perlmutter is Director of the School of Journalism and Mass Communication and a professor and Starch Faculty Fellow at the University of Iowa. He received his B.A. and M.A. from the University of Pennsylvania and his Ph.D. from the University of Minnesota. He is the author or editor of eight books on political communication and persuasion and has written several dozen research articles for academic journals, as well as more than 200 essays for U.S. and international newspapers and magazines.

Sean Reilly is Chief Operating Officer and President of the Outdoor Division of Lamar Advertising Company, an outdoor advertising company headquartered in Baton Rouge, Louisiana. He is a Harvard University and Harvard Law School graduate. He has served Louisiana as a state representative, has served on the boards of the Louisiana Recovery Authority, the Louisiana Community and Technical College System, and the Louisiana Innovation Council, and has chaired Governor Bobby Jindal's Advisory Council on Ethics Reform. He currently serves on many community and nonprofit boards, including the Board of Visitors of the LSU Manship School of Mass Communication, where he taught as an adjunct professor.

David Schultz is a professor at the Hamline University School of Business, where he teaches classes in public administration. He is also a professor of law at the University of Minnesota, where he teaches election law. Schultz is the author of more than 25 books and 70 articles on various aspects of American politics, campaigns and elections, and political communication.

Dane Strother is a national Democratic media consultant. He has worked in the majority of the states helping elect people to office, from mayor to U.S. senator.

Strother is regularly quoted in America's largest newspapers and periodicals. He is credited with creating new political television-commercial formats and has been an early adopter of new media.

Gerry Tyson founded The Tyson Organization in 1983. In ensuing years, the Tyson firm has earned a reputation as one of the most innovative and trusted Democratic voter-contact firms in the country, having played significant roles in some of the nation's most critical, high-profile campaigns, including Obama for America in 2008. As a member of the Obama team, the firm was assigned to the pivotal battleground states of Colorado, Iowa, Michigan, New Mexico, Nevada, and Indiana. Other clients have included dozens of Democratic members of the U.S. Senate and the U.S. House of Representatives, a score of Democratic governors, and mayors of large cities across the country.

Darrell M. West is Vice President and Director of Governance Studies at the Brookings Institution.

Michael Xenos is an associate professor in the Department of Communication Arts at the University of Wisconsin–Madison. His research focuses on how the context and content of political communication influences the quality of democratic deliberation, public opinion, and civic engagement. He is particularly interested in how new communication technologies enable or constrain democratic citizenship.

Index

for television ads, 83–85; self-promotion vs. anonymity, 14–15; size of consulting firms, 16; success or failure of, 13–14
contemporary Christian music (CCM), 230
contracts with consultants, 20–21
contrastive (comparative) ads, 26–27, 83, 187
contributions, regulation of. *See* campaign finance
The Cook Political Report, 268–69
Corax, 126
costs: billboards, 107–8; focus groups, 152; online advertising, 190, 191; social networking, 205; television, 78–80
C-SPAN (Cable-Satellite Public Affairs Network), 53, 270
Cuban Americans, 250–51. *See also* Latino voters
Cunningham, Charles H., 227
Cuomo, Donna, 25
cynicism and skepticism, public, 14, 124–25

daily effective circulations (DECs), 108
DailyKos.com, 271
"Daisy" spot (Johnson, 1964), 24
"Dangerous" spot (McCain, 2008), 29
Davis v. Federal Election Commission, 70
deadlines vs. 24-hour news cycle, 112
Dean, Howard, 1, 194, 206, 236
debates, focus groups during, 145
deceptive advertising. *See* false political advertising
Decision, 232
defamation, 42–43. *See also* false political advertising
delegation by candidates, 17–18
deliberative speeches, 127–28
Democratic National Committee (DNC), 28
Democratic National Convention, 193
Democratic Party: African Americans and, 249; evangelicals and, 228, 235; Latino voters and, 251–54; young voters and, 239. *See also* ideological leanings and partisan divides; *specific candidates and elections*

Dent, Charlie, 81
de Vellis, Philip, 176–77
digital display billboards, 109–10
direct mail: to evangelicals, 235; GOTV and, 172; independent organizations and, 179; younger voters and, 244. *See also* targeting
disabled voters, 171
DISCLOSE Act, 175
disclosure of contributions and expenditures, 65–66, 70–71
DNC (Democratic National Committee), 28
Dobson, James, 231
documentation in ads, 83
Dole, Robert, 26, 215, 252
Donilon, Michael, 28
door-to-door operations: court case on permitting, 70; GOTV, 168, 169, 172; younger voters and, 243–44
Duffy, Jennifer, 269
Dukakis, Michael, 25, 46, 157–58
Duke, David, 106–7
Dvorak, Michael, 39

eagle and ostrich spot (Kerry, 2004), 28
early voting, 164–65, 246
earned media (free media): blogosphere, 122–24; editorial boards, meeting with, 117–18; exclusives, 119–20; letters to the editor, 121–22; local news stations and, 155, 158; monitoring websites and blogs, 122; news conferences, interviews, and photo ops, 116–17; "off the record," "on background," and "not for attribution," 118–19; op-ed pieces, 121; press releases, video news releases, and radio actualities, 114–15; reader or reviewer feedback, 122; research for earned-media plans, 113–14; special events and speeches, 117; talk shows, 118; third-party endorsements, 120–21; trusting relationships and, 120; value of, 124–25; overview, 112–13
economy issue, 29–30
editorial boards, meeting with, 117–18

*Federal Election Commission v. Wisconsin Right-
to-Life, Inc.,* 70
feedback from readers and viewers, 122
Feingold, Russell, 56. *See also* McCain-
Feingold Act
15–15 format, 87
financing of campaigns. *See* campaign finance
First Amendment and free speech: anonymous political speech, 70; disclosure
of membership lists and, 70; express
advocacy vs. issue advocacy, 66–67; false
political advertising and, 41–44, 46–49;
media access and campaign finance, 56
"First Read," 270
501(c)3 and 501(c)4 organizations, 58, 71
527 organizations, 58, 71, 174–75, 176
Florida, 250–51, 261, 263
focus groups: advantages over telephone
surveys, 147–48; costs, 152; effectiveness
in Internet age, 152–53; location and
scheduling, 149; moderator role, 150–51;
questioning routes, 151–52; research
purpose and research questions, 148–49;
screening of participants, 149–50; survey
research vs., 146–47; overview, 145–46
Ford, Gerald, 132
forensic speeches, 127
foundation funding for public journalism, 156,
184
framing of issues, 139
Frankel, Max, 56
Franklin, Shirley, 84
Free Congress Foundation, 268
freelance consultants, 16–17. *See also* consultants, political
free media. *See* earned media
free speech. *See* First Amendment and free
speech
Frum, David, 132
Fulbright, William, 54
fundraising: candidate reluctance, 18–19;
media access as reform for, 56; online,
194. *See also* campaign finance
Fussell, Paul, 7

gatekeeper role of reporters, 58
gender gap, 219
gender issue, changes in, 83
Geographic Information Systems, 108
Georgia, 82, 157–58, 258, 263. *See also* Southern race politics
Germond, Jack, 267
Germond-Witcover Political Report, 267
Gerson, Michael, 132
get-out-the-vote (GOTV) operations: barriers
to participation, overcoming, 170–72;
communicating an effective message,
169–70; high-frequency voters, 165–66;
identifying targets, 167–68; infrequently
voting supporters, 166–67; methods of
message delivery, 172–73; MTV Rock the
Vote campaign, 241, 243, 246; partisan-
ship and early vs. late voters, 164–65;
precinct performance, targeting by,
168–69; statistical models, targeting by,
169; throughout the campaign, 165
Gibson, William, 203
Gingrich, Newt, 55
Giuliani, Rudy, 179, 231
GodTube, 234
Goldwater, Barry, 258
González, Elián, 250
Gonzalez, Nathan, 268
Google News Alerts, 122
Gordon, Bart, 101–2
Gore, Al, 216
Graham, Billy, 232
Greece, ancient, 126–27
gross rating points (GRPs), 79

Halperin, Mark, 270
"Hang On" campaign (E. Edwards, 1991), 106
health care issue, 182–83
Hemingway, Ernest, 99, 102
Henry, Brad, 86–87
Hillary: The Movie (Citizens United), 175
The Hill newspaper, 266
Hispanic voters. *See* Latino voters
Hitchcock, Alfred, 14

Holland, Kim, 86–88
Horton, William, 25
The Hotline (National Journal), 266
House of Representatives. *See* Congress and electronic media
Hughes, Chris, 240
Hybels, Bill, 229

ideological leanings and partisan divides: age groups and, 218–19; *Cook Political Report* ratings, 268–69; earned media and, 113–14; endorsements and, 121; independent candidates, 218; Latino voters and, 251–54; older voters and, 221; younger voters and, 239
"I Got a Crush . . . on Obama" video, 177
image of candidates, 131, 139–40
independent candidates, 218
independent content: in 2004–2010 campaigns, 176–78; dangers and advantages, 180; direct-mail and referendums, 179; 527 organizations, 58, 71, 174–75; on policy, 178–79; Supreme Court decision on corporate funding, 175; overview, 174
information barriers to voting, 170–71
inoculation strategy, 27
insider-oriented publications: on cable and Internet, 270–72; magazines and newspapers, 265–66; newsletters, 267–70
Internet and websites: "anonymous" postings, 124; baby boomers and, 217; campaign websites, evaluation of, 197–202; challenges and opportunities from, 190–91; Congress and, 59–60; costs, 190; disclaimers and accountability not required on, 83; earned media and, 112; effectiveness of, 196; e-mail, 121, 122, 191–92, 241–42; evangelicals and, 232, 233–34; focus groups and, 152–53; independent-source and citizen-produced as, 194–95; insider-oriented content and, 270–72; Kerry's WolfpacksforTruth.org, 28; liberal political websites, 271; monitoring, 122; newspapers and, 90–91, 93, 94–95; news

sites, 51–52; Obama's TaxCutFacts.org, 32; search-engine advertising, 192–93; "shovelware" vs. original content, 162; talk shows on, 118; television and, 77, 105; trends in use of, 30–32; video-game advertising, 194; website advertising, 193–94; younger voters and, 240–41; YouTube, 77, 115. *See also* blogs; social networking, online
interviews: of candidates by consultants, 84; as earned media, 116–17; offering to local television stations, 159
invention, in speechwriting, 128–29
Iowa caucuses, 1, 110, 141, 236
Iraq War, 178
issue advocacy: express advocacy vs., 58, 66–67; McCain-Feingold Act and, 69–71
issue advocacy vs. express advocacy, 58, 66–67

Jackson, Jesse, 260
Jefferson, Thomas, 40
JibJab, 195
Jindal, Bobby, 39, 233–34
"Joe the Plumber" spots (McCain, 2008), 29–30
Johnson, Lyndon, 24, 258
Joint Committee on Congressional Operations (1973), 53
joint ventures, 162
Josh Lee Lecture Series, University of Oklahoma, 33
Jude, Tad, 46
Julian P. Kanter Political Commercial Archive, University of Oklahoma, 33
Justice, Charlie, 102–3

Kaine, Tim, 235
Kanter, Julian P., 33
Kauffman, Greg, 39
Keeter, Scott, 143
Kefauver, Estes, 52
Kennedy, John F., 128, 130
Kerry, John: 2004 television ads, 27–28;

to campaigns, 205–8; candidate failure to conform to expectations, 200–201; defined, 203; election results and, 208–9; evangelical, 233–34; history of, 204–5; younger voters and, 240–41, 243

Social Security, 216, 217, 219–20

soft money, 69–70, 174–75

Somit, Albert, 222

sophists, 126

South Carolina, 260. *See also* Southern race politics

Southern Baptist Environment and Climate Initiative, 229

Southern race politics: black mobilization, 259–61; changing South and age factor, 261–63; continuity and change, 263–64; white racial resentment, 257–59

Spanish-language media, 254, 255

special events, 117

special-order speeches, 55

speeches and speechwriting: in ancient Greece and Rome, 126–27; ceremonial, deliberative, and forensic speeches, 127–28; classic examples, 128; as earned media, 117; five canons of rhetoric, 128–31; media context and, 131–33; Obama's speech welcoming Pittsburgh Penguins (2009), 133–35; one-minute or special-order, 55; training for speechwriters, 127

spouses of candidates, interference by, 19

"State of the News Media" (2008, Pew Center Project for Excellence in Journalism), 60–62

state regulation of campaign finance: overview, 64–65; local regulations, 72–73; Supreme Court decisions on, 65–71; variety of, 71–72

state regulation of false political advertising, 44–47

statistical models for GOTV targeting, 169

Stephanopoulos, George, 27

Stephens, Mitchell, 131

storytelling, contextual, 161–62

Street, Debra, 218

Strider, Burns, 235

subsidies. *See* earned media (free media)

Supreme Court, U.S.: on campaign finance and expenditures, 65–71, 72, 175; on free speech, 42–43, 44, 46; on media access, 47, 48

surveys. *See* polling and public opinion

Swift Boat Veterans for Truth, 176, 195

Swingstateproject.com, 271

swing voters: Latino, 249, 252; older voters and swing states, 217, 225; percentage of electorate, 164

talk shows as earned media, 118. *See also* radio; television news, local

Tangle.com, 234

targeting: billboards and, 107–8; buying airtime and, 79; with Geographic Information Systems, 108; for GOTV, 165–69; Latino voters, 249, 255; microtargeting models, 170; newspapers and, 93, 95; seniors, 216–17

TaxCutFacts.org (Obama, 2008), 32

"Tax Cutter" spot (McCain), 31–32

taxes issue, 31–32

Taylor, Kathy, 85–86

teaser spots, 110

telephone communication: cell-phone use and polling, 143, 147; GOTV and, 172–73; younger voters and, 243–44. *See also* targeting

television: cable and satellite, 51, 61, 173, 270–71; Congressional proceedings opened to, 52–53; evangelical, 231–32; first use as campaign medium, 55–56; high-definition, 78; Internet and, 77, 105; presidential use of, 53; Spanish-language, 254, 255; speeches and, 131; talk shows, 118; viewership, 51

television advertising: beginnings and growth of, 23–24; broadcast television, importance of, 78; Bush's national security focus and Wolves spot (2004), 27–28;